The Desert Kingdoms of Peru

Endpapers: Mochica runners, or chasquis, whose function
was to carry messages from place to place. A drawing taken
from a recurrent motif in Mochica pottery

Victor W. von Hagen

The Desert Kingdoms of Peru

New York Graphic Society Publishers, Ltd.
Greenwich, Connecticut

Contents

CONTENTS   6 THE CONQUESTS

Acknowledgements

The author and publishers are grateful to the Museo de Antropologia, Lima, and the Museo de Rafael Larco, Lima, for permission to reproduce photographs of objects contained in their collections. They are also indebted to the following for permission to reproduce photographs: Bibliothèque Nationale figures 124–26; British Museum 57, 130–37; Museo de Brüning, Lambayeque 63; Museo de Gallerie Nazionale, Naples 3; Dr Fairfield Osborn 6; the Wenner Grenn Foundation 7, 91, 95, 97, 100–102, 107–10, 112, 122.

The following illustrations were photographed by the author: figures 1, 8–12, 40, 55, 56, 61, 62, 65, 66, 92, 98, 99, 105, 106, 111, 113, 114, 116, 117, 119, 120; by Abraham Guillen 13–22, 24, 25, 27–39, 41–46, 48–51, 53, 54, 58, 63, 74, 77–90, 103, 104, 115, 121; by Shippee-Johnson 91, 95, 97, 100–102, 107–110, 112, 122; by George Holton 59, 60, 64, 76, 118, 123; by Charles Dougherty 47; by Modeste von Unruh 93; by Aerial Explorations Inc. 7.

The line drawings reproduced in the text were made by Alberto Beltran and based on motifs taken from Mochica and Chimú pottery.

Maps

1 The Rediscovery of the Kingdoms

A people is like a man; when he has disappeared nothing is left of him unless he had taken the precaution to leave his imprint on the stones of the road. – ELIE FAURE

OF ALL of the many and varied tribes that preceded the Incas, none have left a greater impression upon the history of Peru than the desert kingdoms of the Mochicas and the Chimús. The physical remains of their past – cities, temples, pyramids – even though destroyed and half-covered with sand, are still impressive. Graves have yielded and continue to yield their golden hoard, and with it, feather ornaments, superb weavings and carvings, and above all, the fine, realistically moulded pottery, a pottery so graphic that it is interpreted as their language. Despite the pathos of distance and the destruction brought on by man and time, there are remains of roads, fortresses, defence walls, vast irrigation projects and step-terraces – an eloquent monument to a people who have left their imprint on the road of time.

The Chimús (who succeeded the Mochicas and were called the Kingdom of Chimor) were the last of the tribes to be conquered by the Incas, before the latter were themselves overwhelmed by the Spaniards within the next fifty years. However, before the Incas could effectively stamp out the cultural memory of the Chimús, through their technique of selective manipulation of remembered history, they were themselves involved in a civil war, the struggle between Atahualpa and Huascar for the Inca Empire. This was quickly followed, in turn, by the Spanish intrusion. Here, then, is the reason that much of the Chimú and the Mochica remains are known to us today.

The Mochicas and the Chimús have had a continuous archaeological history, which began roughly in the third century BC and went on (with a hiatus between the years AD 1000–1250) until the year 1461, when they were overwhelmed by a full-scale Inca invasion. This was followed by the final quietus by the Spanish, and so the rest became silence. These 1400 years of continued existence, on a high cultural plane and within the same geographical area, an area of titanic desolation marked only by

COLOMBIA

River Amazon

B R A Z I L

ECUADOR

Tumbes

Sechura
Desert
Motupe

Chiclayo

Cajamarca

Chicama R. *Moche*
Chan Chan R. *Virú*
Trujillo
Virú

Paramonga

LIMA R. *Rimac*
Pachacamac

Cuzco

Ica

Nazca

B O L I V I A

Titicaca

Tiahuanaco

Tacna

CHILE

PACIFIC OCEAN

PERU
LIMA

Area of
Map

South
America

███ Irrigable Areas

SCALE
50   0   50   100 Miles
50   0   50   100 Kilometres

MOUNTAIN, DESERT AND IRRIGABLE AREAS OF
COASTAL PERU

river-oases paradises, is one of the most prolonged in America's cultural history; only the Maya civilization of Middle America has had a longer duration.

The impression that the Mochicas, and later the Chimús, have left on Peru is timeless, since the ceramics recovered from their graves are so exact that their tribal customs, their lives, loves and deaths, can be read as a pictorial history. The desiccating quality of the Peruvian coastal desert has preserved this culture. Their dead were buried along with their possessions, and their very corpses were preserved in so fine a state that one can often observe such subtleties as the effects of arthritis, the wear of teeth and the pruning of nails.

Where all else has perished, there are the ceramics. These are unequalled anywhere in the Americas. With a penchant for realism, their potters have left lifelike portraits of warriors, priests and courtiers, the possessed and the unpossessed, the halt and the blind. Diseases which afflicted them are exhibited in this pottery with clinical exactness. Most of the facial features – the piercing of the ears and the nose septum, the squint of the eye, the hook of the nose – are depicted in this sculptural pottery. All food cultivated or obtained is effectively and realistically presented. The landscapes which are often found painted on the pottery are as detailed as Persian miniatures: one sees the sun glare down upon the wasteland; the desert flora and the dry mountains loom up beside; the plants grow in the cultivated greenness of a river oasis; maize fields bend tasselled heads which sway in the off-shore winds. There are also figures in the landscape, running and dancing, while war is presented with all its rapine and slaughter. Animals and birds, which formed so intimate a part of their lives, are moulded or painted on these ceramics with a warmth of feeling rarely found in other American cultures. Woman, when she appears in the pottery, is handled tenderly, a rather unusual feature in early American art, for her lot was that of an unequal concubinage and a weary servitude. There is also here in this iconographic parade a realistic and engagingly candid picture of their love life – at times so shockingly sexual that it disturbed even the Incas, their latter-day conquerors. No culture in the Americas and few others in the world have left so graphic a picture of the intimate and libidinous details of sensuous love.

This pottery record naturally has its limitations: the Mochica-Chimú gods are nameless, since their vases do not bear, like those of the Greeks, the name of the represented god. Nor do their paintings have the rows of talking glyphs that the Maya often inserted to give us a date. There are no

13

subtleties here, no nuances; beyond the graphic, one must surmise and deduce. It was only after the 'study of the antique' gave way to scientific archaeology that scholars were able to link the creators of this vivid pottery with the widely scattered remains of pyramids, roads, fortresses and vast irrigation works, and thus gauge the impressiveness of the Mochica civilization. This Mochica culture had developed before the Christian era – the earliest Carbon 14 date is 267 BC – and endured despite a massive onslaught from without to emerge later as the Chimú Empire.

CHARLES III OF SPAIN AND THE DISCOVERY OF THE MOCHICA-CHIMÚ CIVILIZATIONS

The first important event in the discovery of the Mochica-Chimú civilizations can be precisely fixed: on June 17, 1771, Charles III of Spain was summoned to the rooms that contained his 'Cabinet of Natural History and Antiquities', in order to inspect some boxes that had just arrived from Peru. These contained the remains of someone who once had been, like himself, a 'king'; the flesh, like a piece of parchment, still clung to the bones: teeth, hands, nails – even the head-dress was intact. Fragments of the mummy's feather robe suggested the opulence of the burial. Beside it was a wooden baston, delicately carved, which Charles III saw to be an allegorical wreath of plants held in the hands of a maize-god. A feather-fan and delicately wrought golden ear-spools were part of the cache, and with it were a number of superbly made effigy vessels which pictured graphically the lives of the people over which this man had once ruled. On each piece was written *17th June 1771*, the date of its arrival; then they were placed in the Cabinet of Antiquities next to the artifacts taken from the ruins of Pompeii.

Far more than most in Europe, Charles III was in a position to appreciate this find from Peru, for it had been he, when King of Naples, who ordered the first successful excavation of the buried ruins of Pompeii. Under the direction of the Italian engineer Rocco Dioacchino de Alcubierre, workmen had dug through fifty feet of volcanic ash and laid open streets and houses. In the course of these excavations they found the fossilized cadavers of people overwhelmed in the act of escape; bowls, tools, even wall-murals had been preserved. The inexorable clock of time had been stopped for 1,700 years, for here, by the accident of volcanic action which had snuffed out in a few hours a whole living city, the ash had preserved that which would have perished in the normal passage of time. Before him now, though of different circumstances, was material from Mochica graves from Spain's kingdom in Peru which had also been preserved. The Mochicas were culturally, according to tradition, approximately the same age as Pompeii – 1,700 years. In distance the two were separated geographically by 6000 miles. Yet, when Charles III compared the artifacts of the two cultures represented in his Cabinet of Antiquities, Pompeii of the Romans and the Mochicas of Peru, he soon grasped the many analogies between them. Bronze chisels from these unrelated civilizations were so alike that they might have come from the same mould; ivory and bone ornaments were also similar, and the paintings on Mochica pottery were as illustrative of their life as the murals of Pompeii were in depicting the foibles of Roman society.

The man who sent the Mochica relics to Charles III was Feyjoo y Sosa, who had taken over the post of Corregidor of Trujillo in Peru in 1760. Within three years he issued a book dedicated to Charles III and printed by the Council of the Indies. Herein one read that the province was almost void of people. There were only 2,513 Indians in the several valleys that formed the area, and these were engaged in agriculture, mostly sugar, and in the upper valleys they worked in cloth-factories. The reader was informed of the large *haciendas* in succeeding valleys, with vast stretches of desert emptiness between them. Geographical and archaeological evidence showed that it was not always so; remains of huge temples still stood, and there was also evidence of vast engineering works, some of which still brought water from the mountains for use in colonial agriculture. The immense number of graves that yielded mummies, gold and pottery gave evidence as to how populated the valley once was.

In 1550 the *cacique*, whose given name in Spanish was Antonio Chayque, had revealed to one of the residents the treasure of the pyramid-*huaca*, called Lomayahuana, on the condition that part of the recovered treasure would go to relieve the poverty of his people. The Spanish complied and an immense cache was found. The site was revisited in 1563 and gave up even more gold. In 1566 García Gutierrez de Toledo, a citizen of Trujillo, opened up the *huaca* which now carries his name, and for a period of over fifty years it yielded gold to the amount of one million *pesos*. Another, Escobar Corchuelo, opened up the *huaca* which he called La Tosca; it enriched him by 60,000 *pesos* of gold weight. After that other citizens of Trujillo, seeing the drift of things, formed a company to exploit yet another vein of Mochica gold. On the edge of the Moche River, in the valley of the same name, are the ancient *huacas* of the Sun and the Moon. They had been

15

erected as early as AD 400 and were by all accounts the largest man-made structures on the coast. The gold-seekers diverted an arm of the Moche River, at high flood, directly into the side of the Temple of the Moon; it caused a large section of it to fall, constructed as it was with sun-baked adobe bricks, and within the multitude of tombs they found gold to the value of 800,000 ducats. All this supported the documentary and archaeological evidence of how prosperous and highly populated this area once was. In the same valleys, wars, disease and inadequate medical science had decimated the population; moreover, the natural resources had been reduced to the point of complete disappearance.

In 1767, Charles III expelled the Jesuits from all his American possessions; it was a most courageous step. The executor of the Jesuit expulsion was Count Aranda, the powerful Minister of State and a friend of Voltaire. This action had a direct bearing on the history of archaeology, for most of the educational institutions in Peru, as elsewhere in the Americas, were under the direction of the Jesuits; the other ecclesiastical orders had, at best, the second choice in the land. Yet the expulsion was unfortunate, for many first-class minds were lost to Spain and most of the Jesuits' missions and institutions were sacked and destroyed. It did, however, for such is the train of circumstances of this extraordinary history, bring into focus the ancient desert kingdoms of Peru, for it brought there Don Baltasar Jaime Martínez de Compañón y Bujanda.

Martínez de Compañón, born in Spain in 1745, came down from the University of Salamanca in his twentieth year as a Doctor in Canonical Law. Even at this early age he had been brought to the attention of his king, who sought then for enlightened minds with the aptitude to officiate in the New World. While he was in a high post at Santander, Spain, the Jesuits were expelled and he was sent to Lima. In five years, that is by 1773, he was already secretary of the Lima council, giving a good display of his organizational ability. Two years from the day that the king had received the mummy of a high-placed personage of the ancient desert kingdoms of Peru Martínez de Compañón was appointed and consecrated as Bishop of Trujillo. He took possession of his See on May 13, 1779 and was instructed by his sovereign to put right the situation in this province by using the powers of his office to change the social and economic conditions.

As pictured in the report of Feyjoo y Sosa, the official who had forwarded the mummy with all its appurtenances, the population of these northern desert valleys had shrunk, and land was held in vast latifundias by only a sprinkling of aristocracy, while the people, mostly Indian or mestizo descendants of the Chimú and Mochica empires, were living on the bare edge of penury. Martínez de Compañón undertook long and arduous journeys over this Brobdingnagian landscape to find out the facts. In a letter to Charles III, dated May 15, 1786, he reported what he found. A year later, in another letter, he explained how he intended to improve the situation. As he worked to establish schools and introduce the latest methods in education, he also, with funds supplied to him by the Crown, employed a number of self-taught native artists who were given the task of recording the pattern of their lives: agriculture, hunting, weaving, dancing and the costumes that were part of it. At the same time Martínez de Compañón carried on extensive archaeological excavations. He made plans of Chan Chan, Inca roads and other ancient structures; he had his copyists limn the mummies found in graves complete with their artifacts, and this was doubtless the first time that opened tombs in America had their contents recorded. This unpublished and illustrated material is encyclopaedic[1]: birds, fish, animals, trees, fruits, cultivated plants, medicinal roots and vines. The collection consists of 1,400 coloured drawings. In addition to this, the bishop collected 600 specimens of pottery, textiles, carved wood, gold, shell and feather-weavings, and other 'Curiosities of Art & Nature'. All this was for the King's Cabinet of Antiquities, and was transported in twenty-four large boxes on board the ship *La Moza*, which sailed in November 1778.[2] Their arrival in Madrid a year later caught Charles III in the midst of world crisis; even then he wrote the bishop a moving letter of gratitude.

One has to project oneself into the thought of those times to appreciate the impact all this had on the mind of Charles III. It is a demonstrable fact that, up to this time, so far as Europe was concerned, the great American cultures – Aztec, Maya, Inca – had been effectively blotted out from human memory. The early excitement that attended the conquests of Cortés in Mexico, Montejo in Yucatán, and Pizarro in Peru had been almost forgotten; the mass of gold and silver ornaments yielded by these conquests had long since been melted down and was circulating in the coinage of Europe. In the New World, the old yielded to the new: the Maya edifices of Yucatán became the source of building material for the conquerors, just as the remains of the Roman Empire in Italy became nothing more than quarries for Renaissance man. The many early sixteenth-century publications which explained those wonderful civilizations were seldom consulted,

17

B

and had long since fossilized in the libraries of the learned. Similarly, the fulsome histories written by the Spaniards about the conquered lands in the later part of the sixteenth century were dismissed, in general, as typical Spanish braggadocio. As such they were summarized by the historian William Robertson, who at that time was writing *The History of America* (1792): 'Neither the Mexicans nor the Peruvians', he wrote, 'were entitled to rank with those nations which merit the name of civilized.' As for the reported palaces, 'these were more fit to be the habitation of people just emerging from barbarity … moreover they convey no high idea of the progress in art and ingenuity.' The lack of general information on these cultures was so profound that Robertson insisted that 'if these buildings corresponding to such descriptions had ever existed in the Mexican or Peruvian cities, it is probable that some remains of them would still be visible … it seems altogether incredible that in a period so short, every vestige of this boasted elegance and grandeur should have disappeared.' His conclusion is that 'the Spanish accounts appear highly embellished'.

To broaden further the horizons of American pre-history, the king's Capitan-General in Guatemala had forwarded in 1773 a report of an astonishing discovery: an Indian had discovered and reported to the local *cura* a ruined city, which they called 'Palenque', at an altitude of 1,000 feet in the jungles of Chipias. It seemed of the greatest antiquity, since the whole of it was covered with the root tentacles of stranger-fig trees. The walls inside and out were covered with hieroglyphics 'which doubtless reveal the history of the place'. There were also immense palaces decorated with dancing figures moulded in stucco, while stone towers outreached the highest trees. Palenque was the second Maya site made known to the Spaniards since the conquest. It is no hyperbole to say that Maya history would be reborn at this site.[3]

The King of Spain was, as usual, deeply involved in world politics at this time. It was the very eve of the American Revolution, and France was pressing Spain to adhere to the Family Compact and use the moment of England's embarrassment to make war on its Empire. Still (and this is an intellectual index of the man), he gave ear to these reports. He ordered that the Italian architect Don Antonio Bernasconi be despatched to Guatemala to explore Palenque. Plans were made, the site was cleared, and preliminary excavations commenced. The commission was under royal orders that they carefully preserve everything found, so that they might illustrate a work the King was projecting in his mind: *An Ancient History of the Americas*.

Following this discovery, El Tajin, another immense ruin, which lay

seventeen miles inland from the Caribbean Sea and 125 miles north of
the port of Vera Cruz, was discovered in 1785. El Tajin would prove to
be not only a city; it was a tribal culture, whose origins stretched back to
1000 BC and continued until it was snuffed out by the Spanish conquest in
1521. It is famed for its clay figures, 'the laughing heads', quite unlike
anything else in the mass of littoral Mexican cultures.

This astonishing news of El Tajin, another mosaic in the American
history which the king contemplated writing, came to him just as the boxes
containing the Mochica and Chimú artifacts arrived from Peru. A map was
made of Spain's America, so that the king could see how widely dispersed
were all these recent discoveries: Chan Chan in Peru, Palenque in Guatemala, El Tajin in Vera Cruz. All these confirmed the reports of the
grandeur reported to the Crown during the Spanish conquests and
explorations of the sixteenth century.

Unfortunately, Charles III was on the point of death when yet another
archaeological discovery was added to the gigantic archaeological anagram
of the Ancient Americas. In Mexico City, on August 17, 1790, workmen
discovered, while strengthening the foundations of the Cathedral, the
Aztec calendar stone. It had been carved and set up during the reign of
Tizoc (1481–1486), the seventh Aztec 'King', and was a large cylindrical
block of trachyte, eight feet in diameter and weighing more than twenty
tons: the sacred *tonal pohualli*. This ritual calendar, carved with symbols
of Aztec day signs, had a profound effect on those who saw it. In any other
century this symbol of paganism would have been broken into building
stone; yet now that the lure of the antique existed, the Viceroy of Mexico,
Count Revillagigedo, upon viewing it, ordered it set up in a museum.

The successor to the Spanish Crown on the death of Charles III was
the well-meaning Charles IV, who inherited an empire beset with troubles.
Spain had no other choice except to declare war against France after its
revolution. Later, when that revolution had spent itself, choked to death
by its own contradictions, and produced by way of reprisal a Napoleon,
Spain again, although it was not to her advantage, was forced into unending
wars and battles. Spain was the victim of the most wretched circumstances;
an ill-starred man for a King; the Queen's lover, Manuel de Godoy, as its
Prime Minister; the heir to the throne a demented Prince fighting with
his father against his mother and his mother's lover. Yet to Spain's immense, and not often recognized intellectual credit, the Crown continued
to support with extraordinary largesse all the scientific research pro-
grammes which had been initiated by Charles III: the botanist Mutis in

Colombia, the zoologist Azara in the purple land of Argentine, Martínez de Compañón in Peru, and the ornithologist-botanist Mociñon in Mexico.

Meanwhile, Martínez de Compañón was named Archbishop of Bogota, where he went by sea; while at Cartagena he packed and shipped, on December 13, 1790, the last of the collections of the Chimú and the Mochica that he had collected in the desert kingdoms of Peru.

ARCHAEOLOGY IN THE DESERT KINGDOMS

It was Alexander von Humboldt who, nine years later, gave scientific meaning to the various archaeological discoveries in the Americas. He arrived in Madrid in 1799, at the very time that scientific curiosity commanded the minds of people and kings. His birth facilitating what would have been difficult for one less well-born, Humboldt was presented to the king by Baron von Forell, Saxon Ambassador to Spain. He asked and received no less than the king's rubric – in effect, a *carta blanca*, so as to travel 'for the acquisition of knowledge'. Charles IV was fully aware of the young scientist's background. He was born in Berlin in 1769, where his father had been attached to the staff of Frederick of Prussia. Since his mother was a Huguenot, he had been reared in French culture; both he and his brother Wilhelm had attended the best of Germany's universities. Alexander von Humboldt, inclining towards the exact sciences, first worked in geology and palaeontology, and had, in fact, written his first book on cryptogamic plants in 1797. At the age of twenty-three, Humboldt was Inspector of Mines at Fichtelberg, and now, at the moment that he stood before Charles IV, at the age of twenty-nine, he was the author of three well-respected books on geology, botany and physiology. There was no doubt either of his training or of his curiosity; he had visited most of the collections in Spain, and he seemed to know almost everyone connected with science.

On June 5, 1799, when the ship that was to carry him to South America weighed anchor, Humboldt was able to summarize his precise aims in a letter to a friend: 'I shall make collections of fossils and plants: I intend to institute chemical analysis of the atmosphere and I shall make astronomical observations. My attention will be ever directed to observing the harmony among the forces of nature, to remarking the influence exerted by inanimate creation upon the vegetable and animal kingdoms.' Humboldt, with the aid of his friend Aimé Bonpland, botanist and physician, performed precisely that which he intended; and yet more, far more, for in time

20

he wrote and published, at his own expense, thirty volumes on the scientific results of his five years' voyage on botany, physics, zoology, archaeology, cartography and history. It was the most ambitious and costly publication ever to have been conceived and carried out by a single person. After eighteen months in Venezuela, four months in Cuba, and nine additional months in Colombia (not including the six months in Quito), Humboldt, accompanied by Aimé Bonpland and weighted down with telescopes and thermometers, then moved toward Peru.

Humboldt entered Peruvian territory in the month of August 1802. It is at this point that he began to observe the archaeology of South America. His unpublished *Tagebücher* provide evidence of the data he was compiling, for archaeological notetaking continued during the entire nine months and developed further as he crossed the Incaic line near the border of Colombia and Ecuador. Humboldt had found in Quito a vestige of what had been the residence of the Inca Huayna Capac, the same who had finally conquered the Chimú Empire. Its architecture had been made part of the Convent of San Augustin, and from its remains Humboldt made the first really architecturally accurate plan of an Inca structure.

When they took the Inca high road toward Peru four months later, he stopped to take notes on the Inca ruins at Llactacunga.[4] After this, they crossed the hail-swept paramo of Pullal. The path used by the muleteers was below the famed Inca Highway, and Humboldt remembered that 'our eyes were continually riveted on the grand remains of the Inca road upwards of 20 feet in breadth'. This road, which ran between Quito and Cuzco and southwards beyond, led close to the Fortress of Cañar. Inca Tampu at Cañar had been built late, *c.* 1450, and is presumed to have been a royal halting-place, albeit an elaborate one, on the Inca road through the conquered northern provinces of the Inca Empire. Humboldt improved upon the plan made by a previous explorer, Charles Marie de la Condamine, in 1746; this remains the most accurate drawing of an Inca structure down to modern times.

The mule-trains of the expedition, eighteen in number, which carried their instruments, dried plants and manuscripts, entered the territory of Peru, still following when possible 'le grand chemin de l'Inca, un des ouvrages les plus utiles, et en même temps les plus gigantesques que les hommes aient executé est encore assez bien conservé'. It carried them to the village of Ayabaca, where there were remains of Inca temples. Next they came to Chulucanas, where Humboldt mapped the grid-iron plan of the ancient Inca site, and noted, 'les restes de grandes edifices ... j'en ai

completé neuf entre le Paramo de Chulucanas et le village de Guanca-
bamba'.

It is from the pages of Humboldt's *Tagebücher*, which, to the disgrace of
German sciences, has never been published, that one can learn the details of
his trip into Peru. After entering the Upper Amazon at the Rio Marañon,
where they stayed seventeen days, they again returned to the Andes, took
up travel along the Inca Highway, searched the mines of the region, and
in August of 1802 arrived at Cajamarca. For reasons of time, space, and
perhaps out of fear of prolixity, Humboldt ceased his *Personal Narrative*, a
series of eighteen books in the first person singular, at the borders of Peru.
All else about Peru was written in a series of disconnected publications.
The *Aspects of Nature* was one of these, in which there is to be found a
detailed section on Cajamarca, the ancient pre-Inca centre and later Inca-
imposed city, the same site where Atahualpa met his death. Remarkable for
its acumen, this essay is the first really critical appraisal of the whole
drama of the last days of Atahualpa. After five dreary days of mule-journey
down the ancient road through the cordilleras, they reached the Alto
Guangamarca, had their first clear, unobstructed view of the desert-coast,
and then began their ascent.

In Paris, after returning from his five years of epic explorations of the
Americas, he published, among other works, his *Vues des Cordillères et
Monuments des Peuples Indigènes de l'Amerique* (1810), an immensely thick
and unwieldy folio, expensively produced with hundreds of hand-coloured
illustrations. Despite its defects in organization, it is a volume that stands
as a landmark in American archaeology. An immense amount of data,
verified by Humboldt himself if not uncovered by Humboldt himself,
was given the reader: the calendar stone of the Muyscas in Colombia; the
lake of Guatavita; the famed El Dorado of history, never before depicted
and accompanied by compact information on the Chibchas. Inca structures
were, for the first time, accurately put down; the façades of the then
known ruins of Palenque, Mitla and Xochicalco, were redrawn from the
originals given to Humboldt in Mexico. Codices – Maya, Toltec, Mitxec
and Aztec – were illustrated with Humboldt's superb massing of accurate
detail. This unbiased, scientific presentation showed those who read it that
these remains of American antiquity were fragments of history. In time,
however, this volume fell out of use, and it became, as many, a 'classic' – a
work that many admire but which few have examined. Each age received it
as a precious burden to pass on without once glancing at it; like many

works of art, its notoriety survived a long time after it became, for most, unintelligible. However, without Humboldt's masterful assemblage of material, American archaeology would have been set adrift, in the oncoming nineteenth century, in a whirlpool of speculations of its Old World origins; as it is, Humboldt gave to the American historian, William A. Prescott, a place from which to start.

The mere statistics of Humboldt's output are terrifying and will never be repeated again by anyone in a man's lifetime. He travelled by mule or boat 40,000 miles throughout the Americas (Brazil, Venezuela, Colombia, Amazon, Ecuador, Peru, Cuba and Mexico). He returned with thirty immense cases of material: 1,500 measurements used in his *Recueil d'Observations Astronomiques*; 60,000 plant specimens, of which more than 6,000 were new to science. Botany, which is generously sprinkled with plants which bear the initials of HBK (Humboldt, Bonpland and Kunth), was greatly enriched by him. Out of all this he wrote thirty volumes – folio, quarto, decimo (*Voyage aux régions équinoxiales du Nouveau Continent* being his 'personal narrative'), which consisted of over 150,000 pages and 426 illustrations and maps. The engravings alone cost him 600,000 gold francs, the paper 840,000 francs, the printing 2,753 Prussian thalers. The task of floating and seeing these works through the presses in Paris took him seventeen years. He also seems to have been his own bookseller, for he records that his twenty folio volumes were priced at £500, twice the sum that John James Audubon asked for his folios on American birds.

Following von Humboldt, there were many speculative antiquarians, such as Edward King, Viscount Kingsborough, who insisted that the American Indians were descendants of one of the lost tribes of Israel; another, Comte Frederic de Waldeck, held that they were Phoenician, even altering his drawings of Maya monuments to prove his thesis. One who was not speculative was Clements Markham. Markham, because of his association with Prescott, became the next Peruvian historian by a sort of apostolic succession; yet, in actuality, he ground-tested Peru's prehistory, which Prescott, because of his blindness, was unable to do. Born in Yorkshire in the 1830s, during the reign of King William IV, he entered the Navy at fourteen, served on a British ship, and eventually reached Peru in 1845. Having read the *Conquest of Peru* while at sea, he then decided to leave the Navy and apply himself to history. At the age of twenty-two, he visited Prescott and spent ten days with him at 'Fitful Head', where it was impressed upon him that 'no history could be perfect unless the writer was personally acquainted with the geography he described'. Markham had a most distinguished career, wrote and edited many books on the Incas,[5] was

DISCOVERING THE DESERT LANDS

1 Typical Peruvian desert country near Paramonga. Bones from a rifled Chimú burial ground lie bleaching in the sun.

2 A map of the Moche Valley made in 1760 for Feyjoo y Sosa, who had been sent to Peru by Charles III of Spain to bring about administrative reforms. Trujillo is shown as a circular walled town, with Chan Chan (marked on the map as *casas arruindas del regulo Chino*), the centre of Chimú civilization, immediately below it.

3 A portrait of Charles III of Spain by Francesco Leoni. His encouragement of archaeological research in Peru led to the uncovering of the forgotten Mochica and Chimú civilizations.

4 The first drawings of Mochica effigy pottery commissioned by Feyjoo y Sosa in 1760 and sent to Charles III for his Cabinet of Antiquities.

5 Llamas at the base of Chimborazo, a drawing made by Alexander von Humboldt for his book *Vue des Cordillières*, published in 1810.

6 Alexander von Humboldt, the German scholar who was commissioned by Charles IV of Spain to collect scientific and archaeological data in the Spanish American colonies. He reached Peru in 1802 and the mass of information he assembled, including detailed drawings of ruins and settlements, is one of the most important sources of early Peruvian history.

7 The barren desert country on the coastal plain of northern Peru showing *medanos* or sand dunes.

8 An aerial view of a river oasis near the Peruvian coast, showing how the coastal yuncas built their dwellings on the arid slopes, leaving the fertile ground free for cultivation.

9 Scrubland near Motupe in northern Peru, with vegetation in the valley below the parched hillsides.

10 Pabur, a river oasis in northern Peru.

11 The river Chira near Pabur, which supplied the Mochicas and Chimús with a valuable source of water for their cotton plantations.

12 *Guanay* birds gathered on the shore at Mancora in northern Peru. The droppings of these birds were used extensively by the Mochicas and Chimús as a rich fertilizer.

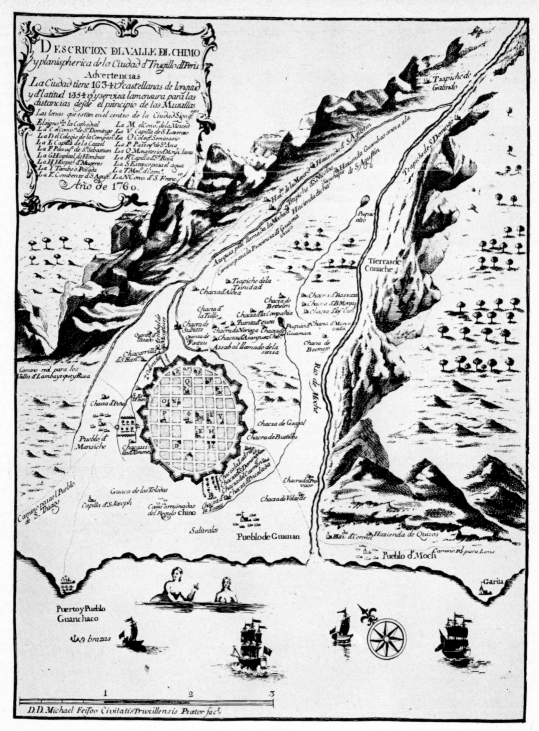

4

5

6

7

8

9

10

11

12

knighted, and became the Secretary of the Royal Geographic Society. However, Markham brushed over the Mochicas and the Chimús and concentrated on the Incas; so again it was an American, Ephraim Squier, who brought the Mochicas and the Chimús into focus with the book, *Incidents of Travel in Peru* (1877).

Squier, who was the first to discern that the 'pottery of the Mochicas is their language', was born in upper New York in 1821. He grew up in gnawing poverty; he was mostly self-taught and was, in turn, surveyor, printer's devil, contributor to magazines, and in charge of the State Journal of Ohio, until he finally found his footing by being the first to gauge and write upon Indian Mounds. He then had, as he wrote, 'an ambition that burns like fire in my veins'. On the strength of this publication, he was made Minister to Central America, and during this time managed to write a series of other books on the archaeology of those lands. Although from his massive governmental reports one wonders how he had the time, Squier studied and then wrote one of the earliest works on Central American archaeology.

In 1862, during the Civil War, Abraham Lincoln sent Squier to Peru with the rank of Minister to negotiate the outstanding differences between the two nations. After his official visit terminated in success, he remained for another year and a half, at his own expense, to initiate the era of dirt-archaeology (distinct from the contemplation of the antique). For the first time, by means of the full employment of a daguerrotype, which cumbersome apparatus his photographer, named Harvey, carried all over the heights and depths of Peru, Peruvian artifacts were correctly photographed and, in turn, faithfully engraved. Squier had done much to prepare himself for his task in the valley of Lima before he arrived in the autumn of 1862 in the land of the Chimú. He went to the Santa Valley and from there to Moche. Trained as he was as a surveyor, his plans of one section of the Chimú capital of Chan Chan are so accurate that an aerial survey made almost a century later does not add much to them.

Squier was indefatigable in his researches, even gathering at Eten a vocabulary of the Muchic language then in use. He then went to Nepeña and gave us the first illustration of the extraordinary Moche ziggurat, or pyramid, called Pañamarca. He studied the vast water reservoir in the upper part of the valley, and went on to map the ruins of Padrejon and the stonelaid ruins of Mora. He left us illustrations of the massive fortress of Chancaillo at Casma; then he went on to Santa, and by the time he came to the heart-land of the Mochicas, the Moche Valley, he had provided himself with the experience to understand what he saw. Unfortunately, financial and marital difficulties prevented him from completing his projected book, *Peru*. Eventually, Squier was assigned to a lunatic asylum. He recovered somewhat and wrote to his publisher that 'mental disturbances have prevented me from finishing *Peru* but I am now pushing it forward'. Still, he had only rare moments of lucidity, and it was his brother who eventually put the book together. *Peru* was published in 1877. It brought the Mochicas and Chimús alive from their desert-tombs and gave impetus to further studies by the author's stressing that 'Mochica pottery is their language'. It was Squier's last audible word.

Charles Weiner arrived in Peru in the same year that Squier's book was published. He wrote of his mission, 'le Ministère de l'instruction publique m'a fait l'honneur de me charger d'une mission archéologique et ethnographique de Perou'. When he had finished his travels, roughly paralleling those of Squier, he published *Perou et Bolivie*, a solidly turned-out volume of 800 pages, 1,100 engravings, 27 maps and 19 plans. A considerable portion of it was given over to the Chimús. Although the reproductions of Mochica and Chimú material are inferior to Squier's, the book was enhanced by plans, since Weiner was able to utilize those which had been previously made by a fellow Frenchman, Angrand, who had sketched in Peru as early as 1837. Some of Angrand's drawings, especially those of Tiahuanaco, the cultural enigma which played so great a part in the drama of the desert sun kingdoms, appear for the first time in the present volume.

After *Perou et Bolivie*, archaeologists nibbled at the edges of the countless *huacas* that dot the desert lands, issuing fascinating monographs, while the looting of the graves was turned into a profession by the *huaqueros*, the grave-robbers. In the Chicama Valley, one Peruvian began to make systematic excavations and collections of Mochica and Chimú pottery. Don Rafael Larco Herrera, the patriarchal owner of a large sugar-hacienda, Chiclin, in the Chicama, began the collection in 1926 and established a museum. His son, Rafael Larco Hoyle, continued the studies, enlarged the programme of excavation and collection, and began a series of studies based on an extensive series of drawings taken principally from the pottery. It was a task that he has never finished; yet his collection of 60,000 pieces of pottery, classified according to theme, will be, so long as it remains an entity, the Rosetta stone of the Mochicas and the Chimú.

While this collection was maturing, the aeroplane was beginning to be used as a technique for finding archaeological sites. In 1931 Robert Shippee, a wealthy young pilot, arranged an expedition to Peru with Lt

George R. Johnson, an outstanding aerial-photographer and the founder of the *Servicio Fotografico Aereo* in Lima. The result of his condor's-eye view of the desert was startling; it gave the whole panorama of coastal history a different perspective, for during the air-expedition they found the great wall of Chimú, made numerous photographs of unknown ruins and agricultural terraces in the Colca Valley, and made an aerial mosaic of the ruins of Chan Chan. Little use was ever made of this photographic material, since there was neither sufficient ground identification of the ruins nor any archaeologist to interest himself in it. This vast archive of films lay for years in a basement, until this author, through friendship with Mr Robert Shippee, acquired the collection and then, during his own expeditions, was able to identify almost all of the aerial photographs geographically. Many of the photographs in this book are reproduced for the first time. The impact of these discoveries from the air has made many archaeologists in these succeeding years turn with renewed interest to the Kingdom of Chimor, with the result that the literature has been wonderfully enriched.

2 The Land and the People

THE GEOGRAPHICAL SETTING

THE MOCHICA and Chimú civilizations originated in a land which is one of the driest in the world. It is, for all practical purposes, rainless; there has been no appreciable climatic change since the littoral was convulsed

Characteristic vegetation from the Peruvian coastal areas, showing cactus, desert succulents and marsh reeds

out of the sea. Even though a sixteenth-century chronicler guessed that the great rains that fell in 1578 robbed the valleys of their earth – a contagious rain that sterilized the soil – still, there is no geological evidence of any great climatic change.

At first sight it appears to be a forbidding land. The utter desolation of it is titanic; the waves break upon shores composed of calcareous sandstone, minute fragments of shells and layers of pudding-stone and shell-marl. Then the sand begins, white-greyish sand driven by south-westerly winds. It covers the horrid desolations and is even carried up as high as 3,000 feet, where sand dunes perch on the craggy foothills of the Andes. On this land the sun beats down with a pitiless, hostile heat, and the reflected glare brings hot sand-blink into the eyes. In the thin air the mountains loom up like dry bones, for the sun seems to enter as a daily tyrant, lording it over this waste landscape. Within an hour from when it claims the sky, it brings a noontide of heat. The desert seems to have what Herman Melville called an 'emphatic uninhabitableness'.

The land seems to be without life, and yet the sands are marked with the prints of small grey lizards, while at night foxes come out to feed on the *Lipe*, a species of Thannus that grows in the wadi-like dry valleys. (They are as fond of these black berries as Aesop's fox was of grapes.) Overhead in the clear, often cloudless skies, there is an occasional blackened form, and a condor glides on the air-currents. 'These deserts have neither water, grass nor trees nor any created thing,' wrote one observant sixteenth-century conquistador, 'no created thing except birds which by the gift of wings wander where they will.'

Where the sand leaves off, rock begins. The whole 2,000-mile coastline is an infinite cumber of rock that has not tumbled in a generation. This distinct note of uninhabitableness begins south of Tumbes, below the line of 3° 30' south latitude, and continues with only occasional geographical contradictions to Coquimbo, which is in Chile, some thirty degrees south latitude; in all, 2,520 miles of desolation. This heat, intense enough to broil one's brains, would be unendurable were it not for the sea with its south-easterly winds. The Pacific rushes onto this desolated coast in huge, unhurrying rollers, agitated by, as it were, a sea within a sea. Driven by wind or current, current or wind, a huge sea of cold water, as wide as a hundred miles and forty feet deep, begins somewhere off the littoral of Chile, below the furthest extension of the coastal desert. This ubiquitous stream, the Humboldt current, brings up in its northern flow a rich and varied sea-life which is, in turn, fed on by many forms of seabirds, in

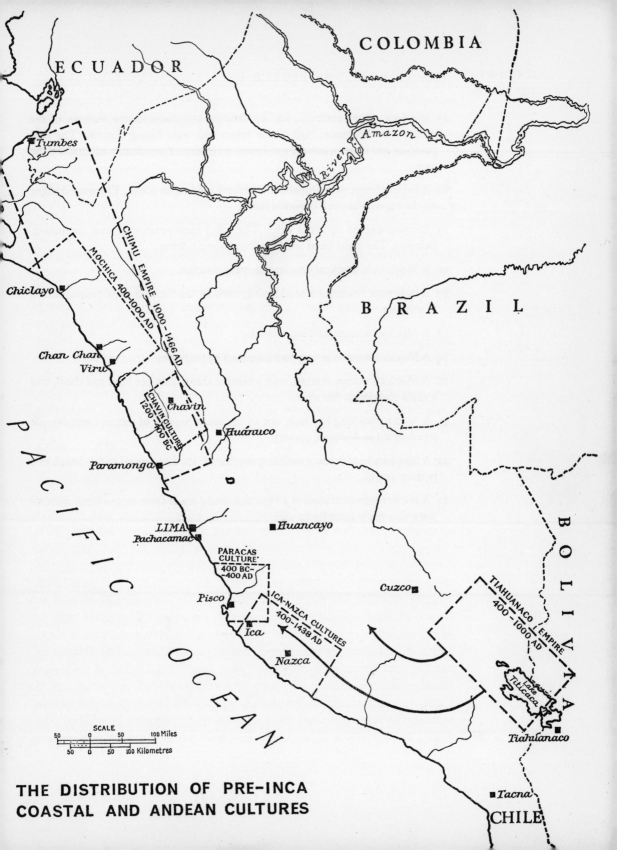

COLOMBIA

ECUADOR

Tumbes

Amazon

River

BRAZIL

CHIMU EMPIRE 1000 - 1466 AD

MOCHICA 400-1000 AD

Chiclayo

Chan Chan
Viru

CHAVIN CULTURE
1200 - 400 BC.

Chavin

Huánuco

Paramonga

BOLIVIA

LIMA
Pachacamac

Huancayo

PARACAS
CULTURE
400 BC -
400 AD

Cuzco

TIAHUANACO EMPIRE
400 - 1000 AD

Pisco

ICA-NAZCA CULTURES
400 - 1438 AD

Ica

Nazca

PACIFIC OCEAN

Lake Titicaca

Tiahuanaco

SCALE

50   50   100 Miles

50   0   50   100 Kilometres

THE DISTRIBUTION OF PRE-INCA
COASTAL AND ANDEAN CULTURES

Tacna

CHILE

THE LIFE OF THE PEOPLE I

13 Mochica effigy pottery *c.* 800 AD showing the characteristic features of the people – hooked nose, high cheek bones and wide flaring nostrils. The face painting and large decorated ear-spools were almost universally adopted by the men.

14 A pottery figure of an important dignitary holding an ocelot. The wave designs on the ear-spools are a common motif.

15 A round-bellied Mochica elder. The effigy incorporates unusual decorative painting. The right hand seems to be holding a drum.

16 A Mochica in a typical daytime sleeping position.

17 A 'wiseman' wearing a headdress formed by the feet and open-fanged mouth of a jaguar.

18 A Mochica woman holding a child.

19 A Mochica woman giving birth, assisted by midwives.

20 A Mochica woman resting, with a burden slung from her head and chest, and a child clinging to her skirt.

21 A woman washing her hair, one of the many aspects of simple everyday life represented in Mochica pottery.

22 A Mochica headdress resembling two hands, used as a motif in the design of a pottery vessel.

23 A pottery representation of a Mochica sandal made from *cabuya* fibre. Sandals were also made from llama skin.

15

16

17

18

20

21

22

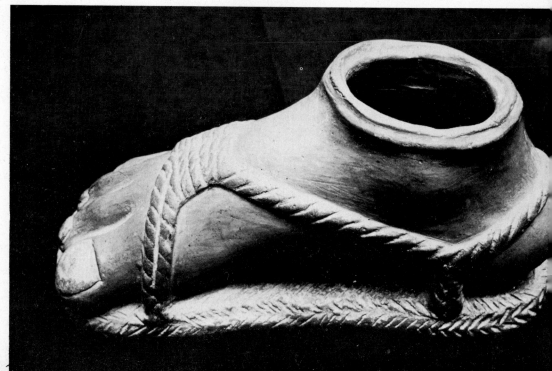

23

numbers so incalculable that at times they darken the sky. They nest on offshore islets, building their nests out of their own feathers mixed with their own droppings, which are the fertilizer, or guano, of commerce. All these phenomena – oceanic current, metazoan fauna, fish birds – have formed into a symbiosis which helped to create this environment for man.

When the sun sets over the desert, it looks as if one were staring into the red-hot mouth of a furnace; yet by the time it sets, the cold night wind is already blowing over the desert. Refrigeration sets in rapidly, and the cold can be as piercing as it is in the high Andes. It is for this reason that one sees in the Mochica pottery figures with bundled heads, breathing through a cloth drawn up under the girdle of the head, so that all one can see are mask-like visages, staving off the cold of the night winds.

The desert is not all sun and hot sand-blink, since for at least six months of the year, that is, between May and November, the cold coastal current becomes colder, causing heavy fog-mists to rise. These roll over the littoral with an opaqueness that makes the days cold and grim. The saturated moisture hangs like unshed tears and increases the intensity of the feeling of cold; a haze overhangs the land during the day and at night hides the glimmer of the stars. Still, the moisture, no matter how slight, is enough to nourish the water-parched plants. Many of the larger rivers descend rapidly from the towering uplands and have cut deep V-shaped valleys; when they reach the coast, these flatten out to form oases. About these, man settled. *Huaca Prieto*, one of the most primitive mounds of the Chicama Valley, which became the centre of the early Mochica empire, shows that man was present as early as 3000 BC, and was cultivating such crops as squash, beans, chili-peppers, maize, yuca, and potatoes. Before 1000 BC, he was gathering the pods of the wild tree-cotton, learning to weave and laying down the social tribal pattern which in the end became his culture of cities.

It is naturally not all treelessness and heat on the coast. The early Spanish navigator who said, in laying down a direction to Peru, 'when you no longer see any trees in Peru, you are in Peru', meant it only as a general statement. There is considerable vegetation. Plants grow even in the rainless desert, under the protection of the *médanos*, immense sand dunes, half-moon shaped and often beautifully symmetrical, formed as they are by the prevalent winds; their convex side turned toward the wind force offers cover for vegetation. Plants that cover the desert are of limited *genera;* most are coarse-leafed branches which are fleshy and full of brine. Even in the *despoblado*, although they are first unnoticed in the overwhelming

33

C

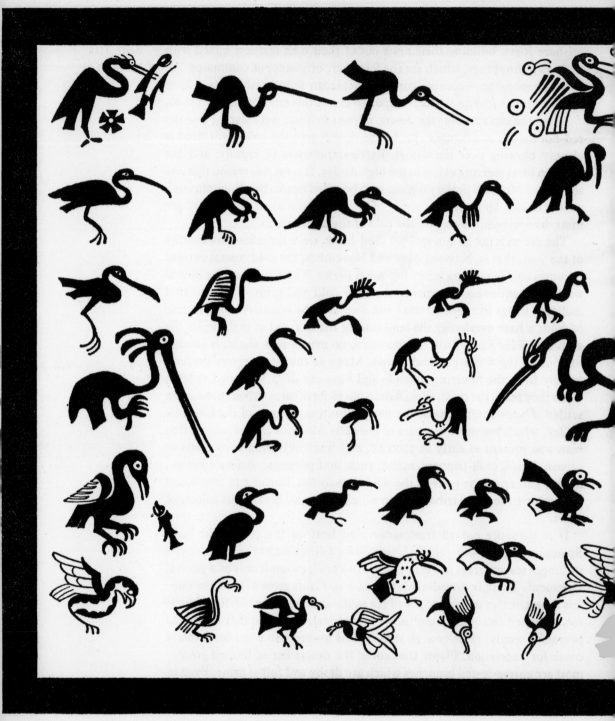

Seabirds and fish,
drawn from Mochica-
Chimú pottery and wall
decorations

35

immediacy of sand and desolation, there is plant-life. The dunes are often capped with the short spikes of the *yuca del monte*, an edible tuber related to the yuca which is cultivated on the coast and in the jungle. There grows here, too, a tuber, distantly related to the sweet potato. Low twisted trees, of scraggy growth, which produce a fruit called *zapote de perro*, always bend in the direction blown by the winds.

The *algarrobo* (carob) is the dominant desert tree. Its bipennate foliage something like an acacia, to which family it belongs, grows tall but never straight; its roots only slightly penetrate the sterile land, for taking too small a hold on the friable earth, it falls, reclines, and in this posture sends out additional roots. Older *algarrobos*, gnarled and twisted, have a fantastic appearance; from their wood the coastal people carved their effigies, taking advantage of the twist in the trunk to depict wrathful sprites of gods. A most useful tree, the *algarrobo* produces a fruit, the *pacai*, a long pendulous and flattish pod which is filled with flat seeds; these lie embedded in a sweetish, mucilaginous, spongy substance and are delectable, now as then, to Peruvians. As they are impossible to cut except with an axe of the best temper, the land is cleared of *algarrobos* by burning. They propagate in such masses that an early sixteenth-century visitor said, 'there are great stands of these carob trees ... so much as to be oftimes impenetrable ... On the Nazca road there are five leagues of these woods so thick that the Inca Highway is the only way to get through them ... one sees nothing but woods and skies.' The *algarrobo*, when matured, secretes a very inflammable gum-resin, which if lighted with a truncheon of wood on its windward side, will take fire and burn through in a few hours to an ash.

The high banks of the rivers are bounded by willows, and on the lower reaches by a tall-growing *vega*, a fifteen-feet-high sedge, from which the Indians obtained the basic material for mats and baskets. *Paico*, a strong-smelling grass, grows here, plus a limited amount of other shrubs and low trees. In these verdured, hot valleys the cicada tingles the ear with its shrillness, from its vantage point in trees which look from a distance like evergreen holly – the *Lipe*, on whose edible black berries foxes feed at night. In the northern part of the coast, that is, the hinterland and eastward, out of the influence of the sterile immensity of the Sechura Desert, trees grow to impressive proportions. Cacti, branched like trees, stud the hills, and when the land height increases to over a thousand feet, the vegetation becomes dense, dominated by the majestic *ceiba*, with spined trunk and brilliant flowers which yield a cotton-pod that has fibre as fine as silk. All of the twenty-four river oases which lay along 600 miles of desert coast, and

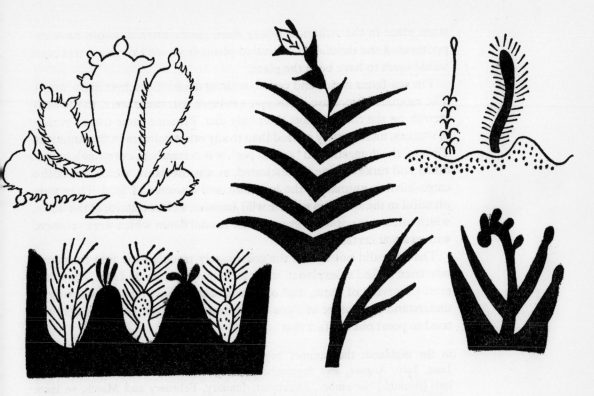

Desert plants, including the edible cactus and, top centre, the cabuya plant from which rope was made

which formed the Mochica-Chimú empires are of a superficial sameness, reminding one of what Charles Doughty said about the carcass of the planet: that it is alike everywhere; it is but the outward clothing that is diverse. The gift of rain, or its absence, makes these valleys differ considerably due to the volume of constancy of the descending rivers on which all depends.

There were many inducements for human settlement and the development of human culture. First, there were the alluvial-rich valleys, refertilized like the Nile Valley with a perennial overlay of silt brought down by the rivers. Then, although cool at night (and in the south, six months of the year generally overcast), the weather was mild and temperate, allowing an almost constant growing season; two or three annual crops of maize was the norm. Also, guano, the most concentrated fertilizer in the world, lay accumulated in almost glacier-like proportions – 160 feet in places – on islets off of the shore, reachable by the totora-grass boats. If there is any

37

other place in the Americas where man, newly arrived, might have experimented and developed cultivated plants from wild varieties, this coast would seem to have been the place.

The sea-fauna is rich and varied, without doubt the richest in the world. The mounds of mollusc shells give evidence that these were, to the early arrivals on the coast, almost their only diet. Proteins came from a variety of sources, more variety offered than to any other cultures in the Americas. The *cui*, the domesticated 'guinea pig', was certainly in everyone's house; ducks and turkeys were domesticated, as was the llama, which was both a cargo-bearing animal on the hot coast and a source of food. Deer were plentiful in the north, as was the wild *huanaco*, a close relative of the llama, which often came down to graze on the coastal llanos which were verdured with grass at certain times.

That rain did not fall on the coast sorely troubled the first Spaniards who tried to find an explanation for it. Pedro de Cieza de León, one of the most observant of them, and one upon whom most rely when trying to understand the nature of Peru in the first part of the sixteenth century, tried to point out the fact that

in the highlands the summer begins around April, and lasts through May, June, July, August, and September; and around October winter sets in, and lasts [through] November, December, January, February and March, so there is little difference in the matter of seasons from our Spain. The fields wither when the time comes, the days and nights are nearly equal, and when the days grow somewhat longer, it is around the month of November. But in these plains along the Southern Sea it is just the opposite of what I have said, for when it is summer in the uplands, it is winter on the plains, for we see that the summer begins in October and lasts until April, and then winter sets in. Truly it is a remarkable thing, this marked difference in the same land and a single kingdom, and what is even more extraordinary is that in certain areas one can come down to the plains wearing a rain-cape which is soaking wet, or, to put it more clearly, set out in the morning from lands where it is raining and before nightfall find oneself in regions where it is believed that it has never rained. For from the beginning of October no rain falls anywhere on the plains except for a light dew, which in many places hardly lays the dust. For this reason those who live there depend completely on irrigation, and cultivate only such lands as can be irrigated by the rivers, for throughout all the rest – because of its aridity – no grass grows, all being bare sand wastes and rocks, and the only thing that grows there are trees having very few leaves and bearing no fruit. Many kinds of thistles and thorn bushes grow, too, but in parts not even these, there being nothing but sand. What they call winter on the plains is only that there are very thick fogs, which look like clouds about to burst, and which let fall, as I have said, a rain so light that it hardly wets the dust. And it is strange that with the sky so heavy with clouds in this season of which I speak, the only rain that falls on the plains in these six months I have mentioned are these fine mists, and for days at a time the sun is hidden by these dense clouds. As the uplands are so high and the plains and coast so low, it seems that the former hold the clouds without letting them reach the lowlands. Thus, in the rainy season it pours in the uplands, and none falls on the plains, where the heat is very great. And when the dews I have mentioned fall, it is in the season when it is clear in the uplands and does not rain there.

Another strange thing is that the wind blows from only one direction along this coast, from the south, and though elsewhere it is damp and brings rain, that is not the case here. And as it encounters no contrary wind, it blows uninterruptedly along the coast almost to Tumbas. From that point, it rains and there are high winds with heavy downpours. We can give no explanation of the foregoing; the fact remains that, as we see, from four degrees south latitude to beyond the Tropic of Capricorn this region is arid.

Another noteworthy thing is that below the line in these regions, some are hot and humid, others cold and humid. But this part is hot and dry, and once one emerges from it, it rains on all sides. This I can state because of what I have seen and observed; whoever can find the reasons for this should put them forward. I merely state what I have seen, nor do I understand more than I have said.

Cieza de León, it should be pointed out, was the first human geographer of these lands, and he described what he saw with exactitude, for as he says of himself, 'I have observed all these things with great care and diligence.' His personal history was a mystery until recent times, but it has now been established that he was born in 1520 in the Villa de Llerena, near the border town of Badajoz on the outer edge of Extremadura province, that harsh and sterile land which gave the New World so many of its hard-bitten conquistadores. He sailed to South America at the age of thirteen as a page to a knight, and arrived at Cartegena de las Indias, which is now Colombia, in 1535. Almost all that we know of the early history of the tribes of Colombia comes from Cieza; he was the first to make a methodical study of the Inca realm and to distinguish between the various tribes within it, pointing out distinct forms of customs, manners and dress. Cieza is not only the best authority, noting each thing down without the bias which was typical of his time, but he was also one of the earliest writers; only a few books about this part of America were published before his. He left Peru on the 18th September, 1550, 'when he was thirty-two years old, having spent seventeen of them in these Indies'. Back in Spain he married

39

24 A vessel with a stirrup cup arrangement of the handle and pouring device is often the setting for Mochica effigy pottery. This example is typical of thousands of pots of this kind that have been uncovered.

25 One of the most amazing features of Mochica-Chimú pottery is the candid and frequent portrayal of sexual themes. Here the potter has modelled the crouching figure of a man in the shape of the male sexual organs – the penis forming the head and body, and the knees the testes.

26 Sodomy was widely practised by the Mochicas and Chimús and is often portrayed in their pottery. Here a man sodomizes a woman as she lies between her sleeping parents.

27 A Mochica pot showing the woollen or cotton ponchos worn by the people. The opulence of the dress reflected rank.

28 Mochica pottery depicting sexual intercourse.

29 A frank representation of the sexual act.

30 A man caressing the breast of a woman while she suckles a child.

31 A Mochica vase showing the practice of sodomy between a man and a woman.

32 Another position of sodomy.

33 and 34 Two Mochica vases depicting *fellatio*. Judging by the frequency with which it is portrayed, this practice must have been fairly common.

24

29

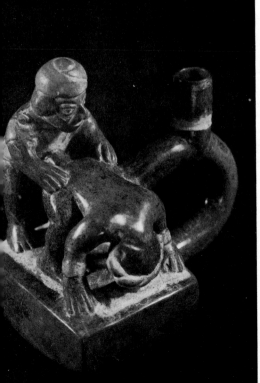

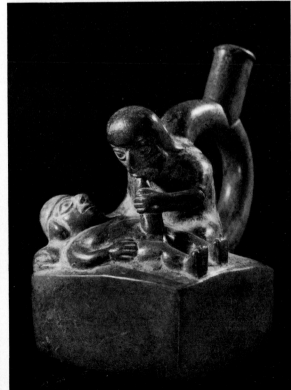

and began to publish his eight histories. The first of these was issued in 1553.[1]

The climatic conditions described by Cieza de León seemed equally remarkable to José de Acosta,[2] the very astute Jesuit who travelled in Peru in 1590. He found that, 'as at Lima and on the Plaines they find the … windes troublesome and unwholesome … yet it never rains … a wonder of

A drawing copied from
a Mochica vase showing
plant and animal life

Nature, never to raine upon that coast and ever to have one winde [from the south] without giving place to his contrary.' The climatic explanation of why rain generally does not fall on the coast of Peru and northern Chile is two-fold. First, geographically, the rainladen south-east trades blowing across Brazil strike the high cordilleras, and the rains fall into the Upper Amazon; the winds, pre-emptied of rain, tumble down on the Pacific coast as cool, dry winds, and reach the ocean again before they can be recharged with vapour. Then, meteorologically, the coast is cooled by the

41

strong northern-moving Humboldt Current, as wide as 150 miles. The cold current (which averages 58°) lowers the temperature of the air that moves across it, and since its capacity for heat exceeds that of the air, rain almost never falls.

Whatever the contradictions – the cold stream within a tropical sea, the lack of rain, the desert, the symbiotic relation of sea-fauna to birds, with the latter's nesting on islands and thus creating guano – all this formed what may be considered, in those primitive times, a virtual paradise. What was lacking in their tribal economy – copper, gold, tin, silver, certain woods, exotic feathers and Andean-grown products different from their own – they could have through their extensive trade-routes, of which there were more than five principal ones within their realm. Although there is no climate that does not have its inconveniences – torrential rains falling at rare intervals and earthquakes – still, the land of the Mochica-Chimú approached the paradisical more closely than any other area in the Americas.

THE APPEARANCE AND HABITS OF THE PEOPLE

'Yuncas' was the broad, general term used by the Incas for all people who lived in the hotlands; yet since those who lived in the jungles were also 'yuncas', the conquistadores, to differentiate between them, called these the 'coastal yuncas'. As Pedro de Cieza de León wrote: 'And as in the course of this work I shall often have to refer to the Incas and also the Yuncas, I shall now explain to the reader what Yunca means ... that the towns and provinces of Peru are situated ... many of them in valleys formed by the Andes Mountains and the snow-covered highlands, and all the inhabitants of the uplands are called mountaineers, and those who live on the plains, Yuncas. In many parts of the sierra where the rivers flow, as the sierras are very high, the plains are sheltered and temperate, so much so that in many places it is hot, as it is on these plains. The people who live there, even though they are in the sierra, are known as Yuncas; and throughout Peru, when they allude to these warm, sheltered regions that lie among the sierras, they say, "It is Yunca", and the inhabitants have no other name, even though their settlements and regions have names. Those who live in the regions ... and dwell in these plains and coastal regions of Peru, are called Yuncas because they live in hot country.'

The time of their first appearance on this coast is unknown, yet, as mentioned previously, at least one date can, with some certainty, be seized upon: it is known that at *Huaca Prieto*, at the mouth of the Chicama Valley,[3] man was living as early as 3000 BC. He lived then in semi-subterranean rooms made of sun-dried brick. The inhabitants did not agree with one another as to their origins, and were as confused as archaeologists are today. The most northern tribes, the *tallanes*, claimed that they were of Andean origin; the same belief was held by the *olmos* further south. Still farther south, in the valley of Lambayeque, near to the original lands of the Mochica, were the yuncas, who said that they came with King Ñaymlap from the north[4] on a fleet of balsa-rafts. He brought his harem, controlled by his wife, Ceterni, court attendants, and with this, *Yampallec*, a green stone idol. Historical truth is not harmed by such folk-tales. Even Livy, when discussing the questionable origins of the Romans, wrote that there is a 'privilege of antiquity to mingle divine things with human so as to add dignity to the beginnings of cities'. However, this mytho-history is far too sophisticated to explain the origin of the coastal yuncas. It is fully probable that the peopling of the coast was perpendicular, that is, moving down from the Andes, for there are ancient and seemingly timeless trade-routes between llano and cordillera; it was also horizontal, that is, wandering from one fluvial oasis to another.

Much as their languages differed and certain cultural traits varied, due to the isolation of tribes in their own narrow corners by the intervening desert, basically the coastal yuncas had a superficial sameness. These coastal yuncas' tribes were organized on congenerical kinship. The unit was the clan, each clan having a totemic name, and these clans made a tribe, bound not so much by land-holding as by blood-ties. Religion was homogeneous and belief animistic; everything in their world, animate or inanimate, was alive, sentient, wilful. Gods, the good and the bad, had to be propitiated, and art-crafts, when they evolved, became dedicated to the metaphysics of this theology, which in these lands was known as *huaca*. *Huaca* was as magical and mysterious as the *numen* of the Romans; *huaca* was a tomb, a pyramid, a natural feature of the land; all worship was *huaca*, and all the dead became *huaca*. It was 'a primordial synthesis in which the conceptual differences of content has never been made analytically distinct.'[5]

The tides of Peruvian cultural inheritance ebbed back and forth between the coastal tribes and the mountain peoples until that which had been the exclusive cultural property of one tribal kin became the cultural currency of all. The Mochicas, who appeared with reasonable certainty about 300 BC,[6] were the inheritors, as most cultures are, of those who preceded them. The earliest of these was the Chavin culture, its leit-motif being an open-mouthed puma, with teeth rampant: the cat-god demon which was to haunt the cosmology of Peru for the next thousand years. This was followed by the Cupisnique,[7] a coastal culture with considerable affinity to the mountain-dwelling Chavins. Another people, without name and called for classification purposes 'Salinar',[8] appeared next, and in the modelling of their ceramics are clearly enough the precursors of the Mochica.

Mochica man, as he pictures himself in his own iconography, was short, thickset, and graced with a longish, dolichocephalic head – a normal head unless distorted by artificial flattening. Their skulls – and there are many extant – which the desert has preserved for thousands of years because of the preservant qualities of the desiccating sands, show that their teeth, like those of most grain-eating peoples, were excellent and usually devoid of cavities. We have an exact and precise knowledge of their faces and general appearance because of the thousands of portraits left to us in their effigy pottery. These portraits have a high level of realism, in which every facial characteristic is shown. The face is round, with high cheekbones, and dominated by a hook nose with wide-flaring nostrils. The mouth is wide and full-lipped, and the dark eyes are almond-shaped and set into the face suggesting a slant, because of the epicanthic fold about the eye, which is, of course, one of the signs of the proto-mongoloid descent. There are a wide range of faces, old and young. Most faces are painted, and one might, from a superficial glance, believe that these are portraits of other peoples than the Mochicas. However, it is not true, as is suggested by the German archaeologist Ubbelohde-Doering (who ought to know better) that these variegated portraits show that it is most 'likely that the [Mochicas'] portraits are representative of the whole of Ancient Peru rather than of a particular tribe only'.

Mochica hair-styles are not clear, since almost all are portrayed – unless they are shown captured – wearing headgear of one form or another. Mostly, it seems, the hair was cropped close to neck length, and cut in bangs over the forehead. All men pierced their ears. A wooden plug was inserted, which was removed for war or festival and replaced by ornamental ear-spools: painted wooden ones for those of the baser sort, or beautifully hammered gold sets with gold, pearl or turquoise inlay if one belonged to the directing classes, for the size and sumptuousness of the

44

Designs of Mochica
face-painting

ear-spool was doubtlessly a status-symbol. In addition to the ears, the nose-septum, the cartilage tissues between the nostrils, was also pierced, into which many inserted a crescent-shaped, golden ornament which hung down to the lips.

Presumably, the Mochica skin-colour was, as it is now in their descendants, a light bronze, varying in colour, dark or light, depending on the place and the individual. However, the true skin colour was never quite discernable, since they invariably painted their face, arms, body and legs. Face-painting was general. No one has ever attempted to explain the pattern of the Mochica face-painting or the reasons for it – magical or indicative of social status – yet individual facial designs must run into hundreds of different patterns. The most common pattern, used by warriors, was the painting in either red or black of both sides of the face, leaving part of the centre of the face unadorned. In some, the eyes were encircled, and long black streams suggested the tear-stains of the 'Weeping-god'. Others made what the early Spaniards thought to be a cross, a cross-bar extending from the top of the head to the chin, and many painted their faces so that the curving lines about the lips and chin resembled beards. A not uncommon design is that of a man, sitting cross-legged, with a 'painted moustache', such as was sported in reality by Chinese mandarins (this has often been grasped at by those who wish to prove a trans-Pacific contact in historical times with Asia).

Face-painting indicated caste, the mark of rank; designs may well have been the equivalent of an escutcheon, as is true of many, if not most of the Amazon Indians. Designs were symbols, yet symbols that were not just something figurative, but very real. As with masks (when an Indian wears a mask of a god, he *is* that god) when a red dye is used as a blood surrogate (for smearing the body with blood has as its aim the increasing of the vital principle of life), then that red dye *is* blood. The Mochicas used, as most, the juice of the plant called *genipa*, which turns blue-black; red was obtained from the berry within the husk of the achiote. The brush was usually a spatula made from a river-reed. Women in many American tribes were, and are, the face-painters.

What was the object of Mochica face-painting? It might reflect on the Mochicas, because 'face-painting confers upon the individual his dignity as a human being; it helps him cross the frontier from Nature to culture, and from the mindless animal to the civilized man. Furthermore, it differs in style and composition according to social status and thus has a social function.' Face-painting was, too, a clan index, since, like most Peruvian tribes, the Mochicas were arranged in a sort of social pyramid, in which the common man, who formed the base, belonged to a sort of earth-cell (the Incas called it an *ayllu*). Land was held collectively by a group or clans related by blood ties. Each had a totemic device – circle, square, animal-head, fish – and if the Mochica vases are minutely studied, it can be discerned that the designs of face-painting are often repeated in ear-spools, on lances or clubs, or even on their shields.

Like most American Indians, the Mochicas had little facial hair, and that which appeared was plucked out; the presence of silver and copper hair-pincers in graves provides evidence of this fact. However, older men

did have straggling hairs, which, with the indifference to personal appearance usual in old age, they probably made no attempt to remove. There is
also in Mochica pottery a mysterious figure of an old man who is bearded
and unpainted. This old man is represented with full white moustache and
broad 'imperial'. His ear-spool decorations are invariable, a motif which
suggests a wave design. If one is to assume that all else represented in their
pottery is of their lives and realistically displayed (except in the sententious
variations of religious themes) – food, sexual positions, costumes, animals
– then what is the reality of the bearded man? What was he?

Mochicas dressed for the climate. This climate, it must be remembered,
was not just hot desert; it was also wind-blown, and the cold of the night
winds caused a rapier-like refrigeration to set in. 'They all went about',
wrote Pedro de Cieza de León, speaking generally about the coastal yuncas,
'attired in shirts of cotton and long blankets.' The Mochicas also left us

A Mochica warrior with his prisoner

in their pottery a very detailed idea of how they dressed. The same Pedro de Cieza de León, assembled with many other knights of the royal army arrayed against Gonzalo Pizarro, spent some time at Tumbes in 1548. There he observed that 'their clothing consisted of a shirt [a form of poncho that looked like a foreshortened version of the Victorian night-gown] and a blanket; they also wore a head-dress which was a round affair, made of wool, and sometimes spangled with gold or silver leads ... known as *chaquira*. The apparel was woven from cotton ... of which they gather as much as they need in the valley [of Tumbes].'

The poncho was a colourfully woven garment, as shown by the designs left on painted ceramics, in which the ponchos are spread out so that the full design can be seen. Underneath, men usually wore a breech clout. As Cieza observed, 'the Indians and their women wear a kind of apron to cover their privities. On their head they wear a kind of crown of small beads which they call chaquira and some use them of silver and others of jaguar or panther skin. The women's dress is a blanket from the waist down and another covering them to the shoulders; they wear their hair long. In some of these villages the caciques stud or fill their teeth with gold ... when the chieftains died, they built a round romb with a vaulted roof, the entrance facing the sun, and buried them together with living women in their arms and other things.'[9]

The Mochicas picture themselves as going barefooted. The impression that they wore stockings comes from the fact that the men, particularly the warriors, painted their feet up to their knees in black. However, sandals made of cabuya-fibre or leather of llama or sea-lion have been found in graves. The focus of attention was the turban. It marked caste and social status. The ordinary man wore an unadorned turban, which was wrapped around the head and tied under the chin. The other piece was a long stole, which when wind or cold demanded, was wrapped about them to bundle up their heads. They breathed through a cloth drawn over the nose that gave them a forbidding appearance, with nothing more to be seen than their dark, robber-like eyes.

Man, amongst the Mochicas, was made for war. Youths grew up in the ceaseless wars between the valley oases or in the limited ones with the mountain-dwellers. The Mochica and the Chimú, therefore, were farmer-warriors, part of an agrarian militia. Each was a member of an earth-cell, a clan to which he belonged by blood-ties, and he wore the totem symbol of his clan on his shield, lance or helmet when he went into battle. He married young; he built his mud house by communal effort; he developed the fields allotted to him by the clan-holdings, communally; and he fought and died in the same manner.

Mochica women, naturally, were of a more delicate structure, although they are often portrayed as heavy-set. Yet the skeletal remains show them to have been very short and delicate, veritable 'Lolitas' in stature and not much more than five feet tall. They were, as the conquistadores found, comely, hard-working and, as their pottery reveals, libidinous. Their hair was long, cut in bangs over the forehead and braided with colourful woollen strands. Mummies have been found with the coiffure so described intact. They used cosmetics (which were often buried with them), combs, and silver ear-spoons to take out earwax; they also used silver depilatory tweezers and mirrors of obsidian or polished turquoise. They did not perforate their ears, but all wore necklaces. Unlike Mochica men they did not wear an elaborate headdress, but like them they went about barefoot.

They covered their brown bodies with a poncho, more delicately woven than the man's, except, said Cieza, that the coverpiece 'was full and wide like a cape with openings on the sides for the arms'. They married young, between fourteen and eighteen years of age. They had, one gathers from the evidence of graves and the pottery, many children, and apparently did not wean them until they were over three years of age. Among the Mayas, Bishop Diego de Landa found the women 'marvellously chaste', but a padre who was in Peru on a similar mission as Landa in Yucatán and was well acquainted with their Muchic language, told Cieza some things about the Chimús' (who were the Mochicas' descendants) sexual behaviour which made him gasp in astonishment: 'The women committed sodomy (i.e., anal copulation) with their husbands or other men even while nursing their own children.'

Women helped in the fields with planting crops and later harvesting them. They educated their children. They also spun cotton and wool fibres and wove most of the wonderful fabrics found in graves and tombs. Doubtless, they made the ceramics cast from moulds. They also made the intoxicating *chicha* liquor by masticating boiled corn, by which process the enzymes of starch were transformed into sugar, and then fermented into a beverage ('it is amazing', says Cieza in an aside, 'how much beverage or *chicha* these Indians can drink, for the glass is never out of their hand').

49

D

Monogamy was general among the lower man in both the Mochica and Chimú communities. Polygamy was reserved for the higher man of the directing class, of whom Cieza observed that 'they had many wives, selecting them among the most beautiful', which of course gave these members of the Mochica-Chimú harem a dubious ending, for the chieftains, when buried, were by custom certain that 'their most beautiful and best loved women' went with them.

There were monogamists in fact, but none of necessity. Even so, it remained the custom of the lesser man. With him, as with the middle classes now, a woman, since she consumed, was regarded as a persistent debit. It really depended on an Indian's wealth whether he had one woman or many. Among all peoples, even the primitive, poverty makes the sexes equal; polygamy is too expensive for one of modest means. Whatever the primitive reason, based either on tribal *mores* or economic status, monogamy was the rule; severe punishments were meted out for those who disregarded it.

Children were born with the aid of a midwife. Their 'speaking' pottery shows a woman being delivered of her child; the midwife stands behind her and presses on her stomach, while another is on hand to sieze the child's head. Various unguents and other primitive *materia medica* are shown in boxes. Woman is treated tenderly in much of the pottery; she is shown nursing her children, washing her hair, making bowls of the intoxicating beverage, *chicha*. A woman had nearly equal rights with man and did not follow the traditional idea that she was mere chattel. Women, in fact, in the coastal yuncas often became leaders of tribes; Pizarro, in his first visit to Peru, in 1527, when near Santa, was visited by an 'Indian woman of rank, followed by a numerous train of attendants of such power that she gave him several men of her tribe as hostages in order to exhibit her sensitive apprehension of her guests'. Divorce was possible, usually by repudiation, but when death ended marriage, the widow had either to wait for a considerable length of time or enter into a levirate marriage with her husband's brother.

The sexual life of primitive peoples is closely tied up with the social life of the community, far more than in most civilized communities. So it is that the Mochica-Chimú pottery is in considerable part preoccupied with sex-life. Certainly the Frenchman who wrote that 'l'animal ignore la diversité l'accumulation des aptitudes; l'homme seul est luxurieux,' may well have had the Mochica-Chimú in mind, for little else disturbed both Inca and Spanish conqueror than the prevalence of sodomy among the coastal yuncas. The Incas, when they finally conquered them in 1460–1470, found most of them addicted to anal copulation, practising it with both men and women. Aghast at such 'waste of seed', for loss of children was loss of people, they regarded this practice as abominable, and tried to stamp it out by destroying families, even whole tribes. It persisted, nevertheless.

The prevalence of sodomy continued far into the seventeenth century, when the Spanish missionaries tried to put an end to idolatry. 'The Indians of these coastal valleys', wrote Padre Calancha, one of the Spanish priests who came to extirpate idolatry and who wrote a great deal on the lives and history of the coastal yuncas, 'are very inclined to sodomy and even up until today [1638] they are not free of this contagious sexual expression. Once they did it with men, now they do it with women. Today many hide their vice under the cloak of matrimony and they prevent human generation by this form of sensuality.'[10] The impact of this on the Spanish was first given full voice by Cieza, when in 1548 he wrote in a chapter of his book (XLIX) the following: 'Of the slightest importance these Indians attach to the virginity of their wives and how they were guilty of the abominable sin of sodomy.'[11] He had already observed that the coastal yuncas were more 'self-indulgent than the Incas'.

It is because of the general trustworthiness of Cieza that we can depend on his observations of the sexual habits of the coastal yuncas, especially since they were reinforced by the information given him by Friar Domingo de Santo Tomás, who spent many years in the yuncas and was the author of the first *Quechua* (Inca) grammar, published in 1560. As Cieza states, 'I set down what I saw … and what I learned from Fray Domingo. And it is true … and I have even heard some of [the yuncas] tell that before marriage the bride was deflowered and they sated their lusts with her.' However, what most interested Cieza, and shocked him at the same time, was the prevalence of sodomy: 'Despite the fact that there were women in abundance and some of them beautiful, most of them were given, so I have been assured, to the abominable vice of sodomy on which they greatly pride themselves.'[12] There are hundreds of pieces of mould-made Mochica and Chimú pottery which portray Mochica women taking great pleasure in this mode of copulation. The depictions of this position of love in Mochica iconography display a seemingly endless array of variations. In some, the woman assumes a position on all fours, then on her side, then again while she is nursing her child. In others, she bends forward, with only her turbaned head touching the floor. Yet, no matter what sodatic position is being illustrated, the potter is forcibly conveying the impression that it is sodomy which is being performed, and not the normal act of love.

This form of sexual mechanism seems to have been widely spread from Ecuador down to and through Peru. On the isle of Puna the Indians had 'certain youths attached to the temples from childhood so that at the time of sacrifices and solemn feasts the chieftains and other men of rank could indulge in the cursed sin of sodomy'. His informant, Fray Domingo, assured him that it occurred in the mountains also: 'In each important temple or house of worship they have a man or two ... who go dressed in woman's attire from the time they are children, speak like them and in manner, dress and everything else imitate women ... and on holidays they have carnal and foul intercourse especially with the chiefs or headmen.' What Cieza could not quite comprehend was that 'they were religiously inclined to it'. However, since ritualistic sodomy, like female temple-prostitution, was venerable throughout the Arab-Hindu world and elsewhere, its occurrence among the Mochica-Chimú was neither new nor unusual. The Koran did not condemn it as severely as the Old Testament, and hence the intense reaction of Pedro de Cieza. The Persians thought it derived from parental austerity; only Zoroaster agreed with the Incas that 'it is a loss of seed'. This, if no other, was the reason for the intense reaction of the Incas' governors, who destroyed masses of yuncas because of this practice. Lazy people, bachelors and sodomists were enemies of the state.

Few people have left for posterity so graphic an example of their sex-life as the Mochica-Chimú. The positions of love, the sophistication displayed during it, and the wide play of the imagination to conjure up new luxuria are extraordinary. The parade of their sexual aberrations in their pottery seems endless; moreover, one cannot call it pornography, since its function, as it was buried with the dead, was to chronicle their lives. There is only one other group of sculptures to which the Mochica-Chimú works might be compared, and these are the stone carvings of the Hindu in Khajuraho and the Sun Temple at Konarak. The Mochicas grew up, as did other American cultures, in splendid isolation; that their expression of luxuria is no less fantastic than the Hindu shows how innately original the human brain can be. Certainly, the Mochica was not the first of the coastal tribes to picture sexual themes; the same appear in Chavin, Gallinazo, Salinar and Viru pottery, of which tribes the Mochicas were the cultural heirs. But none of these equal the realism and vividness of the Mochica work. It has all the *acide* of great art.

Another interesting feature of Mochica erotic art is that the woman was the sex-historian of the tribe: she was the potter. It has been generally accepted that potting, until the introduction of the potter's wheel, was, at the primitive level, a woman's industry, whether in Nigeria, Melanesia, or among the Pueblo Indians.[13] As most of the Mochica-Chimú pottery was mould-cast, a woman could perform these tasks at home in her leisure time. Also, since woman still remains the pottery-maker among all of the primitive tribes in South America, it becomes obvious, even more so by the attention to detail, that the Mochica and Chimú women were the recorders of their own sexual history.

As would be expected, there is considerable attention paid to the male organ; phallic appreciation, if not worship, is evident in many of the Mochica *huacos*. Of the 600 or more that form this section of the collections of Don Rafael Larco Hoyle in Lima, a considerable portion is given to the male instrument. In many of the *huacos*, the phallus (*tef* in Muchic) is shown in full tumescence, exaggerated, however, to an impossible size. The organs of generation, adored for their mysterious fecund power, are naturally a common motif in almost all religions. Among the Moslems, for example, the women addressed a prayer to the penis, offering it respect for the duty it had to perform, and Mochica women seem in their pottery to be doing quite the same thing.

The Mochicas seemed particularly unashamed at a display of their sexual appetites, for the Mochica women have moulded effigy ceramics which display the most intimate of their relationships, running the gamut of love's aberrations. More than this, though, these vases offer excellent details on habits. The position of love was always assumed on a blanket, one end of which was rolled up to form a pillow on which the woman rested her head. This was done when accomplishing the act in a normal position. They are mostly depicted in their pottery as performing the act of love in the nude; in other instances, however, they are under a colourful blanket which has been thrown over them, but which still reveals the sexual organs. These *huacos* are a veritable *kamasutra*, that is, manual of love precepts. They show a young boy mounting an older woman; an elderly man, obviously so since the potterer has put deep lines into his face, is shown having coitus with a young girl. There are others that suggest multiplicity, two men with one woman. Then, a woman is shown pleasuring a man by means of onanism.[14] There is even a unique example, in the Larco Hoyle collections, of two women having a Sapphic relationship, which is one of the Lesbian forms of love.

If everything is proper in love provided that it is moved by the idea of procreation, then this sentiment is not overly apparent in the delineation of Mochica love; for how then are we to understand sodomy and the prevalence of *fellatio* (oral copulation)? Although it is not mentioned by Cieza, or any others who commented on the sexual aberrations of the Mochicas, *fellatio* was the most dominant form of sexual expression after sodomy, as evidenced by the fact that there are more variants of this form in the archaeological collections than of any other. It is obviously the woman who is the active partner in this act, for the potter has been very careful to make certain to the beholder of the *huacos* that she *is* a woman: she is easily identified by her hair, the two long braids which hang down her back to distinguish her from man. The man in these portraits sits back passively in a nobly assumed position, sometimes resting his hands on the woman's head or ears, or again in full prone position, while the woman performs *fellatio*. The pottery shows fully enough, furthermore, that this is not love-play that will eventually bring the two lovers together in normal coition; this is woman portraying herself in the performance of *fellatio* as an end in itself. This, in itself, is unusual, since most, if not all pornographic literature is written by males. (The classic of this type of literature, *The Memoirs of Fanny Hill*, was written by John Cleland in the eighteenth century.) Women, primitive or civilized, are not usually moved to display or record their sexual appetites, no matter how libidinous they are; generally, women maintain discreet silence. Yet here in this erotic pottery the Mochica woman reveals herself in graphic and intimate detail.

Although it is clear that sodomitic relations between Mochica men and women, as commented upon in the early *cronistas*, are archaeologically confirmed through the *huacos*, what is not confirmed is sodomitic love between man and man. This has been emphasized by the early Spaniards even more than the other; yet not in one single instance in all of the erotic pottery (with the one exception of the unique piece demonstrating Sapphic relations of two women) does one find recorded an act of homosexuality. Nor is there a single instance of zoophily, sexual relations between llama and man, recorded in this pottery. The llama, their beast of burden, is modelled in many different ways in Mochica and Chimú pottery: standing, lying down in his peculiar way, scratching his ear, even mating. But there is no record of relations between man and beast. Cieza was aware of this oft-quoted relationship, but he did not actually see what the theologians termed *mores bestiarum;* however, he adds, 'and yet I know that many rational men who know there is a God, heaven and hell, have left their wives and befouled themselves with mules, mares and animals which it grieves me to state'. Because of this assumed relationship between man and llama, a folklore grew up that this was the origin of syphilis,[15] which is assumed to be, and perhaps is, American in origin. Although such relationships are not represented, it does not necessarily follow that they did not occur, for the llama's most distant relative, the camel, is known to lend itself to this activity. A popular expression of El Islam has it that 'the pilgrimage to Mecca is not perfected save by copulation with the Camel', for to the Arabs, bestiality is at its worst mere peccadillo, to the Syrian a matter of taste.

THE 'AN': THE MOCHICA HOUSE

When the Mochica-Chimú married, he put up a dwelling within the clan, which was collectively built and was called his *An*-house. It was constructed of plastic mud. The base was fashioned of a fascine of wickerwork of branches from the willow, which grows along the larger rivers, or bamboo or sedges; these, in turn, were thickly covered with liquid adobe cement. Often houses were built of adobe blocks, which were sun-dried, not kiln-baked. The form of the house varied as to the family's requirements; some are pictured as rectangular or square, while the larger houses of the headmen or their deputies were a house-complex set about a courtyard. As Cieza explains, 'each Lord in this valley has his great dwellings with many pillars of adobe and great terraces and gateways and surrounding his house was a wide square.' Roofs were sharply pitched and thatched with *paico* grass and graced with elaborate roof-combs, which recall the temple structures of the Mayas. The roof was also covered with thick adobe cement and then with ashes, to absorb the light garua mist that falls in the winter months. This form of roof, grass-thatch covered with adobe cement, is still used in the Mochica-Chimú country of Jayanca and Motupe.

The Mochicas left a beautiful record of these domestic dwellings – they were one of the few American cultures to leave such illustrations[16] – in their *huacos*. As usual, they are done with so much realism that all of the variants of individual taste are indicated. The smaller houses for the most part had one entrance. There were no doors; presumably a heavy textile kept out the cold night breeze or gave privacy. Generally there were no windows, although houses are occasionally pictured as having them. Ventilation was usually acquired through vents on either side of the house, below the slanting roof, and always turned towards the sea to get

55

DOMESTIC LIFE

35 A pottery representation of the Mochica house or *an,* showing clearly how the ventilation slits were all turned towards the sea to catch the cool offshore breezes. This is an elaborate three-storied structure with typical painted decoration on the outside.

36 A simpler Mochica structure. These houses were built of adobe mud bricks.

37 A curious representation of a Mochica house with sloping roof. A snake is curled menacingly round it.

38 A Mochica vessel with a painted house and the head of a woman looking in.

39 The coastal yuncas cultivated many forms of fruit and vegetables in the fertile river valleys. A pottery representation of a type of cucumber.

40 The freshwater crayfish was frequently modelled down to the late Chimú period. This example also incorporates a monkey motif.

41 A Mochica figure of a duck.

42 The *cui,* or guinea pig, was an important source of food. It was domesticated early and recurs frequently in Mochica pottery.

43 A Mochica pottery vessel showing a deer resting.

44 and 45 The Mochicas' acute observation of animal life can be seen in these realistic representation of field mice and frogs copulating. Frogs, being a water symbol, were a favourite theme

37

38

41

42

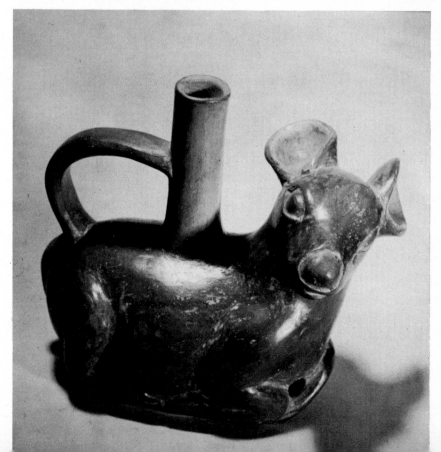

43

44

45

the full effect of the constant offshore winds. This invention of the window turned toward the sea, as with portholes on ships, to re-direct air-wind into the room, is one of the interesting features of their domestic architecture; further, it was adopted by colonial and republican builders throughout Peru. The houses were vividly painted; many, even those of the lesser-men, had murals of the owner's own fancy or fantasy painted about the walls. Since rain virtually never falls on the coast, the mudhouses, when well looked after, were of long duration. (In Nasca, southern Peru, designs drawn on the desert llanos have left their impressions after 2,000 years.)

There is yet to be discovered a Mochica type-site. There exists one for the Chimú, which is Chan Chan, but thus far only the foundations of small unit Mochica houses have been uncovered by excavation. However, the existence of large projects such as temples, *acequiás* and wax earth dams suggests a rather large-scale concentration of human society, and the division of labour presupposes community. Still, the remains of large-scale Mochica villages have not been found, nor a capital such as Chan Chan. There are, however, innumerable Chimú city-sites, and from these, as well as the recently reconstructed ruin (contemporary with the Chimú) of Puruchuco in the Rimca Valley, some sense can be made out of the civic architecture.

The adobes of the Mochica-Chimú were mass-produced. Mud, preferably a silt, was dug out; thoroughly wettened grass was added to temper the mud; then the mixture was well trampled down and allowed to remain so until it became 'sour', that is, tempered. Still today, the methods remain unchanged. The adobe cement is shovelled into a wooden mould, the excess scraped off, taken out of the mould and sun-dried. A man could produce between three and four hundred such bricks per day, and a study of Mochica-Chimú adobes reveals the impress of the corrugated flattened bamboo on the brick, as well as the imprint of the maker's hands. The Mochica-Chimú house, simple and practical, adapted itself to the climate and the availability of materials, for whether a people used stone or adobe was a direct result of environment. In the open valleys the people used adobes; in narrow valleys, where stone was available, stone with adobe-cement was the medium; in the highlands, where good cutting stone was in preponderance, stone was used.

The interior of a Mochica house, judging from the materials they have left, was simple and expedient; in our terms, not overgiven to luxury. The kitchen was at one end; stones placed in the adobe floor became the hearth, and on it cooking pots were placed. Fuel was dried llama dung and hurango-wood, as hard as coal; the smoke drifted out easily through the ample areas of ventilation at the roof purlin. The restored adobe adminis-tration centre of Puruchuco in the Rimac Valley revealed that the Indians employed a raised mud-dais which served as a bed (*chadik*), and on this was placed the inevitable straw mat. The Mochicas and Chimús had pillows of ceiba-tree cotton, and, as they explain in their ceramics, made use of a cotton, or sometimes llama-wool, blanket (which is more than the Greeks used, since their cloaks served also as their bedding). Clothes were hung from pegs or deer-antlers driven into the wall; the festival clothing and personal adornments – ear-spools, earplugs, nose-disks, turbans, necklaces – were kept, as remains of these show, in solander-like, slip-case baskets. There were also elaborately carved wooden boxes for the same purpose. Mats were spread about the mud floor, and the cool, often cold, night air was kept out by a drapery hung in front of the door. In keeping with this bucolic atmosphere, much of their activity was carried on out-doors, when the clemency of the weather allowed.

In the courtyard about the house, which was decorated with ornamental trees and shrubs, the domestic animals roamed at random. Turkeys were bred, as were ducks and *cuis* (guinea pigs); the latter were raised in a darker corner of the kitchen, as they were an important food item. Deer, to judge by the frequency with which they appear in Mochica pottery, were then plentiful, and birds of many types fell to their pellet blowguns. Llamas were used to provide sun-dried beef (*charqui*), and, as noted previously, the sea yielded shell fish of varied forms and fish of endless varieties. The Mochicas also raised dogs, which were barkless and of medium size (*canis ingae*). 'For around their houses', wrote Cieza, 'one sees many dogs different from those of Spain, about the size of terriers ... called *chonos*.' These the Mochicas immortalized in their pottery.

Compared to their contemporaries in Europe, the Mochicas had a fairly wide range of foods. Maize, yuca, and 'a great many beans,' writes Cieza, 'and other edible roots, cucumbers, Guava trees which gave a good fruit were in abundance and planted about the houses, cassia, avocados, *caimitos* ... and in the woodlands of the valleys they grow *carob* beans ... in some regions they make bread of these carob[17] beans and they like it.' Fruits were many: avocado, pineapple, soursop, pepino, lucumas. The woman, as food-preparer, also had a wide range of tubers from which to choose, among them potatoes (which Cieza thought to be 'like a truffle and when cooked is as soft inside as boiled chestnuts'), sweet potatoes (*opoen*), and yuca. Beans (*pecke*) they had in many varieties; earth-nuts were widely planted, and pumpkin and squash (*chun*) were used in soups. Popcorn (*quersu*) was a favourite with them, and they even invented a special corn-popper for it – a flat ceramic with a narrow circular opening.

Maize, as one can gather from the botanical evidence of the graves, was their mainstay – as well as the subject of clay and silver amulets, where offered to the corn-cult. Their fields, when fertilized with guano, yielded two or three crops of maize each year. Maize was also cooked in a variety of ways: when fresh on the cob, it was *ers*; when boiled as hominy, it was *skinnec*; when eaten with chile-pepper, it was *sollermsay*.

The large variety of fish yielded by the sea, which the men harpooned or caught in nets, were augmented by shell-fish, as evidenced by the whitish mountains of shell remains. The Mochica-Chimú were also provided with the richest of game and an abundance of cultivated plants, which were grown in the emerald-green valleys of the fertile river oases. All this, then, provided woman with a sufficiency of foodstuffs, so that, saved from the task of food-gathering, she had considerable leisure time.

Mochica man rose early (he read time by the stars, which he called *pata*), drank a portion of *chicha*, and then went off to whatever was scheduled for the day. If he lived near the sea, he fished communally with his clan. If needed for one of those gigantic public works – the mark of these desert kingdoms – in the erection of temples, roads, or an irrigational project, he laboured communally, too, performing the work-service which was one of their forms of personal tax. The basic occupation, however, was that of farming, and all, we may conclude, who were not of the directing classes, lent themselves to it. Women, when freed of the needs of the house, worked beside their men. They also brought their children, and even the inevitable baby, then as now, to the field, where it lay in the shadows until it cried to be nursed.

Children were plentiful, despite the loss of seed in consequence of their tribal preference for sodomy. The custom of naming them occurred, according to Cieza, 'when they were fifteen or twenty days old, names which they used until they were ten or twelve years old ... and then, or some earlier, they received other names'. Names were totemic: 'the names they give them and which they use are names of towns, birds, plants or fish ... and another called Llama ... and I have seen others called *Piscos*, which is the name of a sea-bird. Some are very proud of bearing the name of their father or grandfather. The Caciques and headmen pick names to their taste ... These Indians considered it an ill omen if a woman gave birth to twins, or if a child was born with some defect, such as six

59

fingers, or something of the sort. And if a woman brought forth twins, or a child with some defect, her husband and she took it very hard, and for-swore pepper with their food, and *chicha*.'

The custom of receiving the coming-of-age names was similar to the Incas' *rutuchicoy*: 'The child was not named until it was weaned ... The name giving was part of an elaborate ceremony, called rutuchicoy, "hair cutting". ... *Inca* names referred to animals the qualities of which were admired, and to natural objects, places, or abstract qualities. A man might be named for his father or grandfather ... He might acquire a nick-name such as "weeper of blood", stone-eye ... [men might be called] tobacco ... haw ... puma ... Women's name were ... star ... egg .... gold ... coca."[18] Cieza says of the Mochicas that at 'ten or twelve years old ... they received other names. When this was to be done, ... most of the relatives and friends of the father assembled, and danced ... and drank, which is their favourite pastime; and when the celebration had come to an end, one of them, the oldest and most respected, cut the hair of the boy or girl who was to be named, and the nails which, with the hair, were carefully put away.'

The training of the child was in the hands of the parents and was effected by instruction and mimicry. There is no evidence to the contrary, for while the realistic ceramics do provide much information, none of the subtleties of child-rearing are given. Neither murals, cast pottery, nor painted pottery supply such information as is found, for example, about the natural life-history of an Aztec growing child in the *Codex Mendoza*, wherein, through graphic Aztec pictographs and Spanish script interpretations, we are given information as to birth, education, punishment, work, and even the maize-cake food allowance for boys and girls. The Aztec clans also supplied a learning of a sort, a school where an old man or well-known warrior taught fighting tactics, rituals and a sort of mytho-history.

LANGUAGE

Despite the lapse of time between the Inca invasion of the Kingdom of Chimor (1466) and the Spanish invasion (1527), Muchic remained the spoken language of the Mochica-Chimú territory. As the Incas wished to be known as the bearers of culture, maintaining that tribes before them were uncultured, their usual practice was to purge systematically a con-quered people of all their tribal memories. After each conquest, they sub-jected the vanquished to a 'sort of editing and selective distortion not entirely unlike the tendentious distortion to which the Spanish themselves subjected Inca history in their turn'.[19] However, because of the civil wars between Atahualpa and Huascar for full possession of the Inca empire (1528–1533), the conquering Incas had not time to eradicate the speech and mytho-histories of the yuncas by their special techniques. Further, since the Kingdom of Chimor was the largest single empire they had ever absorbed, the Incas did not have enough time to implement this programme before the coming of the white man. Muchic, then, lingered on for centuries, and is spoken today in the small village of Eten in traditional Mochica territory.

It was because of the prevalence of idolatry and sodomy among the Mochica-Chimú that something is known of the Muchic language. When the Church discovered, in the middle of the seventeenth century, that idolatry was rampant and that sodomy was again in ascendancy, the crusading padres were sent into the areas once controlled by the Kingdom of Chimor with the purpose of extirpating these evils. More cultural history was destroyed by this act than perhaps by anything at any time since the conquest. *Huacas* and their contents were destroyed in a fierce path of religious zeal. It was similar with the Mayas. In 1562, in the town of Mani in Yucatán, Bishop Diego de Landa gathered all the Maya folding books that he could find, and since 'they contained nothing that was not superstition and lies of the devil ... we burned them all'. Yet Diego de Landa, in bringing about this Mayan *götterdämmerung*, wrote a small book, *Account of the Things of Yucatan*[20] (1566), which is the primary source of our knowledge of the then contemporary Mayas. The extirpation of idolatry among the yuncas brought about more or less the same result, for in the course of his destruction of native culture, Padre Fernando de la Carrera of Reque, in the valley of Lambayeque, wrote and later printed in Lima his *Arte de la Lengua Yunca*.

Three, perhaps four of the spoken languages of the yuncas evolved out of the same linguistic original. One, on the sea-coast, was a fisherman's dialect, which Padre Calancha called 'la pescadora'; its pronunciation, he allowed, was extremely difficult – something akin to the dialect of the Danish fishermen at Jutland, which seems to be understood only by themselves. *Sec* was spoken in the far north by the Tallanes, who were the first to have contact with the Spaniards. Muchic began in the traditional Mochica territory. Then, after the Mochica eclipse, the Chimú revived the Mochica language in a modified form, and spoke still another variation of the same speech; it was called *quingnam* and was spoken from the Moche Valley two hundred miles southward to what is now Lima.[21]

The dominant language at the time of the Spanish conquest was this Chimú, which had been imposed on all coastal dwelling peoples by their conquerors. Thus, when the Incas had, themselves, conquered the Chimús 150 years earlier, their interpreters had had to speak the language of the Chimú, which they called *yunca*.[22]

There remains, if one excepts a few Christian prayers rendered in it,[23] no known literature derived out of the Muchic or yunca language. In Mexico, several pre-Aztec cultures preserved some written evidence of their speech, which was rendered into Spanish. The Aztec literature is richest of them all, with texts transcribed by bilingual padres of the sixteenth century. There also exists a Mayan literature, and, to a lesser extent, one of the Incas. But of the Mochica, nothing exists, unless something lies buried in the Spanish archives.

It would serve little purpose to put down here the vocabulary as translated from *Arte de la Lengua Yunca*, as many of the words are scattered throughout this book. However, it is worthwhile to note the findings of one American scholar, who, on reading Carrera with care and detail, discovered that some fragments of the Mochica kinship system were preserved in their speech. These are listed by John Howland Rowe[24] as the following:

nofaen – man
mecherræc – woman, wife
ef – father
eng – mother
eiz – son or daughter
co cæd – aunt or older sister (man speaking)
uxllur – brother, younger sister, nephew, niece (man speaking)
nier – uncle or older brother (woman speaking)
chang – sister, younger brother, nephew or younger niece (woman speaking)
nang – husband
yquiss – father-in-law, mother-in-law, brother-in-law or sister-in-law (man speaking)
pon – sister-in-law (man or woman speaking)

He goes on to explain that

the terms for ascendants and descendants are the same for both sexes, but for collaterals they vary with the sex of the speaker. There is also a distinction in terminology between older persons and younger ones, and a tendency to class nephews and nieces with younger siblings. The system of classification seems to be roughly similar to that of Quechua, but with many differences of detail. Our information is not sufficient to justify conclusions about the social system, but it does not conflict with other suggestions that women had nearly equal rights with men – an interesting thought, as the position of women was theoretically somewhat inferior among the Incas.

While all this is important, it nevertheless remains that to interpret the Mochica-Chimú cultures, one must always return to their ceramics, which are clear and graphic, revealing a plastic alphabet. For this is a language wrought by hand, a hand far more effective than the human mouth; their pottery *is* in fact, their language.

AGRICULTURE

In areas where there is little or no rainfall, irrigation is inseparable from agriculture.[25] And since the Mochicas' and Chimús' culture originated in one of the driest deserts in the world, the system of irrigation they evolved – and it was a system – easily ranks with the best that existed in the Old World, at least until the appearance of the Roman Empire. There is, however, no such historical record of these engineering feats as exists in Mesopotamia, where there is a large corpus of written documents on baked clay; nor is there a record of the farmer's cycle, as exists in Egypt, where, since agriculture was their life, it was a favourite theme among artists.

The yuncas, lacking entirely the idea of the wheel, or even the concept of lifting water from one level to another by *shaduf* (that is, a horizontal pole with water-bucket, placed on a platform over a body of water, where, by counterpoise, it was raised up to the level of a sloping funnel, into which the water was poured), depended wholly on water conducted through irrigation channels which were made wholly of mud. In their conquest of the desert, by extending the natural limitations of the river-oases, they tapped rivers high up in their sources, and brought down the water in *acequias*, which followed the tortuous sides of the mountains which bordered the valleys. Often the *acequias* twisted and turned for miles (one of these 'miles' lying in a straight line would actually have equalled two). One of the *acequias*, called La Cumbre, was seventy miles in length, the water being taken out from the high level of the Chicama River. Another one of the most famous, because of its sheer mass, is in its lower passage 87 miles in length, eight feet in width, and six feet in depth. It has been calculated that to construct just this part alone, the Mochicas had to move 1,025,000 cubic yards of earth. It is one of the great masterpieces of primitive engineering.

Many of the civilizations that grew up and died about the fertile crescent in the Mediterranean and allied areas, where similar conditions existed as on the arid coast of Peru, brought their water from considerable distances. The Phoenicians,[26] whom the Greeks themselves considered to be the masters of water supply, brought water down from the mountains of Lebanon to the coast. Yet these were trifling distances compared to those covered by the Mochicas. One of the best-remembered aqueducts was built in 691 BC by Sennacherib to bring water to his capital, Nineveh. Even though it was reputed to be as wide as a road and paved with masonry, it was only fifty miles long; and this was considered one of the 'most impressive hydraulic-engineering works until Roman times'.[27] But compared with La Cumbre – seventy miles in length and beginning at 4,000 feet altitude and conducted to sea-level – it is less impressive. Thus, these primitive Mochica engineers can be regarded in an entirely new light.

There are no talking tablets among the Mochicas, as there were among the Assyrians, to proclaim such as the following: 'I, Sennacherib, King of Assyria dug the beds of three rivers in the mountains ... and I made their courses straight.' And, although there are countless ruined canals, many in fact still in use after two thousand years, there is no such map of them as the Mayas were said to have had, nor such as those which we possess of the Aztecs' water-ways. The Mochicas did not, like the Egyptians, have one river, but a half-score of them, and each presented a different hydrographic problem. All of these they met with boldness and considerable ingenuity. In one unique instance, the Mochica engineers in the Nepeña Valley, where the large ziggurat called Pañamarca is located, found in the upper valley a natural depression. They enlarged it, constructed a dirt-dam across it, diverted water from the river into it, and then distributed this water by means of their earth *acequias*.

The system of *acequias*, developed by a people whose material was mud, demanded careful design. The contour of the land, the level and fall of the conducted water, had to be carefully gauged. The water could not flow too fast, or it would erode; if too slow, it gathered silt, in which plants rapidly grow; if neglected, it would cause rapid deterioration of the whole *acequia* system. Since it was made of mud construction, the Mochica system was especially vulnerable to such pitfalls, and any neglect of canal-banks brought agricultural disaster. That parts of this system of water conduction survived far into colonial times and that some of them are still in use after a thousand or more years is sufficient testimony to the ingenuity that went into their conception. Because of this system of water supply, the Mochicas, then the Chimús, opened up arid areas which had never known plant life; they extended the river oases and built up their dry-farming by terracing. By building up the terraces, into which earth and fertilizer were placed, and by creating soil where there was no soil, they created an artificially balanced soil-community and made the exiguous surfaces of earth, rock and sand bear plants. A mere plan or photograph cannot give an adequate impression of the magnitude of this effort to those who have not personally seen it. These very skilful hydraulic artisans used to impound, direct, conduct and then distribute the silt-laden, unruly water into land where water had never reached.

'It is rather curious', questioned Dr John Rowe rhetorically, 'how reluctant archaeologists have been to consider the valleys of Chimor (or indeed any coast valley at all) as possible centres for the origin of Andean civilization. Certainly, compared with the high-mountain valleys or the rain-drenched Amazon forests they would have seemed a veritable paradise to the first inhabitants, and there are few places in the New World that offer such natural inducements to settled life.'[28] The 'natural inducements to settled life' were many: the richly-stocked sea; a soil which, provided it is watered, will grow anything; salt, which was easy to obtain from salt ponds; a reasonably mild climate, in which only four months of the year were overcast sufficiently to dull the glamour of the stars; game – deer, wild pig, guacunos, guinea pigs, turkeys, ducks, birds – all in full abundance; and, moreover, a land empty of any great number of people.

How the land was divided is not certain. If, however, the Mochicas followed the social tribal pattern which they did – and which the Peruvian, in particular, did – then their theory of land tenures was not different from the Incas', as given by 'El Inca', Garcilaso de la Vega. In this system,

each Indian received one *tupu*, which corresponds roughly to one *fanega* and a half of corn acreage, for himself and his wife. For each son he had the right to an additional *tupu*, and to one half a *tupu* for each daughter. When the son married, he kept for himself the *tupu* that his father had been given to provide him with food. The daughters, on the contrary, were not allowed to keep their share when they married: it either remained the property of the father, if he needed it, or reverted to the community to be allocated to someone else. Under no conditions, however, could a plot of land be bought or sold.

The land intended for vegetable growing was distributed according to the same principle.

The nobles, such as the *curacas*, for instance, were given land in proportion to the size of their households, that is to say, according to whether they had wives or

E

concubines, sons, or slaves of both sexes. This law also applied to the Incas, who thus had their own personal land holdings, in addition to those they received from the domains of both the king and the Sun, since they were all considered to be the brothers of one and the sons of the other.[29]

Within the ecology of his land, each coastal yunca was given use of the land by his clan. Man cannot think alone, and in primitive society he does not act alone; he acts as a group. The kin-group, the clan (the *ayllu*, in the Inca concept) is a holding corporation; as a clan, they disperse the arable soils. 'The bonds of kinship can be seen at work not only in the utilization of natural resources', writes Dr John Murra, 'but in exchange of human energy since anyone had ready claim to the reciprocity of his *ayllu* brother in the cultivation, irrigation and improvements of one's land.'

It was common practice among tribes of advanced agricultural communities, such as the Maya, Aztec and Inca, that the periodic reallotments of land were regulated by the size of the family. Each family received a certain specific allotment of land (among the Incas, as cited above, each received a *tupu*), which was enlarged with each new birth. When the family matured, the parents' land-allotment was lowered, and the new couple, the grown children, set up their own subsistence unit. It is not known for certain, but it can be reasonably presumed, that because of the constant interchange between the mountain and coastal peoples, the *ayllu* system of the Inca, which was collectivistic in principle, was, in fact, general throughout the coastal and mountain areas long before the advent of the Incas – although it was the Inca who codified, extended, and rigorously maintained it. As individual members of a clan, they did not own land; large or small, the commune was a social organization – in modern financial terms, a holding company – which administered the land, its fruits, its division and its extension.

Everyone, then, who belonged to a kin-group had an automatic claim to land, based not on any other merit than his blood relationship to a clan. Even those physically absent through war-duty, demented, or incapacitated – all shared in land, unless an antisocial act deprived them of their association with the clan. Such land division was common to most forms of theocracy, whether Peruvian, Assyrian, or Egyptian. When Herodotus made his way up the Nile in *c.* 300 BC, he noted that 'this king divided the country among all Egyptians by giving each an equal square parcel of land,' to which he adds, 'methinks that it is from them that the Greeks learned the art of measuring land'.[30] And of the Greek society, itself, Herodotus tells us that at Athens and in other Ionian cities there were annual celebrations which lasted three days, and on the last day 'grown-up youths were formally admitted as members of the *phratria* or clan'.[31] It is on this principle, then, that the yuncas distributed, organized and developed their land.

As already noted, the first coastal plants under cultivation were squash, peppers, beans. Maize arrived, at least in the coastal graves, about 1000 BC. We know that maize was the favoured plant of the Mochica-Chimú – particularly so since their beverage was made from it. It was Cieza de León who observed that maize was harvested twice a year. There were many varieties and for each the Mochicas had a name. They also cultivated the potato and one of the varieties of 'sweet' yuca (not the bitter yuca, which contains small quantities of prussic acid and must be grated and the poisonous juice squeezed out of it[32]). Beans climbed and entwined the maize-stalks. *Pallares*, which was evolved by plant geneticists into the lima-bean, was also a favourite, and has further speculative interest as being used for a possible form of writing among the Mochicas. As stated above, they also cultivated ground-nuts, camote, aji-chilipeppers, sapallo, squash, pine-apples, and pepinos, the last of which Cieza thought to be 'one of the most unusual fruits I have ever seen, which they call cucumber of excellent flavour'.

Fruit trees were also planted, though perhaps not in a systematic fashion, yet they did cultivate avocados and chirimoyas – which is a favourite with them in their pottery and which was represented so exactly that it seems that a mould was taken of the fruit itself. Also present were the *guanabana* and the *pacai*, the long, seed-filled pod derived from the tree *Inga edulis*, which the Mochicas depicted in their pottery and which is, as mentioned previously, one of the most common fruits found intact in Mochica-Chimú graves. In addition, they grew *granadillos*, *lúcuma*, and, in the humid, moist places far in the north on the upper Rio Tumbes, cacao, which when toasted and ground is our chocolate. It is certain that they cultivated coca, a tall shrub whose delicate tea-like leaves, when sun-dried, are made into a wad and stuffed into the mouth together with lime (to hasten the break-down of the leaf), where they release minute quantities of cocaine. Although the centre of coca-growing on the coast has not been located (it seems to grow best in the lush rain-soaked montaña on the eastern slopes of the Andes), it appears to have been present from the earliest times. The Mochicas have left us innumerable versions of themselves with cheeks pouched as a squirrel's, sitting calmly and dipping their lime-sticks into a gourd filled with powdered lime. Although Pedro de Cieza de León

67

did not specifically say that he saw the coastal yuncas masticating the coca-leaf, he does state the following:

Everywhere that I have travelled in the Indies I have noticed that the natives find great pleasure in keeping roots, twigs, or plants in their mouth. In the vicinity of the city of Antiocha [Antioquia in Colombia] some of them chewed small coca leaves, and in the province of Arma, other plants, and in Quimbaya and Ancerma they cut slivers from a kind of small tree that is soft-wooded and always green, and keep them between their teeth all the time. In most of the tribes under the jurisdiction of the cities of Cali and Popayan they keep leaves of the small coca I have spoken of in their mouth, and dip out of little gourds they carry a mixture they prepare, which they put in their mouths and chew it all together, and do the same with a kind of earth that is like lime. All through Peru it was and is the custom to have this coca in the mouth, and they keep it there from morning until they go to sleep, without removing it. When I asked some of the Indians why they always had their mouths full of this plant (which they do not eat, but only keep between their teeth), they said that with it they do not feel hunger, and it gives them great vigour and strength.[33] I think it probably does something of the sort, though it seems to me a disgusting habit, and what might be expected of people like these Indians. This coca was taken to be sold at the mines of Potosi, and everyone began setting out bushes and gathering the leaves, so now this coca is not worth anything like what it used to be, but it is still valuable. There are those in Spain who became rich from this coca,[34] buying it up and reselling it and trading it in the *catus* or markets of the Indians.[35]

The coastal yuncas did not have to resort to the slash-and-burn techniques employed through necessity by the Mayas; nor the methods of the Incas, where the fields were 'manured with the heads of sardines ... with a digging stick they dug a hole then put a sardine head and two or three grains of corn in each one'. Garcilaso explains that 'the fertilizers they used differed according to the region. In Cuzco Valley ... corn fields were fertilized with human manure which the Indians considered to be matchless for cultivating maize. They collected it carefully throughout the year, dried it and then kept it in powdered form ... around Lake Titicaca in the *collao*, where it was too cold to grow maize, the potato fields extended over more than one hundred and fifty leagues of land, which land was enriched with human manure.'

The coastal people, however, as previously noted, had an inexhaustible source of guano. Because of the system of water-induction, by which the natural river-oases were extended beyond their natural boundaries, and because of guano, they were able to extend their acreage by terracing the lower hills. Long lines of undressed stones were laid following the contours of the mountains, and each wall inclined inward, resulting in a series of horizontal surfaces like gigantic flights of steps. These were then filled with earth and revitalized by guano.

Guano was one part of the coastal cycle. First, it was the cold Peruvian current which was responsible for all the peculiarities and anomalies: the presence of the sea-fauna; the sea-birds; the lack of rain, and hence the presence of guano; and to end the symbiotic circle, the presence of man, himself. Dr Robert Cushman Murphy, in his classic study of South American sea-birds,[36] studied this strange life-cycle and the origins of the current. The latter does not originate in the Antarctic, as might be expected. A wind and current sweeps outward from the west and begins to find force off the coast of Chile, at 38° south latitude. It strikes the steep South American coast line, causing an upwelling of the deep cold waters, and this is then hurried at the rate of .3 to .6 miles per hour along 38° of latitude until the equator, where it makes a full turn westward and, increasing into 1.2 miles per hour, washes and agitates the Galápagos Islands, after which its force is lessened. This current, named after Humboldt who first called scientific attention to the phenomenon, brings up with it a rich metazoan fauna. These are fed on by the varied sea-life, which are, in turn, followed by millions of birds – Inca-terns, boobies, pelicans, penguins, and cormorants, which have followed this pattern for so long a period that, on some islands, their dung has been found to be as deep as sixty yards. The chief producer of guano is the *guanay*, the Quechua word for the cormorant; thus the word guano.

Guano owes its value as a fertilizer (it is over thirty times more effective than ordinary manure) to the manner in which fish in the alchemy of the *guanay's* intestinal tract react to the nitrogen content. The Mochicas and Chimús knew of it and used it. This is known through the discovery of Mochica potsherds in guano, mixed together with bird feathers and fish bones – all at a considerable depth, thus indicating that the men came out to the islet in their totora-grass boats, extracted the manure and used it. It was noted by Garcilaso de la Vega, in 1609, that 'the fertilizers they used differed according to the region ... along the entire coast, from Arequipa to Taracapa, which is a distance of over two hundred and fifty leagues, the only fertilizer used was that of seagulls, unbelievably numerous flocks of which were to be found there. These birds both large and small, live on islands not far from the shore, which are covered with such quantities of their droppings that they look like mountains of snow. Under Inca rule, the birds were protected by very severe laws: it was forbidden to kill a single one of them, or even to approach their islands during the laying season, under penalty of death.

The development of the valuable wealth of these islands was also subject to regulation, each one being assigned, according to its size, to one, two or three specified provinces. In the latter case, the zones reserved for each province were separated by rows of boundary stones which no one who had not the right to do so was allowed to cross, under penalty of death. Lastly, it should be stated that no one could take more fertilizer than was needed for his own fields from the island or plot allotted to him, under penalty of severe punishment for wastefulness. This, alas, is no longer the case today.[37]

With all these factors – water-conduction, terracing, an organized agricultural system, a rich fertilizer, a sun that always appeared in seasoned time – it is very obvious why the coastal gods of the Mochica-Chimú were less ferocious than those of the Aztecs and Maya, who found no other way to cajole their Rain-gods into giving the withheld gift of rain than to offer them a diet of human hearts.

3 Mochica and Chimú Crafts

. . . I do not see how beauty and utility are ever to be syn-cretized into a homogeneous conception. They are too antagonistic to coalesce. . . .

COUNT CALOVEGLIA in *South Wind*

POTTERY

SINCE 'the pottery of the Mochicas *is* their language', their ceramics are the best known of all the Peruvian pre-Inca cultures; first, because they have been so well preserved, and second, because of their realism. No other American culture, with the exception of the Maya statuettes from the isle of Jaina, Yucatán – or more to the point, the Tarascan cultures in North Central Mexico – have left so realistic a portrait of themselves and that which surrounded them as the Mochica-Chimú culture. Every detail of their lives seems to have been recorded. The flora of the desert and the cultivated plants are all depicted in their pottery; the fauna from the sea and the fauna of the land are so faithfully moulded that the species of each is identifiable. The Mochicas and the Chimús lived so close to nature that they had an awareness of all of the exhibiting characteristics of animals, particularly since a considerable part of their subsistence was determined by this knowledge. To this extent their ceramic art was picto-graphic, since there was a desire to convey information. In these sculptured animal forms one sees, for example, a *guanay* protecting its fledgling under its wing; in a moment of tenderness, a llama nuzzles its young, or is modelled scratching its ear. Deer and doe were favourite subjects, and the faithfulness of the modelling shows not only originality, but also the simple enjoyment of line and form.

While all early cultures maintained a totemic relationship with animals, few have left such sympathetic portraits of them. The Mochicas' attitude towards animals is much like that of the early Egyptians, for whom animals and birds also played an active and very vital role in the day-by-day business of their lives. The naturalistic animal portraits sculptured by the Mochicas speak for themselves; yet it is the tenderness, the affectionate manner of moulding or painting them that brings this art of the Mochica and the Egyptian together. The often-reproduced stone portrait of the

71

POTTERY

46 The vast quantity of Mochica-Chimú pottery that has survived is the chief source of information about their way of life. The different varieties of vessels produced by the Mochica potters can be seen on the side of this stirrup cup. On top is the figure of the bat god.

47 A corner of the Museo de Rafael Larco, Lima, showing part of the huge collection of pottery, wooden bowls and figures found in the Chicama Valley.

48 A fine example of Mochica effigy pottery.

49 Mochica potters were fascinated by animal subjects. An ocelot with fanged mouth, resting in a characteristic feline position.

50 A *guanay* bird picking at its feathers.

51 A Mochica hunchback. Midgets and hunchbacks were considered lucky and were often employed as court jesters by chieftains.

52 The monkey is a recurring theme in the pottery of northern Peru. Two pieces from Piura.

53 A pelican modelled by late Chimú craftsmen *c.* 1450.

54 A Mochica wearing a colourful headdress and ear-spools, holding up a woven poncho with spiral and step designs. Much of the information about Mochica weaving is obtained from pottery such as this.

48

49

51

52

53

54

Egyptian mau-cat does not surpass in quality the Mochicas' ceramic of the desert-fox, sitting alert and wily; the artist has caught all the characteristics of the animal that both amused and at times sorely tried these people.

Unrivalled in the Americas as a portrayer of animals, the Mochica artist applied his keen observation to all the animals that inhabited his world. The *cui* was a favourite subject, and the owl, which nested in cactus, also provided a theme of which the potter never wearied. Then there are also many variations of frogs, which symbolized moisture to the Mochicas. They were pictured in many postures, including mating, the position of which was represented with biological accuracy. In addition, they sculptured ducks, heron, *guanays*, and sea-lions – the last of which became, through the Chimús, a whistling jar: a doubled and connected pot with so accurate an imitation of a yelping young sea-lion that the mimicry was to the life. Snails, fish, sharks, molluscs and even octopi were subjects for pottery. The large conch-shell (*Spondylus pictorum*), which is found abundantly in the tropic waters off Colombia and Panama, but not in Peru, was much in demand, as the awesome sound which it emits was used to call down the gods. Since the Mochicas were unable to obtain enough of them, they made a ceramic copy of the shell, even reproducing the particular interior texture that provides the sound-throat for its trumpeting sound – an imitation so exact that only the weight of the ceramic dispels the illusion of its reality.

The jaguar and its lesser cousin, the puma, lived in the humid section, the high forested areas back of Rio Tumbes to the north, and, both alive and dead, were the subjects of a lively trade article. It is possible that they were made into household pets, since a figure of a man in a priestly head-dress and wearing ear-spools with wave-motif, is represented holding one in his lap. These large tropical cats are shown standing, sitting and occasionally, illustrating what superb observers of nature the Mochicas were, lying down with front feet turned back in feline-fashion. In an unusual hunting-scene, a Mochica warrior, using his shield for protection, is hunting a puma with a blow-pipe.

Hunting and fishing scenes were mostly painted on vessels. Hunting, as depicted by the artist, shows men accoutred in turbans that must have reflected rank, as hunting was usually a sport for the directing classes. These men are shown hunting in the same manner in which the Egyptians used to hunt deer: with dogs, attendants, and lassos and nets for capture. In like manner the Mochicas show themselves beating deer into nets and killing them with bola or spear. Their pottery also shows them hunting sea-lions with clubs (they knew that a sharp crack on the nose quickly

Step designs from Mochica pottery

killed the animal). In addition, there are many other hunting sequences in which birds are shown being killed with blow-pipes (whether they contained clay balls or arrows is not certain).

So precise are the representations of their houses that, even though time has obliterated the houses themselves, the ceramics left by the Mochicas give us a clear picture of them. Whereas the Mayas depict only *one* type of house realistically – such as that carved in the beautiful façade of Uxmal, as well as several others in the murals at Chichen Itza – the Mochicas have left a wide range of house-styles, as well as models of temples and fortresses. In addition, they have left behind not only actual artifacts, but also pottery figures shown using these same artifacts: a wooden club, for example, and a piece of pottery showing a warrior with this same piece in his hand; circular popcorn-toasters, both restricted opening and long-handle types, and figures represented holding in their hands miniatures of these objects. Weaving is yet another example of how instructive these ceramics are. Few Mochica textiles have survived, even in the dry desert; yet we know what the designs looked like because of the numerous vessels depicting men displaying their weaving so well that the viewer has a precise idea of the textile's design and colour. In addition, war-weapons and the headgear of warriors – warriors are always shown with their helmets and protective covering – are displayed with fervent attention to the decoration of an ear-spool, and soldiers are seen beating the enemies' heads with war-clubs. The means of transport by sea and by land are also depicted. Transport by sea, by means of their totora-reed boats, 'the little horses of the

74

sea', is presented in many different ways, sometimes moulded to show the small vessel or else painted with a high degree of fantasy or, perhaps, reality.

Ease and disease have an extended iconography in the Mochica pottery. Men with amputated feet are shown riding llamas, while on another vase a 'curer' is depicted trephining a skull with a tumi-knife to relieve the pressure of a dented cranium which presses on the brain. There are hump-backs and harelips, as well as a parade of figurines showing Mochicas afflicted with acromegalia. The representation of the affliction of *verrugas* (a warty disease) is so exact that it can be regarded as a clinical observation. In fact, the different types of diseases are represented so analytically that physicians experienced in tropical medicine have no great problem in diagnosing those from which the Mochicas suffered. And the same exactness holds for all the rest – house-types, temples, dances, drinking and drunks, forms of punishment, and a galaxy of mythological beings.

Of all these motifs, the sculptured ceramic heads are so conspicuous 'and so individual', says Wendell Bennett,[1] 'that they are properly called portraits'. There are heads with painted faces and headgear; there are old men with tattooed faces. Some emphasize ear-spools, or the hanging ear-lobe, which appears so grotesque when the ornament is removed, like the wattles of a turkey. There is one notable piece of an elderly man with a sybaritic face with several cascading chins, and there are so many others and all so highly individual that one is forced to the conclusion that they are intended as individual portraiture. These human heads are not a gallery of heroes; they are Mochica people: in labour terms, the rank and file. Nobles and members of the directing classes are also here, of course, but the bulk of Mochica portraiture reveals individuals, each with his own personal characteristic. It is neither a galaxy of kings nor images, for as they were mould-made – and collections often turn up with numerous duplicates of the vase – it is highly improbable that the head was moulded only for the grave or tomb of the person personified in the vessel. 'Possibly', says one scholar, 'purely artistic motives directed the creation to a large extent, if not entirely, as was true for the effigy vases where the bright and dark sides of life were represented with equal intensity and directness.'[2]

Yet despite these superb sculptural ceramics, by all standards the finest in the Americas and superior to almost all such similar creations in the Old World, only the simplest technical aids were used by the potter. The Mochicas, as well as their inheritors, the Chimús, used only a relatively limited number of vase-forms; the vessels intended for household use –

75

plates and cooking vessels – are also limited in form. They are made of thick clay and are decorated; still, they are utilitarian. The other forms, used mostly for burials, are of a fine thin ware, and feature a tubular handle (called a stirrup because of its appearance) which is at once both handle and spout. The form is not, however, Mochican. The Chavin culture, which antedated the Mochican by perhaps one thousand years, worked out this form; the Mochicas perfected it.

There are many sources of crude clay used in their pottery. The clay, worked as the Indian worked adobe, was tempered with grit or finely crushed rock, then was soaked, kneaded and pounded until pliant enough for shaping.[3] The bottom of the bowl was moulded by hand and was set upon a broken shard which was turned; the vessel took shape, grew and developed by means of long, cylindrical clay strips which were built up by alternately wrapping and smoothing. As already noted, most of the Mochica and Chimú pottery was mould-made, and many such moulds still exist. Fruits such as squash, chirimoya and potatoes were actually cast from the original fruit. Then, when dry, the mould was cut in half and reproductions made from this original casting. Moulds were of the same material as the vases but made much thicker, and prepared with a finely smoothed inner surface before firing. Spouts and handles were cast separately, which suggests mass production. This might well have been the case, although, unfortunately, unlike weaving, there are no illustrations of potters or their techniques. Once the parts were shaped and the two halves put together from the moulds, the joining line was smoothed down and the whole pot burnished, so as to reduce porosity; this was accomplished by polishing the surface by means of a rounded stone. The vase was then sun-dried, so as to allow a uniformity of drying throughout the vessel. It was then coated with slip, a product of the finer washing of the clay; this acted, in effect, as a sizing, on top of which the design was painted. Mochica colours were generally Indian red and a yellowish tint that looks like ivory in the finely cast pottery. Using brushes of various sizes, both broad and delicate, which were made from wild boars' hairs, colour was applied either before or after firing.

The Mochica 'methods of firing', writes the most experienced scholar in this field,[4] 'are not definitely known'. However, whether fired in the open, in a pit, or in some sort of vertical kiln, by using brushwood, grass, straw, reeds or llama-dung, temperatures as high as 950°C can be reached. While none of the higher American civilizations have left us illustrations of these techniques, as the Greeks and the Egyptians did – especially notable are the models from the tomb of Saqqara which show the entire operations of the Egyptians, complete with each detail, from potter's wheel to kiln – the techniques in the latter stages seem almost everywhere to have been similar.

The Mochica pottery was polychromic. The Chimús', which emerged from it, was almost exclusively black. 'The new culture [was] not a pure re-emergence of the old but rather a mixture. None of the technological techniques was lost ... They only differed in application.' Although many of the ancient Mochica themes are repeated, such as effigy portraiture and birds, the moulding is less sure, the detail is often lost and the colour is a lustrous black produced by excluding air in the later stages of firing. Yet in its way, this is fine pottery, and like their precursors, the Mochicas, the Chimús have left us a wealth of ethnographic detail in their pottery. Mochica polychromic styles were not entirely replaced by Chimú black, moreover, for as the authors of an Andean cultural history surmised, the invasion of the Tiahuanaco horizon to the coast – which supplanted and in some cases entirely liquidated the local southern cultures – did not extend to the valleys about Piura to the north; thus, as they also surmised, Mochica styles 'continued to develop locally, perhaps inspired by the residue of Mochica culture'. This was proven by the explorations of the Inca Highway Expedition,[5] through which these pottery collections were widely studied in the most northern section of what was once the Kingdom of Chimor. This pottery remained, until the Inca invasion and beyond, polychromic in colour and Mochica in form; in many examples there are admixtures of Mochica, Chimú and Inca style patterns. All of this pottery is, then, above all else, one gigantic, pictorial history of the desert kingdoms of Peru.

WEAVING

Weaving seems to have had an even older history in Peru than pottery-making: some of the oldest surviving fabrics in the world, c. 2500 BC, come from the north coast of Peru, in the heartland, in fact, of what would one day be the Mochica and Chimú tribal lands. Of all arts, textiles are the most fascinating, and yet, 'if we review the existing literature on the subject it is immediately apparent that proper investigation has only covered a fraction of the subject and that an intriguing amount of research still lies ahead'.[6]

For knowledge of the Mochica weaving, since time has destroyed most

77

Common
patterns of
Mochica
weaving
shown on
ponchos

of their textiles, we have to rely on the details furnished by the pottery and, as well, the contents of Chimú graves, where, as a consequence of appearing much later in history, there is a superb sequence of textiles and textile techniques. The majority of the textiles are not exceptional in design, though technically interesting in the use of double cloth and embroidery. The tapestries, however, are exceptional in quality. Of fibres they had a wonderful sufficiency. First, cotton: there was, it seems, as in Yucatán, an annual tree-cotton, a *Gossypium barbadense*, which was widely cultivated and 'of which they gather as much as they need in [their] valley'. There were two varieties of true cotton, brown and white, both of which are found in the graves. (Peruvian spinners today insist they can distinguish different varieties of cotton in a range of colours from tan to reddish brown.) The Mayas also had two kinds of cotton: an annual, which they sowed every year, and a tree cotton (*Gossypium herbaceum*). This latter seems to have been the original form of cotton. The Assyrians called it 'tree-wool'; it was grown in India as a tree, and the Greek etymology of the

78

word points to the fact that, so far as Eurasia is concerned, its origin was India.[7]

Besides cotton, there was wool. Although llama wool is known to be too greasy for textiles, it was used for braiding rope and for the making of brown sacks in which the llamas carried cargo. The coastal yuncas received alpaca wool by trade, vicuna wool by barter. The latter was the luxury item *par excellence*, for it has more than 2500 hairs to the inch and can be spun as thin as silk, while still providing the warmth of double cashmere. Cottons and wools were spun into such extremely delicate fibres that today they cannot be reproduced even by mechanical means. Three factors were essential in producing fine textiles: the fibre, the climate, and leisure-time. Fine materials cannot be produced rapidly, and the Mochicas' dominance of nature allowed them the necessary time.

The spindle whorl is universal; a spindle stick, ten to twelve inches long, weighted with a pottery balance, is all that was needed. And, although 'virtually nothing is known of the dyeing process', writes Junius Bird, it is known what colours were available: cochineal was widely used, purple was yielded by a bivalve, the *choncholopa*, and the weaving baskets from Mochica and Chimú graves exhibit weavers' pots with red mineral dyes, as well as blue, yellow and black. Their loom was exceedingly simple, consisting of two loom bars with the warp material tied from the lower bar, to be wrapped about the weaver's waist. There is a unique piece of pottery, conserved in the British Museum, with a Mochica drawing of people working at such a loom. Eight men or women, under a single roof, are seen mass-producing Mochica textiles – all using the back-strap loom, while two 'overseers' are served drink. These weavers are following a pre-worked pattern which is suspended from the wall; the artist conveys the idea, if this is carefully studied, that the pattern is faithfully reproduced on the loom. For each colour there is a different spindle; the spindles vary in number among the weavers from five to eight. This drawing is an instructive piece of evidence of weaving techniques.

FEATHER-WEAVING

The art of feather-weaving is another development, a baroque variation of weaving itself. Its presence in Peru is, of course, neither unique nor unusual, for many peoples quite out of contact with each other – Polynesians, Mayas and Aztecs – were masters at it. What is unusual is that in

WEAVING AND METALWORK

55 An example of Chimú weaving. The brilliant colours were achieved by the use of a wide range of dyes, mostly of vegetable origin.

56 Feather-weaving was widely practised by both the Mochicas and the Chimús. The feathers were stitched onto a fabric background by their quills. A colourful example using parrot feathers.

57 A Mochica vase decorated with scenes showing the organization of the craft of weaving. Women are working on backstrap looms following patterns hung on the wall, which are accurately reproduced in the cloth on the looms. The number of spindles lying beside them indicates the number of colours being used. This is one of the most important documents of Mochica industry.

58 A beaten gold ornament in the form of a poncho found in a grave at Batan Grande on the north coast of Peru. Many magnificent gold ornaments have been discovered in Chimú graves and it is known that both the Incas and the Spaniards plundered vast quantities of gold and silver from these sources.

59 A necklace made by Chimú craftsmen, with ocelot heads in beaten gold.

60 Tiny, intricately worked gold objects found in graves at Batan Grande, revealing the delicacy of Chimú craftsmanship.

61 A gold figure of a priest with ceremonial headdress, holding his wand of authority.

62 A gold mask found with a mummy bundle near Batan Grande and dating from the Chimú-Lambayeque culture.

63 A Chimú sacrificial tumi knife with a stone blade and elaborately worked gold handle representing a god. The semi-circular headdress is of delicate filigree work and is inlaid with turquoise. Tiny birds hang from either side and bells from the skirt and legs.

64 The face of a sun god. A detail from a large gold ornament found near Tucume. When it is inverted a second face can be seen.

65 Gold and turquoise ear-spools found in a grave in the Chicama valley.

66 One of a large number of bronze digging instruments that have survived from the Mochica-Chimú civilizations. The narrow shaft was attached to a wooden handle.

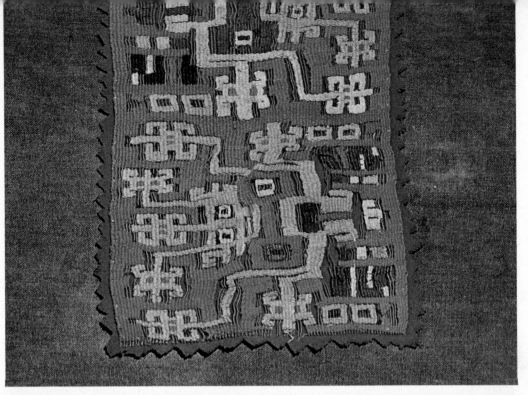

55

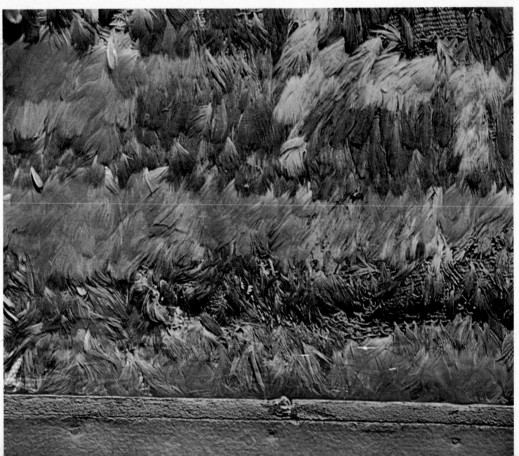

56

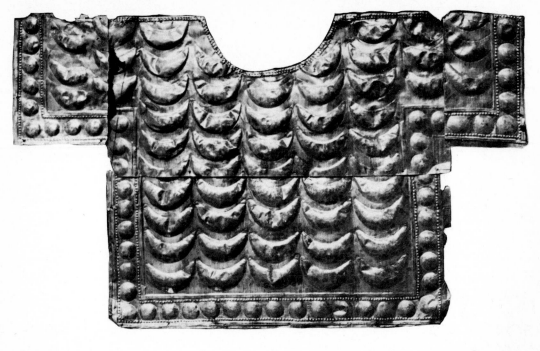

58

59

61

62

63

65

66

Peru so much has been so well preserved. The method and technique of feather-weaving (feather-mosaic is the better word for it) was as follows: the feather-plumes were laid out in a pattern; then they were either stitched to a woven fabric or the quills of the feathers were stuck through the woven weft, tightened, and made part of the fabric. Headdresses, feather back-ornaments that hung down to the waist, poncho-like garments, and costumes were made of feather-mosaics; dancers wore feather-mosaics, even wings, with head-pieces fashioned into bird-heads. Although the graves have not yielded these, the yuncas doubtlessly continued such costumes far into the latter part of the eighteenth century, as the native artists employed by Bishop Martínez de Compañón picture such dances and costumes. 'The Dance of the Pajaros', only one of many dances, is figured with the dancers accoutred in bird-feathers, giving them the semblance of Papagena in Mozart's *Magic Flute*.

Neither the Mochicas nor the Chimús had aviaries such as the Mexicans had in 1450, for which 300 Indians were employed to feed and care for the birds which yielded, without being killed, their plumes for the Aztec *amanteca*, the feather-weavers. There was no need here, for over the agitated sea there were myriad birds at hand; domestic fowl, such as turkeys and muscovy duck, could also yield their share of feathers without being killed. Parrots flew about in thick flocks over their valleys and were trapped or brought down with blow-pipes, in order to be used in feather-weaving. There were also feathers from birds which are not found in their immediate desert kingdoms. Because of this, some writers have posited extended trade-relations with Andean and Upper Amazon tribes. However in the north of Peru, in the upper reaches of the Serran Valley and above, west of Tumbes, the land height is over 3,000 feet and the regions are tropical. Tropical birds, ocelots, jaguars – all figured in Mochica pottery, as well as at least five species of monkeys, another favourite motif of the Mochicas, and especially the Chimús. All these were in abundance, so that they did not have to erect a zoological garden as did the Aztecs. All that was needed was at hand.

METALS AND JEWELS

Gold (which the yuncas called *xllall*) has been called the old, the successful metal. Silver tarnishes, iron rusts, but gold makes life sumptuous; it takes on an effulgent, almost polished light; it heightens pageantry. Early peoples everywhere worked in gold. Of great ductility (a single grain of

F

gold may be drawn into a wire five hundred feet long) and almost as soft as lead, gold can be embossed, cast, hammered, and, even though it is a 'highly bred metal', it can be used to gild silver or bronze. It gives the baser metals effulgence.

The Spaniards were amazed by the gold that they found in the desert kingdoms. Seeing it only whetted their metallic appetites, as they marched through the hot lands in 1532, when trying to find a lateral that would lead them to 'Cuzco', as they first called the Inca whose name and capital they confused. 'It is a marvellous thing to behold', wrote Pedro de Cieza in 1548, 'the vast number of skeletons with their clothing ... buried in the places which they hold sacred, *huacas*, which is a melancholy word ... many of them have been opened ... and despoiled of great sums of gold and silver.' Even before the Spaniards, the Incas had plundered and realized an overwhelming amount of metal from their conquest of the Kingdom of Chimor. Garcilaso de la Vega has observed that the gold taken from Chimú was melted down and recast into life-size golden statues, such as that of the Creator god, Tici-Virachoca, as well as one of Mama Ocllo, the legendary ancestress of the Inca dynasty. They also created a gigantic sun and, in addition, a great wide ribbon of thick gold was wound around the Curicancha, their great Sun Temple. Besides these, a colony of Chimú goldsmiths was installed in Cuzco, where, said Cieza, 'they dressed after the fashion of their own land and could be recognized by the insignia they wore about their heads'.

Metallurgy, so far as the Americans are concerned, doubtless developed in South America, and probably in Peru. It was very late in arriving in Yucatán, for that which they had there was Panama-derived. Gold appears as early as 1000 BC among the Chavins, and presumably the Mochicas were working it within the first century of our era. Its fashioning continued into the time of the Kingdom of Chimor, when it was, as judged by the dross-remains of Chan Chan, a major industry.

The sources of gold were coastal and highland. The nearest source was that which washed from the Rio Tumbes, in the *tallanes*-country, and was given as a tribute to the Kingdom of Chimor. This gold came from a river which had its origin in the gold-bearing quartz mountains at Portovelo [Ecuador]; it was of great fineness. Gold was, too, an important trade item. In exchange for coastal products, the Mochicas and the Chimús traded for metal ores with the tribe in the area about Cajamarca. This tribe, after 1400, entered into a treaty with the coastal empires, for the Cajamarcans controlled the source of several rivers which flowed down to the coast,

and in their territory were gold, silver, copper and tin. Gold mines were
scattered throughout the area, and were worked by Indians before the
advent of both the Incas and the Spaniards. These mines were explored by
Humboldt in 1802 and by Stevenson in 1820.[8] Humboldt estimated that
these had produced, during the years 1771–1802, over 32,000,000 piastres
of gold bullion.[9]

Silver and copper came from Hualgoc, close to Cajamarca, where there
are remains of 5,000 Indian dwellings. Beyond this, there were the mines
of Chupiquiyacu, where crude shafts bore evidence of native workings. At
Curimayu (gold-river), near the Pampa de Navar, lay wire-threads of pure
silver under the rock; at Choropampa there were rich outcroppings of pure
gold and silver; in still other areas the same were exposed like threads.
Gold also came from the Rio Chinchipe, an upper Amazon tributary; this
river, like the Tumbes which flowed into the Pacific, originated in the gold-
bearing quartz regions about Loja. The Aguarunas,[10] a sub-tribe of the
head-hunting Shuara, washed gold which reached Huancabamba in the
sierra by direct road; this same Huancabamba, at 10,000 feet altitude, was
only a two-day walk to the coast, with egress into the valley at Serran.[11] It
is, then, from these sources that the yuncas received their metals.

Metals in general were found in a relatively pure state, although the
Peruvians knew the method of refining copper and gold. They also mined
by sinking shallow shafts, once they had determined the source and could
follow the vein. Much gold was obtained through placer-methods. In the
dry season, when rivers were low, the Indians put stone-riffles across
streams and impounded the gold-bearing detritus during flood seasons.[12]

Copper, in the form of atacamite and found in surface collections, looked
like blue sand. Copper ores from mines were brought up in baskets and
simply crushed with stone hammers. Soft copper will bend to a hammer
easily; it is also easy to melt, ductile and very tenacious. Tin, which is
found abundantly in Bolivia, is less accessible throughout Peru. The early
Peruvian metallurgists, for such they were, did, however, soon find that a
small percentage of tin mixed with copper produced bronze. The sheer
mass of bronze tumi-knives, wedges, cutting tools, and tupu-pins that has
been found in Mochica and Chimú graves gives amazing testimony to the
amounts which were in use, and suggests mass-production. In bronze,
beauty and utility meet: it can be cut under; a craftsman can chisel out
reliefs in it or cast it, like gold; it can resist violent blows; it has splendour,
style, and a distinctive patina. Once the mass of Chimú bronze objects are
seen, one will not repeat with so much emphasis that the Peruvian never

83

left his neolithic horizon. If there ever was a bronze age in America, it was the Peruvian who lived it. The yuncas could cast bronze pieces as large as crowbars or as minuscule as a thumbnail, as seen in their figure of the maize-god; and it was all done with both delicacy and vigour.

To the yuncas, silver was the tears of the moon, for it is a noble metal, elegant, almost elegiac. It was plentiful in Peru, even though rarely found in a pure state, and despite the fact that pure silver is rare and difficult to smelt, the yunca metallurgists used it widely. For example, all the fine Chimú drinking beakers are of silver.

Their metal objects were fashioned in various ways: hammering on moulds, embossing *à la repoussé*, engraving, inlaying with precious uncut stones, plating, soldering, welding, alloying and casting. Casting was witnessed by an early Italian conquistador, Girolamo Benzoni, a Milanese who was born in 1519 and came to Peru between the years 1542 and 1546; he was involved in the civil wars between the Spanish victors fighting over the still valuable carcass of the Inca Empire. He noted down what he believed to be important, and on his return to Italy wrote a book, *La Historia del Mundo Nuovo*, which was published in Venice in 1565. Although the observations were original, the Italianized orthography of names and places on the land bordered on the ludicrous, and it was couched in so threadbare a style that it would have been entirely forgotten but for the sheer chance of its being catapulted into fame through its selection as one of the titles in the *Grands et Petits Voyages* of Theodore de Bry.[13] De Bry, the famous Flemish engraver, fled his country after the Revocation of the Edict of Nantes and went to Frankfurt, where he engraved and published this series of *Voyages*. Girolamo Benzoni's narrative was selected as *Pars Quinta*. Unfortunately, in the process of illustrating it, the baroque style of the original wood-cuts published by Benzoni was not used; nevertheless, observations on the manner in which the Peruvians worked such as the following[14] are contained in it:

In the first place when they wished to smelt the metal, they put it into either a long or round *grisolo* (crucible) made of a piece of cloth daubed over with a mixture of earth and pounded charcoal; when dry it is put into the fire filled with metal; then several men, more or less, each with a reed, blow till the metal is fused. It is now taken out, and the goldsmiths seated on the ground, provided with some black stones shaped on purpose, and helping each other, make, or more correctly speaking, *used to* make during their prosperity, whatever they were commissioned to do; that is, hollow statues, vases, sheep [llamas], ornaments, and, in short, any animal they saw.

84

This process is further explained by Garcilaso de la Vega:[15]

They had [he says] no files or graving tools, nor had they invented the art of making bellows for blast furnaces. They blasted by means of tubes of copper, the length of half-a-cubit, more or less, according as the furnace was large or small. The tubes were closed at one end, leaving one small hole through which the air could rush with more force. As many as eight, ten, or twelve of these were put together according to the requirements of the furnace; and they went round the fire blowing with the tubes. They still use the same method, not being willing to change their customs. They had no tongs for drawing the metal out of the fire, but did this with poles of wood or copper, and threw the heated metal on small heaps of damp earth which they had ready, to cool it. They drew it from one heap to another, until it was cool enough to hold in their hands. Notwithstanding these inconvenient contrivances, they executed marvellous works, chiefly in hollowing things out, and doing other admirable things as we shall see presently. They also found out, in spite of their simplicity, that the smoke of certain metals was injurious to the health and they consequently made their foundries in the open air, in their yards and courts, and never under a roof.

Winds were also used to create high temperatures. The Inca metallurgists practised it with their *huayras*,[16] and we may presume that the coastal yuncas imitated these Andean techniques. Furnaces were built on mountains where prevailing winds produced the necessary draught to obtain a temperature of 1,083°, sufficient to melt copper. Gold needed only a slightly lower temperature. The same object was obtained by blowing through copper tubes. We know that they used charcoal, and it is quite possible they used coal as well, since coal lay in exposed veins, especially at Oyon, high above the Huara Valley.

Casting in bronze, silver or gold was well developed. It was done in both open and closed moulds, and the techniques were doubtless the same as those used elsewhere. The lost-wax process, *à cire perdue*, was one in which the object to be cast, the core, was carved into final shape, coated with wax, and placed in what would be the outer clay mould. The molten metal was then poured in, the wax melted, and the object was cast. It appears to be simple when written in this short sentence, but when one considers the technical difficulties, the real crudeness of their workshops, it is something else. And still, they cast such delicately small pieces, minute, yet with all the vigour of American art and fine enough to receive the accolade of one of the greatest of the Renaissance masters, Albrecht Dürer, who said of the early American art objects, 'I have seen the things which were brought from the new golden land ... all fairer to see than marvels.'[17]

Casting by yunca craftsmen was basically the same as among most of the protohistoric peoples: Egyptians, Celtic or Mexican. The Egyptians have left a record of their goldsmithery on a tomb at Saqqara (*c.* 2400 BC), where they show themselves melting gold by means of clay blow-pipes, in which they force the heat up to the temperature of 1,063° C needed for melting gold. In this illustration, an artisan pours the molten gold from a crucible, while others beat out gold in flat plate with stone hammers. Benzoni, the Milanese conquistador mentioned above, illustrated the methods of Peruvian craftsmen in the same manner, showing them beating out gold with a small black stone hammer. Several of these hammers have been recovered from the ruins of Chan-Chan.

Gold, silver and copper were cold-hammered into sheets of paper-thinness, and from out of this sheet-metal they cut golden mummy masks and pendants. This hammered metal was also coaxed into the shape of tweezers (depilatory devices, since the Indian disliked surface hair, believing it to be unclean) and other objects. Much of the Mochica-Chimú gold work had its design from the embossing of sheet-metal, known as *à la repoussé*, work done in high or bas-relief and executed with controlled hammering on the back. The design was carved on stone or, if it was available, hard wood; then the sheet-metal was beaten with a stone hammer which, with repeated pounding, raised the design and at the same time compressed the metal and pounded it around the surface of the design. But the real art was to bring the two edges together without a seam being visible. After this, planishing and an overall hammering gave a smooth, even finish. Chasing, which is the art of cutting surface decoration on the front of the metal, was also used.

Gilding the baser metals, such as copper, with a thin gold veneer was perfected in Colombia over a thousand years ago, writes a leading scholar in this subject.[18] The gold-copper alloy was known as *tumbaga* among the Colombian tribes, and as *huanín* in Peru, where 'by a combination of heating and soaking in acid, surface copper was removed leaving a skin of gold ... surface enrichment or *mise en couleur*.'

Thus, out of all these gold-techniques – soldering, plating, welding, casting, embossing *à la repoussé* – came the myriads of gold, silver and bronze pieces which, even for the most hardened conquistadors who suffered from a metallic illness which only gold could cure, 'gave their hearts great joy'. In many instances these objects were of such beauty that the Spaniards hesitated to throw them into the crucibles which reduced all of the Lord Inca, Atahúalpa's ransom to gold and silver ingots. Those who were eye-witnesses to the conquest of Peru speak in detail of what they found. Such an account is given of the Curicancha, the golden enclosure or Sun Temple in Cuzco on which many of the Chimú goldsmiths worked after they had been conquered:

...where there was an image of the sun of great size made of gold, beautifully wrought and set with many precious stones ... There was a garden [here] in which the very earth was lumps of fine gold, and it was cunningly planted with stalks of maize that were of gold – stalk leaves, and ears ... Aside from this there were more than twenty llamas and their ewes with the Indian shepards who guarded them ... all of metal. There were made types of gold and silver and emeralds and goblets, vessels of every kind all of fine gold.[19]

Garcilaso de la Vega, whose mother was the grand-daughter of the 11th Lord Inca, Huayna Capac, and whose father was a conquistador, was himself born in Cuzco a few years after the fall of that capital in 1534. Years later, in 1609, while he was living in Spain, he composed his *History of the Inca*, remembering what he had been told as a boy. The goldsmiths' 'imitation of nature', he wrote, 'was so consummate that they even reproduced the leaves and little plants that grow on the walls; they also scattered here and there, gold or silver lizards, butterflies, mice and as well made snakes which were so cunningly placed, that one had the impression of seeing them run about in all directions'. Then there were 'birds set in the trees, as though they were about to sing'. Pipes were made of gold, the walls of the Incas' hot-bath were plated with gold leaf, even 'the Temple of the Sun had molten gold in the place of mortar'. The description of all this is not just highblown sententiousness, for the remaining gold and silver ornaments of the Mochica and Chimú treasures – those which the Spanish missed – confirm all this, and more. There are life-size maize cobs, all of pure gold; a parrot eats from a golden life-size cob; pigeons with fluttering wings hold onto a golden dish. There are golden hair-tweezers ornamented with monkeys, humming birds and spiders; silver ear-spoons are animated delightfully with llamas, deer, crabs and toucans. There are also colanders, dipping spoons, dishes and beakers. All these have been taken and are daily being taken from these graves of the desert kingdoms. Personal ornaments included golden combs, golden fillets for the hair, pendants with precious stones, gorgets of turquoise worked with gold, brooches and *tupos* of filigree. Mummies were buried with outsize golden masks. Gold was used both in a pure state and was also mixed with silver and with platinum.

87

GAMES AND PASTIMES

67 Indians playing a form of hockey, as illustrated in a series of drawings made by a native artist towards the end of the eighteenth century. These traditional games were inherited from their Mochica-Chimú ancestors.

68 *Gallos*, or 'cocks', a game played with a small weighted sack trimmed with feathers.

69 The Dance of the Chimús performed by Indians dressed in ponchos and elaborate headdresses.

70 and 71 The dance of the bears and the dance of the buzzards, both survivals of Mochica-Chimú culture.

72 and 73 The dance of the monkeys and the dance of the rabbits, showing the traditional flute and drum still used by the Indians today.

74 A modern Indian from Cajamarca using a *focedor de clarin*, a long reed mounted with a gourd capable of sounding three notes. This instrument has survived unchanged.

75 An eighteenth-century drawing showing the *focedor de clarin* being used to frighten birds, while corn is being harvested.

76 Modern Aymara Indians from near Lake Titicaca playing reed flutes.

77 A Mochica ceramic trumpet in the form of a jaguar.

78 A ceramic model of a coastal yunca playing a six-noted clay instrument which sounds like an ocarina.

79 A Mochica with painted face and double ear-spools shaking seed pods as a form of percussion instrument.

80 A Mochica stirrup vase depicting a man holding a conch shell made into a horn.

81 A Mochica blowing a conch horn.

82 A Mochica playing a six-noted reed pipe.

67

69

68

7

70

71

72

73

74

75

79

82

The Mochica jewellers used gold wisely, mixing it with precious stones. Turquoise, the *xiuhitl* of the Aztec, was highly prized; it appears as early as 1000 BC in ornaments of the Chavins, the culture which antedated the Mochica by a millennium. Mochicas drilled it and used whole pieces of it separated by golden beads. The imperial purple, which was the colour of *lapis lazuli*, came from Ovalle, in Chile; it was polished into round beads and made into pendants, alternating with gold. Bone was inlaid: mirror-backs were decorated with an inlay of turquoise and shell; wood was sheathed with gold, and in one unique piece, a wooden spear-thrower, is sheathed with finely worked gold.

In addition, the jewellers used, when the materials came to them direct or by trade, quartz, agate, carnelian, blood-stone, serpentine – and emeralds. Emeralds came by the trade routes with the tribes in what is now called 'Esmeraldas' in Ecuador. The rivers Santiago and Esmeraldas are highly auriferous, and from earliest times the amount of gold which came from that area was well-known. (Gold in this area was so plentiful that these Indians even had golden fish-hooks.) The tribes from this area dealt either directly or indirectly with the Chibchas, whose tribal seat was near to the present-day city of Bogotá and beyond, at a land height of 10,000 feet. The Chibchas had neither cotton, wool, nor gold in their lands; their principal trade items were salt from the mines of Zipaquira and emeralds from the region of Muzo. By one of those strange quirks of history, the Chibchas required gold for the purpose of performing an important annual ritual. Each year their 'King'[20] was subject to a ceremony in which he was smeared with an unguent and covered with gold-dust, then wafted on a raft into the centre of Lake Guatavita, where he ceremoniously washed off the golden stuff and became El Dorado. Yet, as mentioned previously, they had no gold-source of their own. The Indians of Ecuador who bordered on the rivers aforementioned, on the other hand, had much gold, which they obtained by placer-methods; however, they had no emeralds, other than those acquired by trade. Contrary to the statement of such a seasoned traveller as W. B. Stevenson, who was there in 1808, that 'the Province of Esmeraldas derives its name from a mine of emeralds, which is found no great distance from Esmeralda-town ... I never visited it, owing to the superstitious dread of the natives who assured me that it was enchanted and guarded by an enormous dragon',[21] in actuality, there are no such mines. Emeralds came to them only by trade.

The Mochicas, then, would have received their emeralds from this source, while the Incas would have acquired theirs perhaps through their connections with the highlands, for their Empire extended into and beyond the borders of present-day Ecuador. And it is, therefore, understandable that all this mass of gold and jewels left the conquistadors 'wrapped in astonishment'.

4 Tribal Life

LEISURE ACTIVITIES

THE ORGANIZED games were those of the children; they had top-spinning and top-whipping, as illustrated by the yuncas themselves. A game of hockey was played with a huge solid rubber ball. They also played a form of tennis, in which a similar ball was struck high into the air with a broad, heavy board paddle, and also a form of badminton, using a weighted object into which three feathers were put, called a 'bird'.

Dancing and drinking seemed to be the principal forms of merry-making for the adults. The various chieftains regularly held banquets which featured singers, dancers and buffoons. Ritual drunkenness was part of the merrymaking; the Indian was expected to drink to excess. This finds testimony in the Mochica ceramics, for the potter has caught the look of drunken stupefaction on the face of a man being led away

A ritual dance

by his two women, and there are many others in which the drunken one is being led away to sleep off his debauch.

Music was bound up with dance and dance with religion, since almost all forms of religious expression involved dancing – doubtless this is part of the collective hypnotism. Masks and costumes were important in all dances. Among the yuncas, these survived far into colonial times, when the artists under Bishop Martínez de Compañón, late in the eighteenth century, left a fascinating record of them. Many of these dances, continuing in what was doubtlessly a corrupt form, were carried on up to 1800. A

A Mochica drummer

list of them, with suggestions as to the costumes, is contained in the still unpublished materials of Martínez de Compañón.[1]

The musical instruments of the Chimú and the Mochica were, as in other Peruvian cultures, entirely bucolic: percussion and wind. Drums were made either of a rim of wood which was covered with llama hide, or of ceramic which was skin-covered. They were beaten with a rubber-covered stick to keep the rhythm. Pan-pipes were various; they made six-noted reed pipes, or, when wood was lacking, they made them, as most other things, of ceramic. All these were common throughout Peru, with the exception that some of the tribes of the eastern montaña made them so large that they had to rest on the ground; these produced a horrendous sound.

The conch horn, called by the Incas *potóto*, and used by every theocracy throughout the Americas, was the shell of a marine mollusc, one not found in Peruvian waters. It was one of the most sought-after trade items, and those in Peru doubtless came from the warmer northern waters of Ecuador and Colombia, especially off the islands of Gallo and Gorgona. As mentioned before, their scarcity was such that the Mochica potters succeeded in making a ceramic substitute. (There is no lack of illustrations of these in Mochica and Chimú pottery.) In addition, there were pottery horns, five feet long and similar to those which appear on the Maya murals at Bonompak, Chiapas, Mexico; they are usually twin trumpets, blown in unison and set in different keys. However, they were also made of wood and copper-silver. (A number of these horns still survive in Cajamarca.) Then, to give depth to sound and beat, there were gourd-rattles, silver, copper and golden bells, as well as seeds which were shaken by hand to the time of the beat or were tied to the ankle and wrist.

Such was the merrymaking of sound, and, as Cieza stated, the Lords were entertained 'continuously with music and song'. This, together with the heady drinking, tended to relax human *mores*, and more often than not the men and women, in their drunkenness, did not know who were their spouses. As is so often the case in our own society, merrymaking often led to extra-marital relations – one of the major causes of disputes.

CRIME AND PUNISHMENT

If we judge human actions by the pain and pleasure they cause us, then justice and justification, like crime and punishment, take on new social hues: morality is here a gaudy thing. Among the Mochicas and the Chimús, punishment was exactly proportioned to the crime; their justice had not for its object that which was just, but that which was useful. Theft was deemed an aberration, since, as a member of a clan, no one had need for it. It was, therefore, punished with great severity. Hands or feet were cut off (one sees such amputated cases on Mochica pottery), or else a thief could even be hanged for the most petty robbery. Even worse, he could lose his clan-rights, which meant a life condemned to slavery and penury. Moreover, anyone who harboured a convicted thief was given the same punishment as the culprit himself. There were no prisons, and no appeal from the sentence, which, when pronounced, was immediately carried out.

In these kingdoms, sexual intercourse between unmarried tribesmen disturbed no one, but adultery was disastrous. The men were buried alive or, says Padre Calancha, brought to the edge of La Horca, a precipitous slope that looked over the place where the Rio Fortaleza debouches into the sea (near to the fortress of Paramonga), 'and pushed over into the sea'. Even more strict was the attitude of man towards the Moon Virgins, 'who are just like our nuns,' says Calancha in passing; 'it was death to those who even used the same roads as the Moon Virgins'.

Sodomy, which was a yunca tribal pleasure, was not a crime until the arrival of the Incas, and although the latter destroyed whole families and even tribes in their attempt to stamp it out, Padre Calancha still found it rampant when, in 1640, he and others were there to try and put an end to idolatry on the coast. He found the yuncas 'very inclined to sodomy and even until today they are not entirely free of this contagious sexual expression'.

Since these kingdoms were functional theocracies, where rulers in a confused palingenesis were both temporal and spiritual, any form of blasphemy was fatal to the one who committed it. 'Those who did not respect the temples or *huacas*', wrote Calancha, 'or observe the laws of their leaders were buried alive among the bones of those who had before them committed these infractions. The names of all such condemned were *ramar*.' It might well be noted, of course, that such gothic barbarity persisted also in the Old World well into the late eighteenth century, when thieves were hanged, murderers broken on the wheel, traitors torn apart in their four extremities by four horses, all pulling in different compass directions; when those who debased coinage were boiled in bubbling metal, and atheists, sorcerers and sodomites were burned alive.

The language of pottery, of course, has its limitations; nothing is here in abstract. However, the obvious that is in the pottery has been supplemented by the personal observations of the priest-chroniclers, from whom, for example, we learn that a clan-chief set up to judge could not punish a malefactor who did not come within his jurisdiction of *marca*, or tribe. The accused had to be handed over to his own people for judgement.

And if the tribal laws were severe with the common man, they were no less so for a chieftain. In fact, often the punishment meted out to an official was all out of proportion, since an act pardonable in a common man became unpardonable in a chieftain, who should have known better. It was equally difficult for those who practised medicine, for should the patient die through what relatives judged to have been carelessness, the 'doctor was tied to the buried man and exposed to the elements and carnivorous birds'.

'The Doctors', stated Padre Calancha, 'are called here *Oquetlupuc* ... and are very much venerated, receiving great favours from the public and given many social privileges. They cure with herbs, powders and waters. But should they kill their patient through ignorance, they themselves are killed and buried with the man that his malpractice has killed.' The murdered and the murderer belong to one another.

The diseases which made these coastal regions at times a troubled paradise arose out of the very nature of the land. The contrast between the daily heat of the desert and the bitter cold that set in as soon as the sun set and the night winds swept over the sands brought rheums and phlegms of various forms. If some modern researches are to be believed, even tuberculosis was present. Certainly, catarrhal complaints were many and infantile mortality presumably high because of it. Arthritis has been found in the skeletal remains of mummies, and, like modern man, the yuncas had their full share of tumours of the eyes, neck and brain. All of these have been faithfully mirrored in their ceramics. Asthma, then as now, claimed many, and the Incas, at least, had a name for it: *karacay-uncoyniyoc*. Mochica pottery also exhibits harelip. Pott's Disease, or vertebral tuberculosis, is often met with in this clinical display. And there are blind men (either through accident or tumours), Siamese twins, water-heads, humpbacks. They also suffered from the common cold, yellow fever (this is endemic in the Americas and is often carried in the intestines by the spider-monkey), and malaria, which was tropicopolitan in its distribution. There are also quite a few ceramics which show people undergoing *acromegalia*, a form of glandular disturbance which causes abnormal growth of the hands and face. And, as previously noted, all of the symptoms moulded on Mochica pottery are so exact that those who specialize in tropical medicine seem to be untroubled in diagnosing the diseases.

One of the terrifying diseases, then as now, was *uta*, often called cancer of the Andes, although it is not, in fact, confined to that particular area. It was (and is) a form of *leishmaniasis* which attacked the nose septum and the lips, until ultimately pus ate away the whole of the nose and the upper lips, exposing the teeth and leaving the one who escaped death from it with a face frozen, as it were, in a horrible, perpetual grimace. (The Incas called it 'red-fringed clouds', in reference to the bleeding red walls of the face ulcer.) The Mochica pottery realistically depicts this affliction in all its horrible detail. *Verrugas* was also greatly feared, both by Indian and, when he arrived, by white man, alike. Transmitted by a fly-bite, the bacilli enter the blood stream and emerge as an eruption of red pimples that increase in size and become suppurating *carbunculi*; the disease is accompanied by high fever, and the warty, corrugated excrescences continue to bleed and erupt until the afflicted eventually becomes exhausted and dies. It was the first disease given to the Spaniards on their arrival at the periphery of the Kingdom of the Sun. In the spring of 1531, Pizarro's expedition en route to Peru stopped at Coaque (now in Ecuador), which was, says one of the *cronistas*, 'a large town full of gold, silver and emeralds'. It was also full of *verrugas*. Many of the would-be conquistadors fell sick with 'eruptions all over their hands and legs'; many died from the white man's first contact with this disease.

There was yet another complaint, which the Spaniards called 'buboes'. Cieza, who became acquainted with it in the isle of Puna, near Guayaquil, said it was 'a pestilential disease'. To rid oneself of it

there is a plant which grows abundantly on this island...called sarsaparilla.... The root of this plant is good for a number of ailments, especially for the pain which buboes...causes. Those who wish to rid themselves of this ailment should remain in a room where the air and cold will not reach them, physic themselves, take only a light diet, and drink the water in which these roots have been boiled for this purpose, which comes away clear, and is not unpleasant to taste or smell. Drinking this, without any other medication, the malady is purged so effectively that in a short time the person is healthier than he was before, and his flesh firmer and without scar or trace, as often happens with other cures.... Many who had rotting flesh by simply drinking the water of these roots became well and had better colour than before they were sick. Others, with advanced cases of buboes all over their bodies and whose breath was bad, were cured by drinking this water the necessary length of time. In a word, many who were swollen and others covered with sores have gone home well again. It is my belief that this is one of the best plants or roots in the world, and the most useful, as is apparent from the number of people it has cured. *Sarsaparilla* is found in many parts of the Indies, but it has been discovered that it is not as good or all-healing as that which grows on the Island of Puná.[2]

Like most desert people, whose eyes were generally filled with hot sand-blink, the yuncas were also troubled with ophthalmia. This, in fact, was the reason that the Spaniards moved their first settlement on the coast at Tangarara, near to present-day Pirua – 'since the location', says Cieza, 'was unhealthy and the Spaniards contracted certain diseases'. One of these was syphilis. On this subject there is no definitive conclusion: only this, that neither the disease nor its symptoms were known in the classical world or in Europe until the return of Columbus from his first voyage to the Americas. Physicians and anthropologists who have examined the mummified bones of Peruvian Indians insist that in these they can see the lesions of syphilis; beyond this, it is a fact that the pure Indian who contacts syphilis does not suffer the deleterious effects that the white or half-caste man does – which might be negative evidence of the native's acclimatization to a disease which is distinctly American.

Mochica pottery, in some of its clinical series, does display the types of sores common to the latter stages of syphilis, and there is no doubt, historically, that the disease appeared in Europe for the first time in Naples, in December of 1494, twenty-one months after Columbus' return from America. It was one of the most momentous events in the Renaissance. A Spanish physician, Rodrigo Riaz de l'Isla, first observed it on sailors arriving on Columbus' ship, the *Niña*; Oviedo, the official historiographer resident in the Indies, later confirmed it. The symptom was a formation on the exterior of the genitals of a small tumour, which was not at first painful. Then it disappeared. Afterwards, there was an eruption inside the mouth and a festering of malignant ulcers on the legs and other parts of the body (which is, in passing, precisely that which the Mochica pottery depicts). Since French troops were in Naples at that time, it became instantly known as the *morbus gallicus*. However it was not quite confined to the French, since the Spanish medico, Dr Gaspare Torrella, who was employed at the Vatican as resident physician, treated seventeen distinct cases of it during the months of September and October of 1497, including that of one person who should not have had it – His Holiness Pope Julius II. As is well known, one of the brilliant and witty scholars of the Renaissance, Frascastoro Girolamo of Verona, gave the disease its name, which he published in a didactic medical poem in 1530.[3]

Some medical historians insist that syphilis existed before America's discovery and that it was carried to the Indians, who, as they did with smallpox, developed a bacillus so virulent that they gave it back to their givers in a violent form. Others insist that it is American. In any case, it is one of the unsolved riddles of sexual history, and the literature is vast.[4] This much, however, is certain, that if American in origin, syphilis was not the result of sexual contact between man and llama, which is part of the folklore of these studies. The Mochicas, who show every sexual aberration in their own sensual catalogue, give no indication of such contact in their

G

pottery, and, from its positive side, no llama was ever found to harbour *Treponema pallidum*, the spirochete of syphilis.

The Mochicas, and, one gathers, the Chimús, called their cure doctors *Oquetlupuc*. They had, as suggested earlier, a high place in their society. There is no evidence, however, of such specialization as seems to have occurred among the Incas, who differentiated between the master curer (*Hampi camayoc cuya*), and one who made sacrifices to effect a cure (*ccamascas*), and those who used suction to suck out the diseases (*soncoyoc*). Diagnosis among the yunca curers was by pressure and 'laying on the hands', as seen in Mochica ceramics; the patient is shown in a prone position while the curer feels him. Doubtless, there were those who specialized in skull trephining or in diseases for which they had found a specific. Such was certainly the case in ancient Egypt, as seen by Herodotus: 'The practice of medicine is so divided among them that each physician is a healer of one disease and no more.' In Babylon, Herodotus observed that diagnosis was far more specific: 'They carry the sick into the market place; then those who have been afflicted themselves by the same ill as the sick man's or seen others in like case come near and advise him about his disease and comfort him, telling him by what means they have themselves recovered of it or seen others so recover.' In the Mochica ceramics, doctors may be seen blowing into the patient's mouth, though for what precise reason is not revealed. In one particular ceramic there is an illustration of the doctor applying his lips to the body of the patient to suck out the foreign substance which, it is believed, has caused the disease.

Naturally (for it is natural to primitives), the Indians thought that all disease was caused by the supernatural, and the curer had to resort to the same medium in order to determine the cause. The denizens of the humid jungle drank the hallucination-producing drug called *caapi*. A vine, a malpighiad – and the only narcotic vine on record – *Banisteria caapi* was drunk in an infusion by both doctor and patient, and as it produced visions, these were seized upon to divine the trouble. Witch-doctors also acquired through trade a seed which, when ground, was taken as *niopo* snuff,[5] giving both witch-doctor and patient the visions needed to effect a cure. Tobacco was used for both cure and divination, and as early as 1535, the royal astronomer of François I, the famed André Thevet, wrote about the virtues of tobacco as a curative as used among the Moxo Indians of Amazonic Bolivia[6] – even though he, himself, had not seen it. There is no doubt that the coastal yuncas, as their contemporaries, the Andean dwellers, had a wide knowledge of drug-yielding plants; many have entered our own pharmacopoeia (such as quinine, coca (from which cocaine has been derived), ipecac, belladonna, curare, etc.). But what plants were used to cure what diseases has been lost to us.

Medicine among the Mochicas and Chimús was, as it should be with us, hygienic and preservative rather than curative. Thus, their own witch-doctors were perhaps less dangerous to them than were those 'Sangrados' and 'Macrotons', as portrayed by Le Sage and Molière, to their patients. For example, *guayusa* was taken, by the jungle Indians, at least, as an emetic. The *guayusa* pot, in which leaves and water were combined in a greenish concoction, was always simmering on the fire. The drink caused anyone who took it to vomit all food which had not been digested during the night. Thus, they practised medicine on a sort of primitive Hippo-cratic principle.

There was an intimate and spiritual relationship between doctor and patient; anyone afflicted could be certain that, if a curer were called in, he would do his utmost to effect a cure, because his own life depended on it. As Padre Calancha states, 'if they show ignorance in the cure and the patient dies when he need not have died, the curer would be judged as having actually murdered the patient'. The 'murderer', then, 'was killed by beating or stoning and when the dead one was buried, the doctor was connected by a rope which passed through the grave to the other cadaver and his body left to be consumed by carrion-eating birds'.

THE CULT OF THE DEAD

The Dance of Death among these yuncas was as real as it was during the time of the plagues in Europe in the sixteenth century. As seen in their ceramics, cadavers dance hand in hand, in a mimicry so exactly like Hans Holbein's *Totentanz* that one would be compelled to believe that it came from the same atelier. Skeletons playing pan-pipes scurry about with all the merrymaking of a devil on two sticks and with a breezy robustness of humanity; they dance with the living, dance by themselves, and drink – showing boundless joy at their state.

Death was a preoccupation among the Indians. In the south, around the peninsula of Paracas, there are people who have neither name nor history and are called, after the locality, 'Paracas'; they performed elaborate burials of their dead and robed them so sumptuously that museums are anxious to display such fabrics and weavings when they are acquired. Of the regions about Lake Titicaca, where once lived the *Collas*, Cieza wrote that

the most extraordinary thing to be seen here in the Colla is, in my opinion, the graves [*chullpas*] of the dead ... And truly it amazes me to think how little store the living set by having large, fine houses, and the care with which they adorned the graves ... as though this constituted their entire happiness ... the great tombs are so numerous that they occupy more space than is given to the living.

The coastal yuncas' cult of the dead was, if possible, even more dedicated to the practice of giving to the dead such thorough reflections of the life left behind that they would not return to carry the living off. 'The Indians', said Cieza, 'bury with the bodies of the dead all those possessions they most prized, and certain of their most beautiful and best-loved women ... They ordered these deep, magnificent tombs built ... into which they laid the dead man with all his possessions and women and servants and a great quantity of food ... and his arms and ornaments ... it was the general belief among all these Yunga Indians ... that the souls of the dead did not die, but lived forever, and came together with one another in the other world ... And firmly believing this, they buried with the dead their best-loved wives, and their closest vassals and servants, and their most prized possessions and arms and feathers, and other ornaments of their person.'⁷ In the chapter entitled 'Of their burial rites and the mourning which attended the obsequies',⁸ Cieza rightly notes that preparation of the graves 'varies greatly, for in some places they were deep; in others high; and in others, flat'. As for the desert lands of the yuncas, Cieza thought it 'a marvellous thing to behold the number of dead there are in those sand dunes and desert uplands; and separated one from the other, one sees a vast number of skeletons and their clothing ... They call these places, which they hold sacred, *huacas*.'⁹ He goes on to describe a burial ritual:

And when the chieftains died, the headmen of the valley assembled and carried on great mourning, and many of the women cut their hair completely off, not leaving one. To the accompaniment of drums and flutes they marched around those places where the lord most frequently took his pleasure, singing sad songs to move the listeners to tears. And after they had mourned, they performed other sacrifices and ceremonies, carrying on their conversations with the devil. And when all this had been done, and some of the wives killed, they laid them in the grave with their treasures and abundant food, firmly believing that they were going where the devil had said. And they waited, and even now they generally do so, some four or five days or ten before putting them in the grave, depending on the rank of the dead man, because the more important the lord, the more honour they do him and the greater sorrow they profess, mourning him with loud groans and bewailing him with sorrowful music, relating in their songs all the things that had happened to the deceased while he was alive. If he was brave, they recount his feats in their dirges as they bear him along; and as they lay his body away, they burn certain of his jewels and garments beside him, and put others in with him. Many of these ceremonies are no longer used ... because little by little these people are coming to know the error of their forefathers, and how idle were these pomps and honours. For it is enough to bury the dead in a simple grave, as the Christians do, without attempting to take with themselves anything but good works, for all serves only to increase the power of the devil and lay more and more grievous weight on the soul descending to hell. But it is my belief that most of the older chieftains arrange to be buried in secret, hidden places, in the manner I have described, where the Spaniards can neither see nor know of them. That they do this we know from what we are told by the younger people.

Were death and life but aspects of the same thing? It seemed that they were, for in the Elysian fields, where the dead conversed, no one seemed to know the real nature of the soul: to some it was material and figurative; to others it was incorporeal and immortal; and to the Stoics it was merely a temporary manifestation of the will. Some averred that death caused

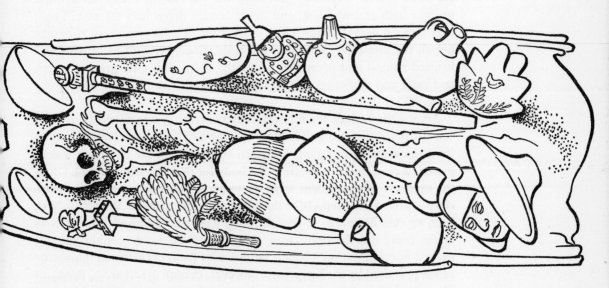

A reconstruction of a tomb showing how the dead were buried with their possessions and provisions for the after-life

beings to re-enter into God, like a sound that vanishes in the air. Nor could those in the gardens of Epicurus even agree on the nature of the hereafter: 'What is life?' someone asked; 'Life is death,' was the reply – for it is true that the dead spoke of death as if they knew nothing of it. This, no doubt, was because the dead remain human and mortal in considerable degree (and especially so to the Mochicas and the Chimús), for when they have entered immortality, they would neither speak nor think any more. 'They would be like the gods.'

'The souls do not die' – nor does the body, either. At least the yuncas were partially convinced of this. The Mochicas prepared shallow graves, often lined with adobe, and placed in the niches the stirrup-shaped vessels filled with *chicha* to nourish the dead. It is because of this practice that we have the wonderful sequence of their pottery. The dead were also wrapped in their own *mantas*, the quality of which depended on the owner's station in life; high-ranking Mochicas were customarily buried with their head-gear, which signified rank.

The mouth of the dead was often stuffed with cotton. However, mummification, as classically understood, was rarely practised by the Mochicas or the Chimús. The earliest description of this practice comes from Herodotus, who apparently witnessed it in Egypt in *c.* 450 BC: 'If they do this in the most perfect way, they first draw out part of the brain through the nostrils with an iron hook, and inject certain drugs into the rest. Then, making a cut near the flank with a sharp knife of Ethiopian stone, they take out all the intestines, and clean the belly, rinsing it with palm wine and bruised spices; and presently, filling the belly with pure ground myrrh and casia and any other spices, save only frankincense, they sew up the anus.'[10]

Among the yuncas, the intestinal cavity certainly was not removed, nor was the brain. Yet mummification, or a form of body preservation, was in Peru the same as in Egypt, a magico-religious act, for its object was to provide a reasonable facsimile of the body for the return of the soul. Often the cadavers of the yuncas were wrapped in many layers of long, white cloth – thirty yards seems to be the maximum. There seems, though, to have been no definite rule as to how the body was to be disposed. The dryness of the coast and the desiccating character of the sand brought about a natural mummification which is far different from the artificial mummification practised by the Egyptians; however, in both desert areas, Peru and Egypt, it was the heat of the sun and the sterile, porous quality of the sand that provided the preservative.

The Mochicas and the Chimú were Moon worshippers; in contrast, the
Incas were Sun worshippers. The reason for this is meteorologically
obvious and needs no recourse to the abracadabra of primitive mysticism.
The sun warmed the mountain-dwelling peoples; when it disappeared,
cold appeared. To the coastal dweller the sun was constant, almost a
tyrant in the sky; so, it was the lesser God, the Moon (which they called *Si*)

The crab god

DEATH AND THE SUPERNATURAL

83 Animals were invested with totemic significance by the Mochicas and Chimús. A lively representation of a fox, dressed in a man's tunic and holding a plate.

84 A Mochica with his lime gourd, wearing a headdress which suggests he is a cure doctor. Lime was used to hasten the breakdown of coca leaves, which were chewed to release minute quantities of cocaine.

85 A cure doctor or *Oquetlupuc* examining a woman.

86 A Mochica with an ocelot on his shoulder. This animal was apparently used as some kind of familiar.

87 The owl god represented in the shape of a man holding a *macana* weapon.

88 The dance of death depicted on a Mochica vase. Skeletons dance hand in hand, while others play pan-pipes.

89 The skeletal figure of death playing a drum.

90 An elaborately dressed bearded man. Since beards were rare among the Indians, who were usually without facial hair, it is probable that this represents a mythological rather than an actual being.

83

84

85

87

89

The bird god

which they worshipped. Moon worship might well have been the spiritual
bond that held most of the coastal people together, since it represented
opposition to the Incas. The Chimú at Pacatnamu, says Calancha, called
their shrine – which was close on the sea – *Si-An*, 'The House of the Moon'
where, as he says, 'five-year-old children were sacrificed while lying on
beds made of coloured wool or cotton'. In the Moche Valley the Mochicas
built two temples, one to the Moon and the lesser one to the Sun; these
are the largest man-made structures on the coast, or perhaps in the whole
of Peru. And all such phenomena as the influence of the moon on the tides
and the phases of the moon which coincide with woman's menstrual cycle
were not lost on them.

In the lonely hours of the night, it was the stars which attracted them.
In their remoteness, stars seem always to have aroused primitive man into
a play of fancy. The yuncas based their calendar upon the setting and
rising of stars: 'they do not count the lunar months nor the sun's course,
yet only by the march of stars … by those they call *fur* and we Cabrillas.'
Stars, too, were gods; about the constellation of Pata, which is the constellation of Orion and his belt, they wove a quaint tale of one miscreant
star which was being held captive by the other two. To water, which they

105

called *Ni*, they offered as tribute 'white maize flour and other worthless things'. The water-cult grew out of their closeness to the sea, for they were dependent upon it and in a great measure it ruled their economy. So, anthropomorphized gods emerge which run the gamut of sea-spawned creatures. Each phenomenon had its god, which is something primitive people everywhere have in common. As Calancha said, '[they] even adore certain rocks which even today [he was writing in 1630] are called *alecpong*,

The fox god in flight

which means "Gods of the Rocks".' And since the yuncas envisaged themselves as part of, rather than apart from, the sphere of animals, totemism was also a part of their religion. The whole world was alive and sentient; everything, everyone had a soul. Every Chimú and Mochica had, as his Inca contemporary, a guardian angel, a *Hauqui*, a shadow, a 'soul' which was good friend and counsellor.

At times, overmuch has been made of the impact of religions on man and that which shaped him. The Aztec who expressed himself in the statement, 'We do not believe, we fear!', was expressing, in essence, the fundamental *raison d'être* for all this concern with death and its consequences: 'We fear!' This, because death did not conform; it was quite unlike anything else in the experience of the primitive. Death was contagious, because the dead did not want to go; and if the body were improperly sent off – without its life appurtenances, food and drink, and, if life's station permitted, women and servants – it just might not go, or might, perhaps, carry off some of the living to assuage its loneliness. Above all, the clan was maimed by death. The Indians thought as clan, lived as clan, and acted as clan. These people, while living, drew upon the reservoir of other living men, for that which is made by another or an experience lived by another had the aura of his personality; if one man was invested with the quality of strength, then a mere shadow was enough for one of lesser being to absorb the mystical transference of his power. Death, however, caused an individual to be lost to the clan; he was no longer communal, he was individual.

'We fear!' At the beginning of all feeling there is a fact irreducible and incomprehensible in itself; common reasoning starts from feeling to explain the fact. Take, for example, the fact of death. The dead were sumptuously buried, and, as Cieza opined when he saw the magnificent tombs, the Indians seemed to live only in order to die. Since man, in his own general opinion, does not die (the refusal to accept that end, whether in primitive or civilized man, is a human illusion – that there is neither beginning nor middle nor end in the series of causation), then in this concept, the essence of the dead must go somewhere. And this is where, in the Mochica and Chimú theogony, the 'vertical and horizontal gods' appear.

The fish god holding a tumi knife

Mr Keith, in Norman Douglas' novel *South Wind*, liked the classical Greek gods, because they were invented by 'intellectuals who felt themselves capable of maintaining a kind of comradeship with their deities ... practically on a level and walked hand in hand with them over the earth'. These were, for him, the horizontal gods, 'the downstairs variety'. The vertical gods, to which category those of the yuncas' faith would belong, were 'the upstairs variety'. Worshippers of the upstairs gods, Keith felt, were motivated by what he considered to be the fact that the lower man (he actually said 'proletariat') loves to humiliate himself; these lower men grovel, exalting a diety at such a distance that they abase themselves.

Mankind [his observations continued] remains in direct contact with the downstairs variety. That simplifies matters. But the peculiar position of those others – perpendicularly overhead at a vast distance – necessitates a troublesome code of verbal signals, unintelligible to common folk, for the expression of mutual desires. You cannot have any god of this kind without some such cumbrous contrivance to bridge over the gulf and make communication possible. It is called theology. It complicates life very considerably.[11]

It certainly complicated life and death for the Mochica and the Chimú. Still, let their fears be praised, for it is because of this that they left buried in the security of the desiccating sands enough artifacts of their lives to enable us to draw from them yet another piece of the mosaic of life's multitudinous forms.

5 Tribal Organization

All fables have some real foundation – ALEXANDER VON HUMBOLDT

THE 'CIE': THE DIRECTING CLASSES

'THE LORDS of these valleys were called *Cie*,' one chronicler set down, and Pedro de Cieza de León goes on to explain that the ancient rulers, before they were subdued by the Incas, 'were greatly feared and obeyed by their subjects, and were served with great pomp ... surrounding themselves with buffoons and dancers who entertained them, and with others who continually made music and sang ... and each lord, in his valley, had his great dwellings, with many pillars of adobe, and great terraces and gateways, covered with mats, and surrounding this house was a wide square, where they performed their dances and *areitos* [ceremonies].'[1]

This small paragraph is all there is – the only pertinent, actual contemporary observation on the tribal organization of the yuncas just before the Inca conquest. All the rest came later, when that which Cieza saw was gone. But even this early information has been confirmed by archaeology. As each valley was separated from the other by a void of sand and desolation, each had a certain, and often a high portion of, political autonomy. However, as archaeological evidence shows, there was mass labour in weaving and the production of metal objects; remains of the massive public works also indicate mass labour on irrigation ditches, water supply, the terracing of hills, the dressing and hauling of stone, the production of billions of adobe blocks, the raising of pyramids. Then there were wars, hunting expeditions and trading on a large scale. All this, of course, presupposes organization. One must assume, further, that, as the desert kingdoms grew in complexity and the Kingdom of Chimor expanded until it embraced all the lands between Tumbes to the north down to Chancay (close to Lima) in the south, these individual valley rulers became subordinate to the grand Chimú, whose residence was presumably in his capital, the immense city-state of Chan Chan.

The lords-of-the-valley have deep roots. They begin with legend; and, as Humboldt avowed – and which is in essence true – 'all fables have some real foundation'. The following is the yuncas' legend of Ñaymlap.

Once upon a time there was a king named Ñaymlap. He came from the south of Peru on a fleet of balsas. With him were his wife, Ceterni, and his harem. He also had numerous court attendants to care for him; these included the following:

Xam Muchec	keeper of the royal face-paints
Pita zofi	trumpeter on the potóto
Nin-acola	in charge of the royal litter and throne
Nin-agintue	royal cup bearer
Ollo-copoc	bathing master
Llap-chillulli	master of weaving and feather mosaics

The king also had his idol, which was made of green stone and was called *Yampallac*. It acted as an autologos and had directed him to Peru, to a valley called Lambayeque. After his arrival, Ñaymlap named this valley after his stone idol in a gesture of gratefulness for having been led thence. Eventually, Ñaymlap landed at a place called Chot, near to the mouth of the Faquisllanga River. There he established his kingdom, and after many fruitful years of life, he died, took to wings, and flew away.

Ñaymlap had sired many sons. His first-born, named Cium, built a palace, became king, and married Zolzdoñi. Another son settled at Cinto; another, called Cala, settled at Túcume; and still another developed the lands about Collique. It was the master of feather-weaving, one Llap-chillulli, who settled Jayanca.

These kings and their people developed the desert coast. They had the water brought down in *acequias*; they widened the earth-domain, terraced the hills, brought guano fertilizer from the islets off the coast. And they also established weaving on a large scale. Thus established, the dynasty went on. There were, naturally, wars and disagreements, such as, for example, the sin of Fempellec. Fempellec wanted to move the green idol *Yampallac* from its shrine at Chot. Then he had a dream, in which he was seduced by a voluptuous woman. Thereafter, it rained for thirty days and thirty nights, and the land was reduced to utter sterility; whereupon the priests, acting for the people, trussed up Fempellec and tossed him into the sea. From that time the valleys remained kingless until the rise of the Kingdom of Chimor.

It is, grants a scholar who has written briefly of it, 'rather threadbare history ... for our sources are scanty, but fairly reliable to judge by the substantial agreement we find in the fragments. Whole chapters of oriental history are based on less.'[2] And it is perhaps not alone a story of origin, since, with a little juggling of phonetics and spellings, there are actual physical remains whose place-names bear close resemblances to the Ñaymlap story. It may be assumed, upon reading the whole of this 'history' (in which appears names of rulers and their length of reign, and which covers some three hundred years or more), that it is legendary coastal history.

It is indeed remarkable that this legend should have persisted for a century or more after the conquest of the yuncas by the Incas. As previously explained, we have little historical knowledge of many of the pre-Inca tribes because the Incas wished to give the impression that before their advent (and they arrived very late), these peoples were void of material culture. Thus, by a systematic killing off of the official tribal 'rememberers' and by replacing their remembered histories with myths of Inca origin, they eliminated much of the conquered peoples' own history. Yet the Ñaymlap narrative continued, and was still there when Cabello de Balboa arrived after 1576 – one hundred years after the Inca conquest.

Father Miguel Cabello de Balboa was a Jesuit, and one whom Philip A. Means refers to as 'one of the greatest of the chroniclers of Peru'[3] – this despite the fact that his book, *Miscelánea Antártica*, still lies in manuscript form in the New York Public Library, and, save for an atrocious French abridgement, has never seen light.[4] He was born in Spain, near Malaga. After taking Holy Orders, he proceeded to the Americas. He went to Bogotá as early as 1566, and after that settled in Quito. While in Bogotá, he was led to speculate on the origin of the American Indian and to equate it, somehow, with the existing glaring biblical inaccuracies. If all mankind were destroyed in the flood, save those men and animals alone who were preserved in Noah's ark, then how does the Church account for the survival of the American Indian? Friar Juan de Orozcoman, an erudite Franciscan who had already written a good deal on his speculations as to 'origins', gave the inquiring Cabello his answer: the Indians were Jews; they descended 'from Noah through Shem and through Ophir, great-grandson of Noah'.[5] Father Cabello adopted this thesis. While in Quito, he even made a map (now lost) to show these migrations; he was out to prove by inquiry that these Indians springing from the loins of Ophir had reached South America by way of the scattered islands, between India and the Americas, in the Pacific. While highly questionable as anthropology, it was good theology, and the Church approved the thesis, as it made the impossible possible. Thus, Cabello set off, with the Church's blessing, to gather the legends of the coastal peoples.

Cabello had great opportunity for observation. He went to the Province of Esmeraldas, the same place which caused so much confusion about the origins of emeralds; he journeyed into the savage country of the Chunchos, of which he wrote an account. He was also versatile as a writer, producing two comedies in the style of Calderón and a sonnet about the great Amazon tributary, El Marañón – all of which were published. But not this great work, the *Miscelánea Antártica*, with its 800 folio pages of tightly written prose (the New York manuscript is a copy made in 1700 and is believed to be the only record of it left). Philip A. Means has left a complete analysis of the manuscript of this work, and, he says, Cabello's observations and writings of the early coastal peoples 'gives one of the lengthiest, sanest, and most detailed accounts that we have of the peopling of the coast and of the history in long pre-Incaic days of the states there'.[6] It was, for example, Cabello who brought up the voyage made by Topa Inca, *c.* 1460, to the two islands called Wawa Chumpi and Nina Chumpi (which, again, enters the Galápagos-Inca-Heyerdahl controversy). But, however objective Cabello strived to be, he was out to prove his theory that the American Indians descended from Ophir. Therefore, anything that deals with people arriving by balsas from elsewhere must be considered in the light of his possibly adjusted facts to fit preconceived theories.

The chroniclers' legend-histories give us, then, first the directing classes, who arrived with a developed retinue. Each valley had its Cacique (*alaec*), and they, in turn – at least in the later stages of the Kingdom of Chimor – were guided by a lord-ruler of all (the *Cie*). The Mochicas and the Chimús were, as all evidence implies both historically and archaeologically, a theocracy – a natural political growth out of a neolithic economy. It was based on the following system. The land belonged to the directing classes, a king, or real leader, whose power, like the baroque archbishop's, was both temporal and spiritual; land was partitioned out to individuals on the basis of needs. A priestly class constituted the official contact between the gods and mere man. When men were asked, they performed work on the temples as part of their work-service tax, in order to curry the favour, either real or imaginary, of the supernatural forces on which, in great part, their lives depended. The organization of natural resources by means of their labour work-service tax enabled them to bring water from a distance, thus enlarging the areas of cultivation; to terrace the hills, under direction of the directing classes; to collect and concentrate the fertilizers (llama, human and guano) – all of which gave an impetus to agriculture, and which, in time, helped to produce surpluses within this neolithic economy. The surpluses gained from improvement on very primitive agricultural methods were then stored by the directing classes, and these paid for the non-producing nobility and priests, and later, for other categories of craftsmen who were not taxable. This gave rise to a stratified society, one which was class-divided. It had status and status symbols. The type of turban worn suggested office, and emphasis was placed upon the elabora-tion of the headdress. The Mochica-Chimú pottery suggests, and in large part it is corroborated by archaeology, that there were priests, rulers, messengers, warriors, fishermen – all of those which constitute 'society'. It is quite possible, then, to assume (since Cieza confirms it) that the rulers were surrounded, as the legend of Ñaymlap has it, with a keeper of the royal face-paint, trumpeters, royal cup bearers, bathing and weaving masters.

No one knows how this theocracy functioned. It was doubtless hereditary, but not necessarily carried out by primogeniture, since some of those rulers who visited Francisco Pizarro near the Santa Valley in 1527 (one, at least, is historically known) were women – even though, in general, women never seemed to appear at social functions. Entry into the heredi-tary nobility was usually acquired through achievements of war. Such, for example, as General Pacatamú, leader of the armies that conquered the valley now called Pacasmayo (a transliteration of the original name). 'Pacatamú', writes Padre Calancha, 'took its name from him and the great number of ruined edifices one sees today took his name, *Pacatamú*, and in some of these lived the governor of Chimú with his families.'[7]

What was the Mochica-Chimú theory of rule, and how were the lands alienated? A chronicler, when speaking of the Inca-system (*Cobo*) – which cannot necessarily be applied to the coast – averred that after an Inca conquest, land, rivers, llamas, mountains were all declared crown property. However, 'community tenures may have been allowed to function in pre-Incaic fashion … which viewed all peasant holdings as a royal dispen-sation'.[8] Since the Incas were borrowers rather than innovators, and since they arrived late and organized other older cultural patterns – prin-cipally in agriculture and land tenure – it may well be possible that the coastal pattern of rule and distribution of land, and the fruits from it, was similar to the Incas'. Whatever the process, implicit in this theocracy was 'everybody's automatic claim to land, based not on merit or purchase, but on membership in a kin-group. Every member of the *ayllu*, including

H

those absent or obviously unfit, once they were married, could claim a share of the culture's capital good: land.'[9]

The Lords, the *Cie*, were hereditary. They ruled through governors, a large priesthood who were the guardians of tradition. The land belonged to the *Cie*, and newly created arable lands, made such by large-scale irrigation, were his to parcel out in periodic reallotments to the communities. The fruits of the land were divided between the state and the producer. All Indians – except those non-tax-paying groups of the directing classes, rulers, priests and official craftsmen – were expected, in addition to sharing their crops, to give time, in the form of work-service, to build the gigantic irrigation projects, temples, palaces and fortifications. An individual Indian might have occasionally escaped this system, but as a group, they submitted.

RELIGIOUS AND MILITARY ARCHITECTURE

The sheer mass of structures, temples, roads, fortifications, cities, and defensive walls that the Mochica-Chimú have left behind in the Peruvian desert will forever remain a monument to their aesthetic sensibilities – and to their muscular energy. There has been so little systematic archaeological work done on these remains that there is now no clear picture of the various epochs, in human time, that they cover; yet, since the earliest evidence to have been found thus far is the *Huaca Prieto*, in the Chicama Valley, with the grave contents dated as *c*. 3000 BC, we do know that here time and man reach far, far back.

At Tumpiz, called Tumbes, in the northern boundaries of the Kingdom of Chimor (and, when it was conquered, the boundary also of the Inca Empire), the rich agricultural valley was dotted with structures. The most famous of them all – and that which for unknown reasons still survives, amorphous as it is – is the Sun Temple. This temple, of which the Italian Benzoni has left a drawing, was built by the 10th Lord Inca, Huayna Capac, some time after 1490. He, according to one chronicler,[10] 'entered Tumbez where he ordered construction of a fortress, a Temple of the Sun'. The Sun Temple, once connected by a road to the bay, was large enough to have been sighted by Francisco Pizarro and his minions from the sea in 1527. Pedro de Candia, who arrived at the Kingdom of Gold with Pizarro, was the only one to see it and to leave a verbal record of it. Pizarro's ship stood off the shore of Tumbes, and it was Pedro de Candia who volunteered to go ashore:

Sir, I am going alone to see what there is in this valley. If I die, you will have lost only one man ...

He put on a coat of mail that came down to his knees ... and buckling his sword, took up a shield of polished steel ... In this outfit, after begging of his companions to commend him to God, he took leave of them ...

... the Indians were quite persuaded ... that he was a son of the Sun and that he had come from heaven; with the result that they started to worship him as such and brought him to the temple, which was entirely panelled with gold, in order that he might see how deeply they revered their god, who was also his father. They led him from room to room and from treasure to treasure, showing him the living quarters of his brothers, the Incas, their sumptuous bedrooms, the stock rooms and kitchens, filled with gold and silver tableware, as also the famous gardens in which every tree, every plant and herb, every animal, every bird and insect, was made out of a precious metal. And although this Christian had amazed the Indians, they, in their turn, amazed him even more.[11]

Pedro de Candia, a Greek, was born in Crete. He was an immense man, known for his physical strength, as well as for his skill at casting bronze (he cast the sixteen bronze cannons for the Battle of Chupas, 'of such good quality', said one who lost his leg when one of them was fired, 'that they could have vied with those from the workshops of Milan'). Although he was supposed to have written a report on Tumbes, it has never come to light. Furthermore, what he reports sounds more like a description of the famous Curicancha of Cuzco, the golden enclosure which contained all such golden mimicry of life, than of Tumbes. Events proved him to be not especially bright, however, so that his report on Tumbes might simply have been overdrawn. Still, though, in 1536 another conquistador, a *pícaro* of high degree,[12] wrote that

the great city called Tumpiz is inhabited entirely by Indians and close to the shore is a great house belonging to the lord of the country with walls built of adobes like bricks, very beautifully painted with many colours and varnished. I never saw anything more beautiful. The roof is straw, also painted so that it looks more like gold. About a large temple was a garden with fruits and vegetables of the country imitated all in gold and silver. The women wore a dress large and broad like a morning gown, and the chieftains went dressed in mantles and shirts and wore a thing like a turban adorned with gold and silver beads which they call Chaquira.

Nevertheless, by 1548, at the time of the arrival of Pedro de Cieza de León, along with many other knights who came to do battle with Gonzalo Pizarro at Cuzco, the Temple of the Sun is no longer mentioned. This is probably because by that time it was in ruins. The civil wars between the disputants for the Incaship, Huascar and Atahualpa, which occurred between the years 1528 and 1532, while Pizarro was in Spain organizing his conquest of Peru, left Tumbes partly in ruins and the temple in good part sacked.

'This valley was once thickly settled and cultivated,' wrote Cieza de León, 'covered with fine, cool irrigation canals.' Here the Inca road, doubtless laid over the more ancient Mochica and Chimú road, begins; still extant, it traverses the valleys, moving along the areas shaded by immense hurango trees and answering precisely the description of it given in 1548 by Cieza, who spoke 'of a road fifteen feet wide,[13] bordered by a mighty wall more than a fathom high. Throughout its length this road was carefully tended and ran beneath the [hurango] trees ... and all of the trees were alive with many kinds of birds and parrots. In each of these valleys there were large and fine lodgings ... '

The largest of the complex cities of the valley is Apurlé, which, like all of them, is built of adobe blocks and composed of pyramids, dwellings, roads and canals. Apurlé lies between Motupe, a place of ancient mention,[14] and Jayanca. It was watered from the great canals, one of the four eight-foot-wide *acequias* drawn from the upper reaches of the Rio Leche. The whole area, in fact, is laced with canals, and about these are the ruins of what was once an immense centre.

Jayanca, which was in ancient times a Chimú lay-centre, was fully taken over by the Incas. It has many structures, both of adobe as well as of stone set in adobe; most of them, however, are so amorphous that only an aerial view gives any idea of structure and form. Pizarro, when he stalked the valleys, found them well-peopled, and Cieza reported that 'in bygone times this valley was thickly settled ... The chiefs of this valley [of Jayanca] were venerated and respected by their subjects; even today [1548] this is true of those who survived, and they are followed and served by their women and servants, and have their gatekeepers and guards.'[15] It was seemingly in this same Jayanca[16] that the Inca raised a Temple of the Sun; and the importance of this valley is further registered by the fact that the brother of Huayna Capac, the 10th Lord Inca, married the daughter of Jayanca.

Túcume (once spelled Tuqueme), south of the River of Milk (Leche), gives full hint, with its enormous adobe block temples, of its past. Cieza found it 'large, beautiful, and covered with groves and meadows, and despite the fact that its buildings are in ruins and falling to pieces, one can still see what it once was'. Despite four centuries of sack, rain and the insults of time, one can, indeed, still see the immensity of these ruins. There are truncated *huacas*, remains of ramps that lead to the top of them, platforms, walled enclosures; if one gave time to it, there could be found the remains of the dwellings that surrounded it. Close to Túcume are also the graves that have yielded more than three quarters of all of the gold objects which are continually being found in Peru. Túcume, which is 'El Purgatorio' to the natives, since its tremendous walls and rooms may suggest their idea of a hellish labyrinth, is immense – and remarkable.[17] There are no less than eight immense structures; walled-in areas, as at Chan Chan; and a well-built, stone-laid fortress, a *pucara*, which crowns the hill that overlooks Túcume, and from which one can see a number of truncated pyramids in all directions rising above the foliage on the plain, through which runs the Inca coastal highway.

Southward from this administration and religious area is the immense valley of Lambayeque. No less than sixty-one ruined sites have been recorded there, and of particular interest, since they give substance to the legend of Ñaymlap, are the ruins of *Huaca Chotuna*,[18] which are covered with an ornamental adobe frieze of Chimú-Lambayeque style. (It is at Chot, as previously mentioned, that Ñaymlap was said to have settled.) The valley of Lambayeque is divided into three parts, all of which are filled with ruins. One of the largest of these is *Pútapo*, which is thought to have been formerly called Cinto and has been described as a lay-centre,[19] an administration centre for the area about. Like much of the Chimú style, it is characterized by high adobe walls, palaces, houses and storage areas; the rock-bound hills are studded with fortresses. Through it the Incas placed their coastal highway. Within this area, Cieza wrote, there was 'another exceedingly beautiful valley, by name Cinto'. However, he also found that by then, in 1548, 'most of the natives have disappeared as a result of the wars the Spaniards waged against each other. The evils and hardships these wars occasioned made an end of them.'[20]

At Pacasmayo, separated from the valley of Lambayeque by thirty miles of desert, is the Rio Jequetepeque. Since Pacasmayo was very fertile and well populated, it contains the remains of countless sites, all Chimú or Mochica. The largest is Pacatmú, a vast complex of buildings with both Mochica and Chimú features, which lies on a high bluff overlooking the ocean, above the Jequetepeque River. The length of the ruins, which include pyramids, courts, burial grounds and palaces, is at least three quarters of a mile, and the width is about half that. It is smaller than Chan

Chan, although it preserves many of the same city features, and doubtless, as the graves reveal, was first a Mochica site. Cieza, even in his time (and it was, as he said, a bad enough time for the Indians), found it 'most fertile and thickly settled, more than all those I have described, whose natives, before they were dominated by the Incas, were powerful and feared by their neighbours, and had great temples where they performed sacrifices to their gods. All is now in ruins.'[21] Padre Calancha wrote of it: 'This city was named Pacatamú after the Chimú general who made a conquest of the valley.' (The valley was later called Pacasmayo.) 'It was this Pacatamú who built', avers Calancha, 'the great edifices and dwellings in which he and his family lived when he was governor.' This, then, seems to be the only ruin site which is associated with a historical personage; all the other ruins retain the names given to them by the Spanish colonists.

The Chicama Valley, the next one southward, is considered to be the heartland of the Mochicas. (However, as Cieza himself said, 'the reader must realize that between one valley and another … lie sand wastes and arid stretches of rocks where no living or growing thing is to be seen, neither grass nor trees'. It is true that in the void between the valleys, there is nothing, although often there does arise a pyramid, and one is forcibly reminded, when one sees the remains of an *acequia*, from what distances the Mochicas and the Chimús brought water in order to make human habitation possible in an area in which nature created superhuman obstacles for life itself.) Chicama, if one wishes to rely on the folk history, could be a corruption of 'Chacma', who was the wife of the first Grand Chimú; it is possibly a survival of that name. The valley is studded with ruins, though none as large as those in the next valley of Moche. And although in this place one might hope to find the remains of a city which tradition insists was the capital of the Mochicas, there is no such evidence. It is, however, fully obvious from the collections of Don Rafael Larco, upon which most of the deductions have been drawn, that the valley was dominated by the Mochicas.

It is on the periphery of the valley that the Mochicas become architecturally conspicuous. At Chiquitoy, just where the Chicama Valley asserts its fertility and the desert begins, there are splendid remains of a truncated pyramid, a walled enclosure, and, as well, clear evidence of a road which was part of the Chimú road system until it was absorbed by the Incas. Near to the pyramid of Chiquitoy was a large walled structure with all the evidences of having been an administrative centre for the surrounding area.

118   The ancient coastal road, which runs through a desolation which is

overwhelmingly arid,[22] becomes, when it approaches the Moche Valley and the great city-state of Chan Chan, a sixty-foot-wide processional road, with metre-high walls to give it dignity; at a dry river bed, there are guard houses and a flight of stone-laid steps which, despite the centuries of cultural rapine, can still be clearly seen. Chan Chan was the political and economic centre of the Kingdom of Chimor, and is metropolitan in character. It was built on the sterile edge of the Moche Valley at its north-west corner, a six-miles-square complex of buildings which extended to the very edge of the sea. Within the city, as revealed by Robert Shippee's remarkable aerial photographs taken in 1931, there were ten distinct clan or tribal units; the largest is 480 by 375 feet. Outside the walls, as the aerial plates show, was a veritable sea of small houses, built with no apparent pattern.

Everything here is on a large scale. Immense walls, forty feet high, an admixture of small rock and adobe pressed into forms called *tapia*, separate clan from clan; each unit seems to have been a complete entity. Towering above the clan walls are three large pyramidal *huacas*, within the walls or near its peripheries, which complete the city. The city was complete with regular streets, houses with gabled roofs, cells, and gardens which were irrigated by special canals. Water was conducted into Chan Chan by the same aqueducts which brought water down from the upper reaches of the Moche River: the same, too, that were cut off by the conquering armies of the Topa Inca, forcing the Minchan-çaman of the Kingdom of Chimor to surrender his city. Water was preserved within the city by stone-lined reservoirs, *pozos*, capable of holding two million cubic gallons. These are immense and well engineered, and, as they are on a low plain, presumably were practicable owing to their proximity to the sea; either they were fed by water brought down to them, or else water was held in them by seepage, which suggests that it would have been brackish. In any case, the whole was planned on an immense scale.

While Chan Chan is greater than anything else on the coast (except Pachacamac, located near Lima) its construction is nevertheless similar to much of the official Chimú architecture. In fact, most of these administrative centres have certain architectural features in common. They are always erected in sterile land (land was too scarce to allow the erection of a dwelling on fertile soil). The centre was walled and dominated by a pyramidal *huaca*, with raised platforms for religious performances; if not within it, then close to it, were immense granaries for storing dry maize, beans, peppers, fish, etc. When the lay-centre was placed in the Andean

ARCHITECTURE

91 A detail of the Temple of the Sun showing the adobe-brick construction.

92 The Temple of the Sun (foreground) and the Moon (background) built by the Mochicas at the southern end of the Moche Valley. These pyramids were the largest structures on the Peruvian coast.

93 The restored ruins of Puruchucu in the Rimac Valley near Lima. This was a pre-Inca and, later, an Inca administrative centre.

94 A section of an adobe-built wall constructed in about 1200 showing the way in which the bricks were laid with adobe cement.

95 One of the walled clan units at Chan Chan, the vast metropolitan complex which was the centre of Chimú civilization.

96 A map of the ruins of Chan Chan commissioned in 1773 by the Bishop of Trujillo for his history of the Chimú.

97 A unique aerial photograph of Chan Chan. This gives an idea of the extent of the city-state, which was six miles square and had an estimated population of over 50,000. The walled clan divisions can be clearly seen.

98 A detail of wall decorations at Chan Chan. At one time most of the interior walls were covered with adobe designs of this kind.

99 An adobe frieze of bird-dragons at Huaca Esmeralda close to Chan Chan.

100 An aerial view of the ruins of a large settlement in the Catalina Valley near Chan Chan. The hillsides have been terraced for agriculture.

101 The remains of the shrine of Pachacamac, the Creator-God, between the Rimac and Lurin Valleys. This was a leading cult centre.

102 A Mochica pyramid and its courtyard at Chiquitoy. The pyramid was composed of four tiers and reached by a ramp. The road nearby was originally Mochica, later Inca.

91

92

93

94

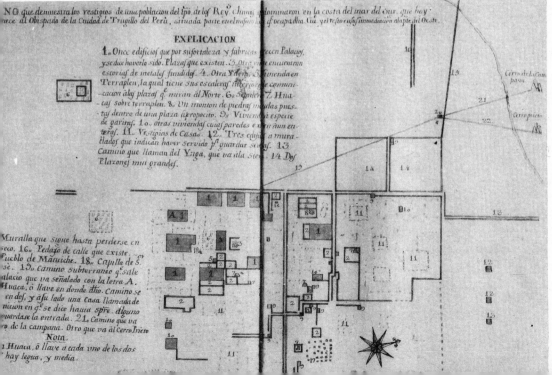

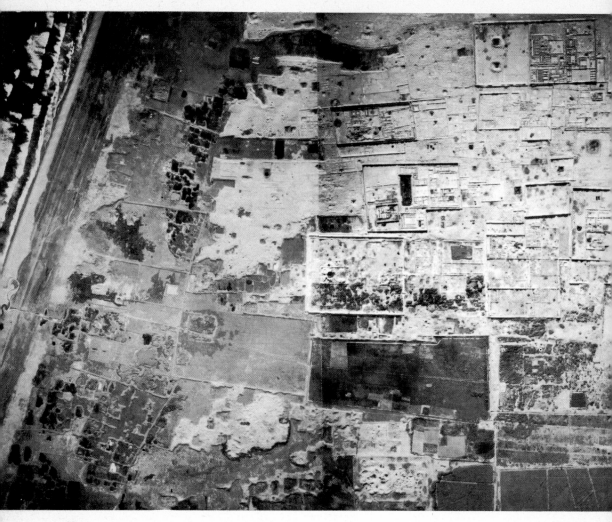

97

98

99

100

101

foothills, there was terracing of the hills either to raise crops or to ease the falling of stone landslides. The planning called for general rectangularity in the combination of the various structures that made up the city. Building materials are everywhere the same: mould-made adobe bricks, standard and mass-produced. The iron-hard wood of the *algarrobo* (which in some ruins has held up after 1,000 years) was used for lintels and wall binders. The adobe walls which divided the clan-lands were coated with liquid adobe, and design was then applied. The Mochicas painted their walls with murals, quite a few of which are still extant, and, although the Chimús also painted their walls, they decorated mostly with adobe frieze. As with the Mayas, all this presupposed a high degree of social organization, for it required numbers of skilled artisans to erect the buildings, map out the highly complex systems within the walls, and apply the decoration as well.

The whole of the interior walls of Chan Chan seem to have been decorated in the Chimú manner. The earliest of the archaeological explorers have commented on these walls, in particular those found in the halls of the Arabesques, of which they also left illustrations.[23] The walls in the Verlarde group – discovered in 1908 only to be completely destroyed by rare torrential rains a few years later – are utterly fantastic: there is an overall design that covers these walls, which are twenty feet in height and forty feet in length, a continuous border of anthropomorphized birds carrying fish, scorpions, and crabs, and a fret of swimming fish. The wall friezes seem to have been mould-produced, and the numerous *huacas* lying about Chan Chan that reveal these, plus new discoveries, whether by *huaqueros*[24] or archaeologists, provide a continuous stream of material for study.[25]

Chan Chan was the largest prehistoric coastal city of South America. It is calculated to have had upwards of 50,000 inhabitants; however, if one merely counts the scattered dwellings that lie outside the walls of Chan Chan, assuming the norm of each family to be six, the estimate of 50,000 is too modest. The aerial mosaic of Chan Chan, made in 1931, gives the first accurate plan of it. It confirms, too, the earlier theory that the walls were not made for defence; they do not have parapets from which defenders could hurl down destruction. It was Squier whose instincts led him, in 1866, to presume that these were walls that separated clan from clan, and that within these barriers were specialized workers in metals, weaving, pottery, wood carving, etc. There is now no reason to negate his deduction. One may still see immense masses of the dross from the operations of the gold-workers and copper-workers. Weaving within Chan Chan was done in mass. Pottery, predominantly black-ware, was mass-produced from moulds, and gold ornaments were cast by craftsmen. The immense amount of Chimú ornaments, drinking beakers, earplugs, necklaces, crowns, and diadems seen in the various public and private collections gives an idea, no more, of the almost Arabian Nights splendour and other-worldliness of Chan Chan.

Although archaeological sites were and still are found throughout the Moche Valley, Mochica history itself is bound up with the Temples to the Sun and the Moon, which are located at the southernmost part of the valley, at the edge of the desert. As previously stated these are believed to have been the single largest man-made structures on the coast of Peru: that of the Sun was 145 feet high, with a base platform of 75 feet by 450 feet, and with five stepped terraces that were reached by a ramp, which, itself, is 290 feet long. When first systematically investigated,[26] these temples were found to have once been extensively covered with murals of seven colours, all Mochica in style (a style not dissimilar to that of the figures painted on their vases). The Temple of the Sun, which has been calculated to have contained 50,000,000 adobe bricks, was built of columns of adobes, sun-dried brick held together by adobe cement, with no attention to binding. Over this, the mass was plastered with thick, liquid adobe and then painted.

At the base of the Temple of the Sun is the Moche River, the same river which was turned out of its course in 1602 by Escobar Corchuelo in order to secure the treasures buried within the *huaca*. Across from the river is the Temple of the Moon, terraced against the side of the bare mountain. It is smaller than the Sun Temple (which seems strange, in view of the importance given to the Moon by the coastal-dwelling yuncas), and connected with it are numerous remains of what may have been living quarters for priests and women attendants, Virgins of the Moon.

A people use the material which is available to them; thus, plastic mud was the medium of the coastal peoples. The use of sun-dried brick does not necessarily make the work inferior in concept to that produced by those who worked in stone. Other ancient cultures, such as that of early Mesopotamia, also worked with sun-dried brick.[27] In addition, they used solid walls of rammed clay mixed with potsherd and gravel, which they called *pisé*; the same techniques were employed on the Peruvian coast, under the general term of *tapia*. Geological and geographical environment has, naturally, a marked influence on the evolution of building materials, and a specialist in these cultures of the fertile crescent has pointed out that 'the two greatest centres, the Nile valley and Mesopotamia, show a regional conservatism in technology which was impervious to political or military upheavals'.[28] The same thing may be said of the Mochicas and the Chimús. Their civilization spanned perhaps more than 2,000 years of continuous occupation of the same land, but their techniques never changed; they never thought of turning mud-brick into kiln-dried brick. There seemed no need. For all practical purposes, it never rained, and, if it is kept under constant repair, re-cemented and painted, adobe keeps well. The following description of the making of sun-dried bricks in Mesopotamia[29] is comparable, in all its details, to the techniques of the adobe-makers of Peru's coast:

The brickmaker works on a prepared piece of ground, with the mixture stacked on a mat beside him. The mould, which often consists of two brick-sized compartments, is filled, and the surplus mud is smoothed off with the hand. The mould is then removed by handles projecting on either side, and the bricks are left in place to dry, for a period which varies according to the heat of the sun. They are then turned over or tilted together for a further period. A more liquid form of the same mixture is used as mortar, and as plastering for both internal and external wall-faces.

Thirty miles south of Moche is Virú. Virú has a long, involved and interesting history for so small and so confined a valley, and has been the subject of one of the most intense and co-ordinated archaeological projects in Peru. It is notable for the diversity of its sites, and particularly for a fortress known as Tomaval, 'the boldest ruin on the north coast'. Built into a stone hill, it dominates both the upper valley and the river. Of further interest is the fact that the gnarled and twisted trunks of the *algarrobo* tree are used as binder.

It is at the Santa Valley that both Mochica and Chimú put in their most sustained architectural efforts. The river, which draws its immense amount of water from that which runs between the White and Black Cordilleras and drains a large portion of the central Andes, is the largest coastal stream, although, until its waters were systematically canalized by the Mochicas and the Chimús, its natural oasis was one of the smallest. Santa Valley is separated from Virú by the same hiatus of desert and arid desolation which separates the other valleys. Before it is reached, as Cieza pointed out, 'one crosses a small valley having no river'. This was Salinas, which was (and still is) one of the major coastal salt-producing areas. It lies about two miles back from the sea, and ancient rectangular shallow beds have been dug, into which sea-water filters; when the water evaporates, workers remove the salt. It is now, as then, a large-scale operation. In times past, a pre-Inca step road led from this valley to the highlands, and the Chimús built a high wall, part of the great wall, to defend it. Remains of a large Chimú village lie close upon the salt pans; its agriculture was fed by an *acequia* which followed for many miles the tortuous convolutions of the low-lying hills, in order to bring water to the community, whose sole purpose was to work the salt. And finally, when the Incas conquered the coast, they ran their road close to the village and again developed a community of *mitamaes* to maintain the highway.

Although the remains in Santa were extensive, well known and distinctly visible, it was not until 1931 that archaeology became aware of the wall. It was discovered by Lt George Johnson and Robert Shippee:

While we were still operating from the base that we had established at Trujillo for the mapping of the well-known ruins of Chan Chan, we made a flight with the photographic plane inland as far as the Marañon River and, on the return, circled southward around Mount Huascaran and then followed the valley of the Santa River to the coast. Our course was over the edge of the foothills bordering the narrow upper valley of the river on the north. Johnson, co-leader and photographer of the expedition, watching for photographic subjects, noticed what appeared to be a wall flowing up and down over the ridges beneath the plane, wondered for a moment as to the purpose of such a structure, decided that it was worth recording, and made a number of photographs of it.[30]

On the second flight they noticed forts at irregular intervals. They crowned the hills; some were round, others rectangular, and still others square. All were of *pirca* construction, rock cemented with adobe, but none were connected with the wall. Most of the fortifications, of which more than fifty have now been counted, lie on the right, or south bank of the Santa Valley and the river; all are placed on top of the highest hills. The wall at times follows the crest of the low spurs of the Andes that border the Santa; it often crosses and recrosses dry river beds. Only recently, in a thorough investigation of it, an American explorer, Gene Savoy, found that the wall, which at places rises to a height of ten feet and is fifteen feet thick, is forty miles in length, running from the sea to the land height of 1,500 feet and ending at the Hacienda de Suchimancillo. (Immense stone-laid *pucaras* were found here, pottery which the discoverer said showed 'Chavin influence but to be Mochica in essence'.) As the wall has not been connected with the fortresses, could not be manned, and could be easily pierced or climbed, it was perhaps a boundary marker

124

rather than, as assumed, a defence barrier. There is, however, no doubt of the character of the fortresses; they were for offence and defence.

The Mochica-Chimú agricultural effort in the Santa, now almost totally destroyed, was on an immense scale, with land reclamation and water conduction to reclaim or better develop the lands which had not been intended for cultivation. Cieza, when he travelled there, found that '[it] was very heavily populated, and there were great warriors and native lords there ... [who] dared to measure their strength with the Incas ... They ordered great lodging and many storehouses erected there, for this valley is one of the largest ... It is crossed by a large and turbulent river[31] ... There used to be many thousands of the natives, but now there are not more than four hundred left, a sad thing to consider.'[32]

Mochica and Chimú influence, despite the wall and the extensive chain of fortifications, did not end at the Santa Valley. The next valley to the south, which is reached by crossing a void of sand and desolation, scoured by the powerful off-shore winds that blow with the force of a hurricane, is the valley of Nepeña, formerly Huambacho. In pre-conquest times, Nepeña was a two-day trek from Santa. Still, there was extensive Mochica and Chimú occupation, and both have left considerable architectural remains: the Chimú, one of the finest preserved altars, with exquisite decorated pillars; and the Mochicas, one of the best-preserved of their temples. The latter, known as Pañamarca (which is not a Mochica word), is a six-tiered pyramid with a temple situated on its eighty-foot height, surrounded with walled courtyards. It was reached by ramp-stairways, six in number, which brought one to the temple. In size and structure, it may be likened to the ziggurat at Ur, the famed Sumerian temple which was built c. 2000 BC.[33] Constructed of the inevitable adobe and covered with the inevitable liquid adobe cement, it was painted with murals exhibiting a wonderful flow of Mochica imagery. What time has left intact shows prisoners, neck-bound with serpents; fanged men, who prance menacingly; winged fox-gods making offers of *chicha* in silver goblets; and priests with panoplies consisting of elaborate headdresses, finely woven stoles, and feathers, who stride about either in an attempt to cajole the gods or to frighten the beholder. The whole valley, too, is full of Mochica and Chimú remains, with an elaborate system for the disposal of the water which comes down perennially from the towering Andes, which can be seen in all their power from the valley.

From this valley and southward there is a falling-off of Mochica-Chimú influence; however, there is still evidence of it in the next valley of Casma and throughout the desert-void that next appears – fifty miles of unin-habitableness, save an occasional surface seepage of water, where there are, nevertheless, remains of dwellings and extensive graveyards. ('The thing that struck me most when I crossed this valley', remembered Cieza, 'was the multitude of graves to be seen ... [even in] many remote spots, laid out in their own fashion, all covered with bones of the dead.') Beyond this is Huarmey, which one seventeenth-century chronicler placed as the southern limits of the Mochicas and the later Kingdom of Chimor; Padre Calancha puts it still further south, at the next valley of Paramonga. However, as the son of a Chimú king, called Minchan-çaman, was living at Huara, which is far south of this, it may be assumed that the Chimús had control of all these valleys, even though nominal rule was that of their own 'lords of the valley'.

Most authorities agree that Paramonga, known in its heyday as Para-munca, was the final boundary of the 620-mile-long Kingdom of Chimor, which extended from the north of Tumbes through all the stretch of desert and oases. It was, as kingdoms go, not unsizeable; Egypt, at its height, did not occupy any larger area. The number of structures which these two cultures, Mochica and Chimú, erected over the span of years between 200 BC and AD 1460 is staggering: so much so, in fact, that no one has ever attempted to catalogue the number of *huacas*, pyramids, temples, lay-centres, *marcas*, administrative centres, etc. that dot these lands within the 620 miles. Just to the south of Paramonga, in the Lurin Valley, was the shrine of Pachacamac, the centre of a cult which had great influence in the lands of the Chimú. The cult of Pachacamac (this is an Inca designa-tion; the yunca word for it seems to have been lost) was originally a cosmogonic legend of the coast. Pachacamac was the creator-hero of the Moon and the husband of Mamacocha, goddess of the sea. This cult seems to have drawn pilgrims from many of the tribes along the coast.

Paramonga, the best-preserved site on the coast, is a double structure built on low-lying rock outcrops next to the river. It was first seen by Europeans when Hernando Pizarro, on the day of Epiphany, 5th January, 1533, set out 'with twenty horse and a few arquebusiers' to traverse the Inca road from Cajamarca to the fabulous shrine of Pachacamac. Miguel de Astete, who served as the scribe for the expedition, wrote the following: 'Marching along the banks of a river [Fortaleza] they stopped for the night at a village called Huaracanga [Huariconga] ... Next day they stopped at a large place called Parpunga [i.e. Paramonga]. It was a strong house with seven encircling walls painted in many devices both inside and outside with portals well built like those of Spain, with two [painted] jaguars at the principal doorway.' Paramonga commands a view of the coastal road and the sea, and was served by a complex of buildings nearby. Its base is about 900 feet by 600 feet, and it is built into the sandstone outcrop with adobe bricks. As Miguel de Astete asserts, it was painted, but although the walls still carry some elements of colour, the animals and birds seen by early observers such as Cieza de León have long since vanished.

It is a tradition that Paramonga was built by the Chimús under their chief, Minchan-çaman, as a bastion of defence against the encroaching Incas. However, the existing remains of Paramonga are of Inca construction (perhaps over a smaller Chimú structure not as yet explored), and are not, as Garcilaso states, a fortress. Dr Arturo Jimenez Borja, who restored some of the adobe ruins in the Rimac Valley and made the restoration of Paramonga in 1961, believes it to have been, like Pachacamac, a shrine. Certainly, on close inspection, it would seem that it was not designed as a fortress, since it is without parapets or defence walls. Moreover, by the time that it was finally finished, c. 1460, the Incas dominated the entire coast, and there was no longer any need for such a fortress. Nevertheless, whether Chimú or Inca, Paramonga seems to have been the southernmost end of actual Mochica-Chimú construction; within this relatively vast waste-land were thousands of structures which follow a definite coastal architectural pattern.

COMMUNICATIONS

Roads, formal roads twenty feet wide, held the Kingdom of Chimor together. No one knows how ancient the Peruvian coastal roads are, since, in most parts, the Incas laid their own coastal *capac-ñan* over these.[34] As the Incas did not use the road-bed (there being no need, since they did not employ dray animals and did not have the wheel), stratification studies to determine road techniques in the Peruvian desert have not been rewarding. But, just as the Romans learned their road-building techniques from the Etruscans and, after 146 BC in Africa, from the defeated Carthaginians, so the Incas learned from those they conquered; thus, when they emerged into the desert after their conquests, they imposed, when possible, their roads on those of the Chimús.

The roads that the Mochicas and the Chimús first cut through the earth were mostly of a comparatively short length and linked up valley to valley. It is to be recalled that each river-oasis was separated from the other by a fierce desert, waterless and treeless, where a pitiless sun beat down most days of the year and the sands were swept by off-shore winds strong enough, at times, to move the *medanos*, the halfmoon-shaped dunes, before one's eyes. To prevent the road from disappearing then, they built metre-high walls of adobe blocks and cemented with mud. This kept out the sand-drift. And the Incas, when they entered the land, copied this technique, as Cieza observed when he rode along the Inca highway: 'Walls flanked this road on both sides; when the sand became so deep that it was impossible for the Indians to built a foundation for them, to keep the traveller from losing his way ... long poles of even length, like beams, were sunk at intervals. And just as care was taken to keep the road clean and to repair the walls if they became worn and needed mending, so they were on the alert to replace any of the poles or piles in the sand if the wind blew them down.'[35]

Transport along the roads was mainly by foot. When it was domesticated, perhaps as early as 5000 BC, the llama served as the principal burden-bearer. The llama could be utilized in a variety of ways. As a means of transport, it could carry up to one hundred pounds at about a pace of ten miles per day. Llama meat (*charqui*), when sun-dried, could be preserved for some time; its wool, while too oily to spin and weave for ponchos, could be used for those famous brown llama-bags into which cargo was placed. Finally, the llama was also used for divination, after it was killed and disembowelled. As one chronicler relates this practice,[36] 'they looked for omens ... examining the heart and lungs ... [they] took out the heart, lungs and all the interior organs, taking care that they should be whole and all in one piece ... [then] they would blow air into the viscera; then, holding the end tight between their fingers, watch the way the air filled the lungs even to the tiniest vessels, and the more they blew, the better that omen became.'

Llamas were to these people what the camel was to the Arab. Both alive and dead, the camel provides almost everything useful to man. Llamas differ physically from camels in their lack of hump, sternal knee, and hock callouses, and most important, in their weight, height and carrying capacity: camels grow to 2,200 pounds, llamas to 400; the camel can carry 800 pounds, the llama 100. But it is their mutual adaptation to varied climates and their general usefulness to man that is their greatest link and closest similarity.[37] They are both equipped to endure climatic extremes: camels can withstand the heat of the Gobi desert, which rises to 140°, and, as well, the almost arctic cold; llamas can withstand the cold of an altitude as high as 18,000 feet and, as well, can acclimatize themselves to the coast.

The llama, contrary to both popular and considerable archaeological opinion,[38] was adapted to the coast. They are found mummified in graves; they are widely portrayed in Mochica and Chimú vases; they are painted on rock murals in Chile. The Mochicas, in particular, were very explicit about how they lived. They are portrayed with their heads covered with a fringed woollen sun-shade that hung over their eyes to keep out the hot sun-blink, thus giving them the appearance of Scottish sheep-dogs. They are shown being loaded, and are also depicted in mating positions. Further, at Pachacamac, llama dung is found lying ten feet deep, indicating that this was accumulated for fertilizer. There are many places along the coast where light rains fall, where grass grows, and where the climate is equitable for llamas to mate and foal. Obviously, then, there were llama-herds; each llama guided by a cord which perforated the ear, they passed throughout the length and breadth of the coast.

But, then, what happened to the llamas? First, they were slaughtered by the hundreds, and herds were not renewed. Also, since llamas must have Indians to guide them through their lives, and since the coastal Indians as a community were exterminated, so the llama also perished. It was the civil wars, the last phase fought between the King's forces, led by La Gasca, and those of Gonzalo Pizarro, in 1548, which was the actual exterminating force. Gonzalo Pizarro, one learns from his letters,[39] used a scorched-earth policy as La Gasca approached from Panama; his lieutenant, Villalobos, in a letter dated from San Miquel de Piura, April 15, 1547, assures Pizarro that he 'sent ten cavalrymen to Maycabilca [the name of the chieftain at the city of Poechos], burnt the *tambos* and fields and sent all the llamas away'. Another of Pizarro's instructions to his captains, in that same April, was to 'take all food supplies and llamas, induce the Indians to rebel ... do not leave anything'. In the seventeenth century the Spaniards, realizing their mistake, tried to remedy the desert transport problem by bringing Arabs, camels and date-palms to the coast. It failed, and all that is left now are the bones of the camel and fruiting date-palms.

Ever since man became man, he has attempted communications in one form or another: drums, shouting, smoke signals, relays of horses, carrier pigeons and, among many civilizations, the courier.[40] The last of these was highly developed under the Incas and was known as the *chasqui*. Pachacutic, the 9th Lord Inca, is said to have been the inventor of this system. The

I

Quechua word *chasqui* means exchange, give or take, and this is precisely what the *chasquis* did; they received a knot-string record, the *quipu*, which was accompanied by a verbal explanation of what each row of knots meant (men, potatoes, llamas, bridges, etc.), and this was transmitted in a relay system from post to post in the following manner: '[the *chasquis*] lived in groups of four or six in two thatched huts, located a quarter of a league apart along these roads. They were all young men who were especially good runners, and it was their duty to keep permanent watch of the road, in both directions, in order to catch sight of messengers from the other relays, and hurry out to meet them, before they had even covered the distance assigned to them.'[41] Our most reliable source, Pedro de Cieza de León, who actually witnessed the *quipu* system in action, assures us that messages were carried in relays and that each *chasqui* ran two miles at top speed; further, that in this way a message could be carried from Quito to Cuzco, a distance of 1,250 miles, in five days![42]

A representation of a *chasqui* as a winged runner

The *quipu*, as described above, was simply a knot, a mnemonic device. It was both simple and ingenious. It consisted of a main cord, ranging from a foot to two yards in length, from which hung smaller strings, some of which were coloured. It has been shown that it was used to record numbers in a decimal system, including a symbol for zero, which was merely an empty space. Knots were tied into the strings to represent numbers so that if, for example, a governor wanted to know how many able-bodied Indians were captured in a newly won *marca*, this could be read from the knot-string record.[43] The different colours of the wool threads apparently had meaning; the mode of intertwining the knot or twisting the thread or the distance of the knots from each other gave nuance. With these *quipus* the Inca had the numbers of tribes, llamas, women, old people. Beyond mere numbers the colours of the smaller threads, the green, blue, white, black and red, could, it is believed, express meanings and even, it is asserted, abstract ideas. When Pedro de Cieza de León in 1549 talked to some of the old 'rememberers', they explained that these

knots counted from one to ten and ten to a hundred, and from a hundred to a thousand. Each ruler of a province was provided with accountants, and by these knots they kept account of what tribute was to be paid...and with such accuracy that not so much as a pair of sandals would be missing. I was incredulous respecting this system of counting and although I heard it described, I held the greater part of the story to be fabulous. But when I was in Marca-vilca, in the province of Xauxa [i.e., central Peru, near to present-day Huancayo] I asked one of them to explain the *quipu* in such a way that my curiosity would be satisfied ...the *quipu-camayoc* proceeded to make the thing clear to me...he knew all that had been delivered to Francisco Pizarro, without fault or omission, since his arrival in Peru. Thus I saw all the accounts for the gold, the silver, the clothes, the corn, the llamas and other things, so that in truth I was astonished.[44]

With all this, however, the knotted strings had to be accompanied by a verbal comment, without which the meaning of each string knot would have been unintelligible. That, of course, is why those *quipus* which have been recovered from graves are to us, the living, only so many knotted strings.

Unfortunately, no one has ever found any such *quipus* as were illustrated by the Neapolitan nobleman, Principe di Sansevero, who issued from his private press in 1750 the first work on *quipus*, entitled *Lettera Apologetica dell Esercitato Accademico della crusca di contenente La disesa del Libro Intitolato Lettere D'Una Peruana Per rispetto all supposizione de*

QUIPU. The authorship was attributed to an anonymous 'Duchessa Di S ... ', but was actually written by himself, Raimundo di Sangro, Principe di Sansevero. He illustrated *quipus* with miniature pan-pipes, moon-symbols, gold, rainbows, slings, the symbols of Pachacamac, of Viracocha, of the sun (*inti*), of lightning (*illapa*), which were fiery-red strings in burst; it was, in other words, a dictionary of contrived Inca symbols. It was however doubtless a mutation as a result of the author's reading of an Italian translation of 'El Inca' Garcilaso's history of the Incas, which was largely responsible for the 'noble-savage' theme which for a century haunted much of the literature on the American Indian and still hangs like a miasma over some of it to this day. As such, Sansevero's book played a dubious role in the attempt to form a history of the early Americans. Neither this nor any subsequent attempts, however, were actually able to prove that the Incas had a form of writing.

Did the Mochicas actually have writing? Rafael Larco, one of the pioneers of Mochica and Chimú studies, insists in the affirmative, and he has done a considerable amount of research to prove that the Mochicas had a form of hieroglyphic language. To begin with, Larco insists that the *chasqui* system was invented by the Mochicas. There are innumerable running figures in Mochica pottery portraying men with a special head-gear running over the desert and carrying pouches in their hands. Larco found such a pouch in a Mochica grave. It was a well-tanned, soft piece of llama hide, and in it were painted *pallares*, a form of the lima-bean. These, he believes, were used by the Mochicas' messengers (or *chasquis* – which system, he contends, was borrowed from the Mochicas by the Incas), and he further contends that they actually wrote on the broad surface of these *pallares*.

All this could be possible. There is no doubt that the Mochicas and Chimús had some system of communication, although no one saw it in operation and there is no given word for it; aside from the runners on the vases and the hieroglyphic-bean theory, there is little else. Moreover, there is little evidence that either the Mochicas or the Chimús used the *quipu*, the only known form of writing in South America. The absence of writing in any form among these advanced South American cultures is at once a puzzle and a problem, for it is a cultural hiatus almost without parallel. The Aztecs had a form of pictographic writing and had reached the stage of syllabic phonetics, at which point they were snuffed out as a cultural unity by the *conquistadores*. The Maya system was far advanced, and certainly, even the North American Plains Indian tribes had a form of rebus writing through which, by puns, positions, colour and drawings, they were able to convey ideas.[45]

Larco advanced his theory in a very short paper.[46] In it, through illustrations, he attempted to draw an analogy between the Maya glyphs and those of the Mochicas. Some of the comparisons are ingenious: a Mochica fox is seen handling what are obviously *pallares* painted with different symbols and the Maya figure of a fox which has glyphs painted above it; even more convincing, the Mochica figure of an anthropomorphized bird painting symbols on beans and, in comparison, a figure from a Maya Codex doing more or less the same thing.

The marked-bean theory, as an idea, however, has never been carried beyond this stage, although much manuscript material remains to be published. That the marked beans constantly occur on Mochica pottery is

Marked *pallares* beans with a man's body growing out of one of them, apparently in the act of speaking. The other symbols are a shield, mace and spears

true, though many archaeologists believe that these can be explained as representations of divination or gambling, and that the pictures of the runners with bags containing marked beans represent a game. The important question is, if the courier carried in the leather pouch a number of marked beans, how could they be read as a message by the receiver? They would not serve, as the *quipu* did, as a good mnemonic device unless they were strung together. Nor is there, as there is for the Mayas and the Aztecs,[47] any study by one of the early chronicler-priests which could give us a clue as to the meaning of the symbols on the marked beans (unless, of course, one should turn up from the archives). Because of the lack of clear-cut evidence, then, explanations seem vain in these matters; they divert the curiosity without satisfying the reason. And until Rafael Larco can, by continuing his studies, bring about a more satisfactory answer and provide an explanation out of the corpus of his unpublished material, we are still at the same point as the first chroniclers of Peru, who made note that 'they [the Peruvians] have no form of writing'.

The ship is almost as old as society. Yet it took man a long time to know how to use it effectively. Indian history never mentions the sea in its own story until just four hundred years ago, and the Romans, until they defeated Carthage, hated it and called it 'the pasture of fools'. For many millenniums all sailing was coastal navigation; it took centuries before man broke past the pillars of Hercules and the symbol of *ne plus ultra* ('go no farther') and dared to pit himself against the waves beyond. The really great merit of Christopher Columbus is that he broke the barrier in man's relation to the sea and set out boldly into the unknown.

In the Americas, the boldest adventurers of the sea were the Arawaks and those who replaced them, the Caribs; they sailed the fierce-tempered Caribbean seas in dugouts as large as forty feet in length. While the legends of the mainland from Mexico to Peru are filled with tales of gods and men arriving by sea, there is no archaeological evidence of such. So far as we know, the only advanced Middle American culture that used the sea consistently was the Maya; they travelled in outsized canoes as long as sixty feet and carved from a single tree, using them for extensive coastal navigation from Tampico to Panama, a distance of 2,500 miles. However, as they were out of contact with islands such as Cuba – and this only one hundred miles from Yucatán – their navigation, as all primitive early navigation, was essentially coastal.

There was also coastal navigation in South America, mostly with large balsa-tree rafts between Tumbes and Tumaco. The first historical note

The faces of masked men growing out of marked *pallares* beans

of this comes from the famed Bartolomé Ruiz, the first white navigator to sail 'below the line' in the Pacific and an important figure in the discovery and conquest of Peru, who was later given the title by the King of Spain of *Piloto Mayor de la Mar del Sur*.[48] In 1526 Ruiz was sailing southward in a small caravel to bring help to Francisco Pizarro, who was stranded on the Isle of Gallo, off Tumaco (now a coastal port in Colombia). Here, at about two degrees north latitude, their ship discovered off the coast a large balsa of about thirty tons burden sailing northward; aboard were twenty men and women. It had a cotton sail and no deck house. It was sailing out of Tumbes with an impressive cargo comprised of gold and silver objects, weavings and beads called *chaquira*. The *tallanes* of Tumbes (by this time the Inca dominated the entire coast up to Ecuador) were going on a trading expedition.

After this description by Ruiz, there followed many descriptions of the balsa-log rafts. Benzoni, who, it will be remembered, was in Peru during the last of the civil wars in 1548, left the first illustration of such a balsa raft, which more or less fits the description by Ruiz. And numerous other white men left their impressions.[49] But – and this is the important point to remember – neither Mochicas, Chimús, Incas, nor any other Peruvian coastal tribes ever left an illustration of a balsa-log raft. A good description of the first balsa boats is given by Garcilaso de la Vega:[50]

The only tall trees in Peru being of a hard wood that is as heavy as iron, they did not carve out canoes as is done elsewhere in America, but constructed rafts

135

WAR

103 A jet-black effigy ceramic of a Chimú warrior adjusting his headgear.

104 A pottery representation of a duel between Mochica rivals. The weapon being used is a heavy club or *macana*.

105 A Mochica vase depicting warriors with their prisoners, who have been stripped and are being led by ropes round their necks.

106 Mochica pottery showing a prisoner being led into captivity.

107 An aerial view of the Great Wall of Peru, which runs through the Andean foothills north of the Santa Valley. This probably formed part of the Chimú defence system against the Incas.

108 Ruins of a fortress, which formed part of the Great Wall of Peru, overlooking the Santa Valley.

109 A double-walled fortress, probably of Mochica construction, built on a stone outcrop in the Viru Valley.

110 Tamboreal, an immense fortress on the south bank of the Santa River. A recent survey has discovered over thirty similar fortifications in this area, which was the site of the Chimús' last stand against the invading Incas.

111 Paramonga, an elaborate construction traditionally believed to have formed part of the Chimú defence system. Some scholars, however, claim that its function was that of a shrine rather than a fortress.

112 The ruins of Huarco in Southern Peru (now known as the Cañete Valley), a centre of local resistance to the Inca invasion. Later the Indians from this area allied themselves with the Incas in the conquest of the Chimú.

105

106

109

110

III

principally, made of a tree very commonly found in the mountains, that is no thicker than a man's thigh and as light as a fig tree. These rafts were usually built of five or seven tree trunks tied together and cut in such a manner that, on either side of the central trunk, which was the longest of all, they gradually became equally shorter. Thus, in front as well as in back, these rafts had the same pointed shape. They were connected with the banks by two ropes which, when pulled, made it possible to cross over.

The balsa tree, the *Ochroma piscatoria,* is the most buoyant species and the one which is most frequently used commercially. It grows in the rain-drenched coastal jungles about the Guayas-Daule river system. Balsa grows plentifully, and provided the conditions of water, heat and jungle-humus are met, it can grow from a seedling to a tree forty feet tall, fourteen inches in diameter, and relatively branchless in eight years. The centres of the balsa-trade were Guayaquil and the island of Puna, which was controlled by the Huancavilca tribes, the principal traders in balsa logs.

As there was no wood, the other boats used by the coastal Indians in Peru were made from the tall cylindrical reeds which grow in the swamps about the river oases on the Peruvian coast. Although the form of construction differed somewhat from those made by the people who dwelt in the Lake Titicaca region, they were essentially the same. The classic description of them was written by José de Acosta,[51] following his long visit to Peru:

They [the Indians of Peru] make as it were faggots of bul-rushes or drie sedges well bound together, which they call *Balsas*; having carried them upon their shoulders to the sea, they cast them in, and presently leape upon them. Being so set they launch out into the deepe, rowing up and downe with small reedes of

Coastal yuncas on a balsa-log raft

eyther side, they goe a league or two into the sea to fish, carrying with them their cordes and nettes uppon these faggots, and beare themselves thereon. They cast out their nettes, and do there remaine fishing the greatest parte of the day and night, untill they have filled up their measure with the which they returne well satisfied. Truely it was delightfull to see them fish at Callao off of Lima, for they were many in number, and every one set on horsebacke, cutting the waves of the sea, which in their place of fishing are great and furious ... beeing come to land they drawe their barke out of the water upon their backes the which they presently undoe and lay abroade on the shoare to drie. There were other Indians of the vallies of Yca which were accustomed to goe to fish in leather, or skinnes of seawolves, blowne up with winde, and from time to time they did blowe them like balles of winde, lest they should sinke.

This type of balsa raft made of reeds is widely illustrated by the Mochicas, the Chimús and others; the illustrations of totora-craft are found both painted and moulded on stirrup cups, showing Indians – seldom more than two or three in a single boat – fishing or paddling. These boats were considerably seaworthy, even in the high waves, and the Indians used them to fish far out to sea and to visit the guano islets off the coast.

Along the entire coast of Peru, the Indians go fishing in the little reed boats we have described, and the sea being very calm, they can venture four to five leagues from shore in these light skiffs. But to carry heavier loads they always use rafts.

The fishermen, in their little reed barks, remain on their knees, using as a crude rudder a piece of bamboo split lengthwise, which thus ends naturally in the form of a shovel. They row, first on one side then on the other, so skilfully in fact that they may attain to astonishing rapidity. They fish with harpoons, on a cord thirty to

Fishermen in tortora-reed boats

A mythical figure in a reed boat struggling with demons

forty spans long, the end of which is tied to their boat. When their harpoon gets caught in a big catch, they loosen the cord and maintain their equilibrium by putting both hands in the water, until the fish wearies of towing them and they can pull it on board.[52]

The Mochicas also illustrate more elaborate reed boats, with the bow and stern fashioned into dragon-heads; and, if their iconography can be accepted, one drawing shows several Indians between the decks, where pots and other gear are stowed. But there is neither keel nor any other bottom-side make-weight. It is fully possible, however, that, as these reed boats are usually shown as embarking gods, they could have been, as Means wrote, 'merely aesthetic or mythological compositions'.[53]

The same type of reed boats were used for navigating on Lake Titicaca;[54] they were large, with sail, and capable of holding as many as twenty-five people. They were also used for constructing pontoon bridges, the most famous of which is the one that crossed at what is now called the Deas-guadero River, the only river which flows out of Lake Titicaca. Then known as Cacha-marca, this floating road was laid over reed-balsa boats which were renewed every year.[55] Hundreds of these reed-balsa boats—which, when dry, are of such light weight that a boy can carry one – were brought up from the coast, a direct distance of seventy-five miles from the sea to the Andes, by the troops of the Topa Inca for an Inca amphibian assault on a resisting enemy who had taken refuge on islet-fortresses in the waters of the Lake of Chinchay-cocha (known today as Lake Junin).

There is, then, ample documentation – historical, oral and legendary – of the use of totora-reed craft. It is, however, with the other type of boat, the balsa-log raft, that the real problem begins, since it involves, first, cultural diffusion by way of fleets of balsa rafts; second, the Americans-are-Jews theory; and lastly, Thor Heyerdahl and his theory of Inca and pre-Inca voyages to and from the Galápagos islands six hundred miles west of the coast of Ecuador.[56]

This story begins in 1460, when Topa Inca Yupanqui, the 10th Lord Inca, had pushed the Inca conquest as far north as Quito in the highlands. He then descended to the coast and began the first conquest of the coastal tribes of Ecuador, north of Tumbes. The tale, as given by two chroniclers, both of whose motives are suspect,[57] states that while in the gulf of Guayaquil, the Inca heard of two islands, which were called Wawa Chumpi and Nina Chumpi, some eighty to one hundred leagues[58] westward. He sailed there and remained absent for one year; then he returned with his fleet of balsas, bringing back black prisoners, gold and silver, a seat of brass, and the hide and jaw of an animal which, both suspected sources said, looked like that of a horse.

Where were the islands of Wawa Chumpi and Nina Chumpi? The description of them is significantly vague. We do know of the St Elena and La Plata islands off the coast of Manta; of Gallo, near to Tumaco; still further north, of Gorgona and, off Buenaventura, the isla de Palmas. Where, then, did the Incas go? 'Unless', says Philip A. Means,[59] 'we discard the whole story altogether as merely fabulous, an impossibility in view of the two chronicles which relate it, the fleet must have gone somewhere. Was it only to some off-shore islands such as Gorgona or La Plata? If so, how could it have taken nine months or a year to accomplish?'

It must be remembered that the Incas were a purposeful and pragmatic people. They had found, as is well known, an intensive trade-traffic, mostly of balsa sailing, between Tumbes and the north, presumably as far up as Buenaventura, a port in Colombia at 4° north latitude. They soon became aware of the wealth involved in these lively coastal trading voyages:

platinum and gold came from Colombia, as well as the highly prized conch-shells, which were not native to the colder Peruvian waters; pearls were also an item of trade, and from around Esmeraldas came gold of extremely high carat, emeralds, and, as well, chocolate. It is natural, then, that the Incas would go where their imperial appetites led them in this case. (Hernando Cortes did no less after the fall of Tencochtitlan in 1521, when he found the tribute charts of Moctezuma in which there were listed 371 subject towns; it was to these that he sent his troops.) And, if one wishes to fit in Sarmiento's description of the spoils brought back from the Incas' voyage to Wawa Chumpi and Nina Chumpi, the 'black prisoners' could be coastal Indians who dyed themselves with *genipa* dye; the gold and silver objects are, of course, understandable; the seat of brass – as there was no brass until the Spaniards arrived – would instead have been of copper; and the hide of an animal that looked like a horse – as there were no horses until the Spaniards brought them – would have been that of a sea-lion.

One must also consider and bear in mind the importance of the 'meteorological régime of the region and its bearing upon coastwise ocean currents'.[60] The northerly winds between January and March allow rafts rapid passage between Panama and the Guayaquil gulf, but during the remainder of the year, the breeze beats strongly to the south, so that, as Dr Robert C. Murphy, the world's authority on oceanic birds, states, it requires from two to three times longer to go south than to go north.[61] It was this northern balsa journey, followed by others, that eventually brought to the attention of the Indians about Panama the existence of the Incas, for it was on a muddied shore of Darien, on the Pacific side of Panama, that a chieftain in 1521 modelled in clay for a Spaniard an animal which he meant to be a llama, and explained to Pascual de Andagoya that 'where the people live who have these animals there lies the Kingdom of Gold'. And it was just this same type of rumour that eventually promoted the series of voyages of Francisco Pizarro and Almagro, between the years 1522 and 1527, which led to the eventual conquest of the Incas.

The Incas, as noted, did not have contact with the sea until very late in the empire; to them it was and it remained a *hatun-cocha*: a big lake. The Incas, like the Romans, were earth-bound; they thought in terms of land.[62] In fact, one of the pertinent reasons for the defeat of the Inca Empire, with its three million people, by only 326 Spaniards, was the Inca Atahualpa's belief that once the enemy was defeated on land, they could not get reinforcements from the sea; thus, his strategy was to allow

Pizarro and his small army to advance into the empire and then to liquidate them with a single attack. Further, the Incas had only one name for a boat, *hampu*, which was the word for the totora-rush boat used on Lake Titicaca; and, it has been pointed out, the conspicuous poverty in Quechua of nautical terms 'was a reflection of the general ineptitude of the people for seamanship as a whole'.[63] There was, too, a natural limit to balsa navigation; this limit was set by the force of the Humboldt current. In spite of Thor Heyerdahl's explanation of the use of *guaras*,[64] or centre-boards, which allowed great manoeuvrability of balsa, large balsa rafts did not go much further than 5° south because of the force of the current. Therefore, the balsa-raft trade, because of the insistent reality of geography, was necessarily between Tumbes and Buenaventura.

Insofar as the balsa raft theory of communication looms so large in the Mochica-Chimú mytho-history of their origins (it will be remembered that King Ñaymlap was supposed to have arrived from the south on a fleet of balsas to occupy the northern Peruvian territory), it is necessary to examine it carefully. First, there is no such thing as 'direct archaeological evidence' that balsa navigation extended at least to the Chimú area.[65] However, Thor Heyerdahl, being stuck with his theory that the Incas populated Micronesia and Polynesia, having arrived there by balsa rafts, has reached out even further to the Galápagos to show that pre-Spanish navigation was not alone coastal, but that there also 'appears to have been an unbroken tradition of visits to these islands by native fishing rafts from as early as coastal Tiahuanaco [AD 1000] to quite recent historic times'.[66]

This is pure hypothesis. The Galápagos islands, lying across the equatorial line and six hundred miles directly off the coast of Ecuador, were found to be uninhabited. Tomás de Berlanga, Bishop of Panama, was being sailed to Perú in 1535; as navigators always did in the southern seas, they were hugging the shore line. When, at the line, the sails were suddenly emptied to wind, 'something' took hold of the ship and they drifted westerly. On March 10th, 1535, after drifting for two weeks, the vessel came in sight of islands. It was an outlandish place, strewn with sharp-pointed basaltic lava that rang, as the sailors walked over it, with a metallic sound. Cacti held their spiny arms aloft. Birds, myriads of birds, swooped down upon them. Reptiles – nightmarish creatures, more out of the brain of a Hieronymus Bosch or a Jacques Callot than out of nature's largesse – crawled over the sun-hot lava stones. It was enough to waken all the half-slumbering superstitions of the sailors. The islands made a deep impression upon the amiable Bishop of Panama, for, when he at last got his ships back to Ecuador, he wrote his liege, Philip II, 'of the island filled with *galapagos*'.

Your Imperial Catholic Majesty:

April 6, 1535

It seems eminently correct to me to allow Your Majesty to know of the progress of my trip from the time when I left Panama, which was on the twenty-third of February of the current year, until I arrived in this new town of Puerto Viejo [Ecuador].

The ship sailed with very good breezes for seven days, and the pilot kept near land and we had a six-day calm; the currents were so strong and engulfed us in such a way that on Wednesday, the tenth of March, we sighted an island; and, as there was enough water on board for only two more days, they agreed to lower the life-boat and go on land for water and grass for the horses, and once out, they found nothing but seals, *and turtles, and such big tortoises that each could carry a man on top of itself,* and many iguanas that are like serpents. On another day, we saw another island, larger than the first, and with great sierras; and thinking that, on account of its size and monstrous shape, there could not fail to be rivers and fruits, we went to it, because the distance around the first one was about four or five leagues, and around the other ten or twelve leagues, and at this juncture the water on the ship gave out and we were three days in reaching the island on account of the calms, during which all of us, as well as the horses, suffered great hardship.

The boat once anchored, we all went on land, and some were given charge of making a well, and others of looking over the island; from the well there came out water saltier than that of the sea; on land they were not able to find even a drop of water for two days, and with the thirst the people felt, they resorted to a leaf of some thistles like prickly pears, and because they were somewhat juicy, although not very tasty, we began to eat of them and squeeze them to draw all the water from them, and then drank it as if it were rose water.

On Passion Sunday, I had them bring on land the things necessary for saying Mass, and after it was said, I again sent the people in twos and threes, over different paths. The Lord deigned that they should find in a ravine among the rocks as much as a hogshead of water, and after they had drawn that, they found more and more. In fine, eight hogsheads were filled and the barrels and the jugs that were there on the boat, but through the lack of water we lost one man, and two days after we had left that island we lost another; and ten horses died.

From this island, we saw two others, one much larger than all,[67] which was easily fifteen or twenty leagues around; the other was medium; I took the latitude to know where the islands were, and *they are between half-degree and a degree and a half south latitude.* On this second one, the same conditions prevailed as on the first; many seals, turtles, iguanas, tortoises, many birds like those of Spain, but so silly that they do not know how to flee, and many were caught in the hand.

COMMUNICATIONS AND TRANSPORT

113 Part of the Inca coast road running for several thousand miles along the western seaboard. Many of the Inca roads were based on earlier Mochica and Chimú road systems.

114 A pottery vessel decorated with a frieze showing a chieftain being carried in a palanquin.

115 Chimú pottery showing a child being carried in a tubular cradle.

116 and 117 The llama was the chief beast of burden. It is frequently portrayed in Mochica-Chimú pottery, often, as in the top picture, with a protective eye-shade against the blazing sun.

118 The llama still plays an important part in Peruvian life today. A modern Aymara Indian from near Lake Titicaca with two llamas.

119 A pottery model of llamas mating.

120 The balsa boat, made from reeds, was used for transportation by water. Here a Mochica potter has modelled a boat in the shape of a fish monster, being paddled by a turbaned fisherman.

121 Mochica pottery showing a llama scratching its ear.

122 Balsa boats on Lake Titicaca still used today by Indian fisherman.

113

116

117

119

The other two islands we did not touch; I do not know their character. On this one, on the sands of the shore, there were some small stones, that we stepped on as we landed, and they were diamond-like stones and other amber coloured; but on the whole island, I do not think that there is a place where one might sow a bushel of corn, because most of it is full of very big stones, so much so, that it seems as though sometimes God had showered stones; and the earth there is like dross, worthless, because it has not the power of raising a little grass, but only some thistles, the leaf of which I said we picked. Thinking that we were not more than twenty or thirty leagues from this soil of Peru, we were satisfied with the water already mentioned, although we might have filled more of our casks; but we set sail, and with medium weather we sailed eleven days without sighting land; and the pilot and the master of the ship came to me to ask where we were and to tell me there was only one hogshead of water on the ship. I tried to take the altitude of the sun that day and found that we were three degrees south latitude, and I realized that with the directions we were taking, we were becoming more and more engulfed, that we were not heading for land, because we were sailing south; I had them tack on the other side, and the hogshead of water I had divided as follows: half was given for the animals and with the other half a beverage was made which was put into the wine cask, for I held it as certain that we could not be far from land, and we sailed for eight days, all of which the hogshead of the beverage lasted, by giving a ration to each one with which he was satisfied. And when that hogshead gave out and there was no relief for us, we sighted land and we had calm for two days, during which we drank only wine, but we took heart on sighting land. We entered the bay and river of the Caraques [Ecuador] on Friday, the ninth of April, and we met there the people of a galleon from Nicaragua who had left eight months before, so we considered our trip good in comparison with theirs.[68]

Berlanga then searched the records carefully and questioned the Indians widely about the islands; yet none at that time (1535) knew anything about such islands. Where, then, is this 'unbroken tradition of visits to these islands'?

Then there is Heyerdahl's recording of 'archaeological sites', these sites being no more than scattered potsherds,[69] all pre-Inca: he wishes to establish the fact that the islands had been purposefully visited since AD 1000. This would thus place the Galápagos within the orbit of pre-Inca balsa-raft navigation – not coastal or accidental, it must be marked, but *purposeful* navigation into the Pacific. And for what reason would these Indians risk this, that which no other Indians in America had purposefully done until the coming of the white man – that is, deliberately sailing out into the most treacherous of waters? Because, states Heyerdahl, the Galápagos were full of fish. But why the Galápagos, it must be asked,

145

K

when the sea all along Peru's coast for one thousand miles is rich with the most concentrated sea-fauna in the world?

These centuries of visits to the Galápagos, according to Heyerdahl, were intermittent and temporary. None were permanent, which is why he found no graves or settlements, only potsherds. Also according to Heyerdahl, Indians came from all over Peru to visit the Galápagos, down as far south as Paracas: ' ... it is evident that seamen of the early local high cultures had comparatively *easy* access to the barren Galápagos.'[70] 'Comparatively easy access': two currents collide at the Galápagos, the Humboldt, strong enough to cause a large ship to drift six hundred miles in ten days, and the counter equatorial current which sweeps down from the north, resulting in a vortex that churns the whole of the Galápagos seas with irregular currents and complex eddies. 'Nowhere', wrote Herman Melville, 'is the wind so light, baffling, and every way unreliable, and so given to perplexing calms.'[71] Melville wrote from personal experience, for, having sailed out of New Bedford, Massachusetts, in December of 1841, on the whaling ship *Acushnet*, he was becalmed for many days between these islands. 'Sometimes it is impossible for a vessel from afar to fetch up with the group itself, unless large allowances for prospective lee-way have been made ere its coming in sight. And yet, at other times, there is a mysterious indraft, which irresistibly draws a passing vessel among the isles, though not bound to them.'[72]

The extensive literature on the Galápagos Islands is filled with tales of ships being caught in this 'mysterious indraft', and in every century since their accidental discovery by Tomás de Berlanga, there has been a series of tragic episodes involving ships drawn by currents into this vortex.[73] In many instances the ships were captained by expert sailors who knew how to manage sailing craft in any waters; yet they were wrecked on the Galápagos. But not Heyerdahl's Indians, for with 'the correct interplay between the handling of the sail and the two sets of guaras ... [they] jibbed and tacked into the wind and in any desirable direction,[74] and set sail back and forth from the Galápagos Islands over the centuries.' Yet all they left behind on several of the islands were pieces of broken pottery. Still no one seems to have asked just where the potsherds really came from or how they got there.

As already noted, there is not a single illustration on any of the pre-Inca pottery showing balsa rafts; sea communication among the Mochicas and the Chimús was confined mostly to totora-reed boats, the same that are still used in those seas today. Further, the balsa, as a tree, grew mostly in the humid areas of Ecuador, and the balsa-raft trade was sailed, because of the currents, no further south than Paita, which lies at 5° south latitude. The Incas arrived late, and, moreover, knew little of the sea. Topa Inca's expedition with 20,000 troops (and, in passing, this would have taken one thousand balsa rafts and 15,000 trees), if there was such a voyage, was to the north. Following the balsa trade, they went to those northern islets, 'where priests and wizards go to make sacrifices', and to the Ecuadorian mainland, where the gold, emeralds, pearls, conch shells and chocolate came from.

TRADE

A wall, like a vacuum, is something that nature abhors. It is, therefore, in the very nature of things that, because of the inequalities of geography and the distribution of its resources, some areas possess things which others do not. The distribution of resources and products, then, is modified by trade, and thus, commerce is organized between different groups of people.

The yuncas were self-sufficient, more so, in fact, than the highland tribes. They had, first, that indispensable item, salt, especially important to grain-eaters (it also served as a preservative of foods), and important medicinally as well. It was also relatively easy to transport. In addition, there was fish, which, in all its variety of forms, was always in demand. As Cieza observed, 'the Indians of Tumbes are great fishermen and make a great profit from it by selling it to the highlanders'. Dried fish, salted fish, sun-dried molluscs and other shell-fish of many varieties were stored as surplus and offered for barter. Seaweed was also an important item, for it yielded iodine, a necessity to the Andean diet, so as to keep down the incidence of goitre. So important was seaweed that the Incas named their bridge to the Pacific the *Chaquillchaca*, the 'seaweed bridge'. This was traversed by the *cunti-suyu* road leading from the heart of Cuzco to the sea-coast. In addition to foods, the coastal people offered cotton in six varieties, a luxury to the Andean dweller, and shells for ornaments; turquoise, lapis lazuli, gold-dust, and the famed *pótoto*, the trumpet-shell which the yuncas got by trade from the people living in Manta and Tumaco. Then there was tobacco, perhaps coca, and certainly cacao, which when roasted and ground became chocolate.

All these things and more formed the basis of barter between the coast and the sierra. Although self-sufficient, the yuncas still had need of minerals, wool, and llamas; llama studs were needed to replace or to reinvigorate their own extensive coastal herds. Therefore trade between these two ecologies became in a large sense vertical; some of the oldest trade routes between coast and sierra were located in northern Peru.

There were two forms of yunca trade: state and individual. Well organized as were both the Mochica and Chimú kingdoms, they still remained, in essence, tribute states. Those subjected to them, through an organized agricultural and fishing industry, piled up for the hierarchy vast surpluses of food-stuffs, as well as shells, minerals, gold and silver. The directing classes, including their priests, used these surpluses as capital for the payment of all the services that were not covered by the work-service tax obligated by the common Indian. Such surpluses were state-controlled and were traded *en masse*, being conveyed by llamas and human carriers to the Andean markets. Roads led down from the Andes to the salt-sources, one, notably, at Las Salinas, 'a small valley', wrote Cieza, 'having no river', but one which did have immense salt beds. Today, salt is still gathered there from shallow ponds, being piled up in such huge white mounds that from a distance the dry plain seems to be covered with dazzling white tepees. The yuncas controlled the salt supply in the area, and since the highland Peruvians did not have in their ecology a mountain of salt as existed, for example, in Zipiquira, Colombia (which was worked by the Chibchas, who sent salt about their kingdoms in small ceramic dishes), they were considerably dependent on the good-will of the desert dwellers.

The surpluses were brought to Andean trade centres, where chieftain bartered with chieftain. Copper-yielding ores were most sought after, for copper was perhaps the first luxury to become a necessity, and since transport was a problem, trade for copper and silver was probably sought in ingots. Llamas for the official herds were another trade-necessity, for the vast herds of llamas used for transport had constant need of replenishing.

The trade routes, all pre-dating the advent of the Incas by a thousand or more years, were many. To the north was an ancient route joining coastal Tumbes to what is now Ecuador. It followed the River Tumbes, which turned north-east into Ecuador, climbed the lower Andes, passed Portobello – famed for its long-lived mines of free gold (continuously worked from pre-Inca times until very recently) – and then continued to Loja. This road was later widened and, in parts, metalled by the Incas.

The second and most important trade route was the Serran-Huanca-bamba-Jaen route which followed the upper Rio Piura and climbed the precipitous Andes by means of a stone-laid stairway road. Only thirty-seven miles in length, it could be walked in three days by an Indian loaded down with seventy pounds of trade-goods. The Huancabamba was a tribe of considerable magnitude which occupied the arable lands of a sharply pitched valley formed by a river (Rio Huancabamba) which, flowing into the Marañón, was thus one of the affluents of the Amazon. Little of its pre-Inca history is known, only that it was one of the myriad of tribes which peopled the Andes. Garcilaso de la Vega, revealing his part-Inca inheritance and echoing the Inca thesis that before their advent all the Indians of Peru were basically primitive, writes that, in *c.* 1450, the 10th Lord Topa Inca

with forty thousand soldiers undertook to conquer the great province of Huanca-pampa, which was like a mosaic of tongues and small nations, with neither leaders nor laws nor cities nor houses. They fought like animals themselves over their wives and their daughters; they also went naked ... [they lived at an altitude of 10,000 feet, with the temperature falling below 20° at night; this meteorological fact should dispose of much which Garcilaso avers, he not having been there himself] ... It is comprehensible, therefore, that it should have been extremely easy to conquer them ... Topa Inca promptly had them assembled and appointed master-teachers to teach them how to live decently ... They also built roads and canals with the result that this province became ... one of the most prosperous opened up in the Empire. It even had a Temple of the Sun and a Convent for virgins.

This was personally seen by Pedro de Cieza de León in 1548, when he rode down the Andes:

Here in Huancabamba there was a Temple of the Sun with many women. From all these regions they came to worship in this temple and bring their offerings ... They wear clothing made of the wool of their alpaca-flocks ... the men of these regions are dark, of goodly aspect ... in certain districts they wear their hair long, in others short ... Those who cannot afford garments of wool use cotton.

It was in this same Chulucanas-Huancabamba region that the soldiers of Hernando de Soto forced out five hundred of these Virgins of the Sun, and while some of the cross-bowmen held off masses of the Incas' army, the others had their turns at having their way with the sacred virgins.[75]

Huancabamba had extensive trade alliances with the coastal peoples. It also was a trade-axis for the jungle; a route less than sixty miles ran from the mountains about Huancabamba down to Jaen, near to the Rio Mara-ñón, one of the tributaries of the Amazon rivers system. This was the heart of the jungle and the milieu of the head-hunting Shuaras, a widely spread

149

Upper Amazon tribe who could trade in rubber, chicle, chonta-wood (an iron-hard palm wood for spears and pipes) and such narcotics as cacao, *guayusa* (an ilex-holly, allied to Paraguay tea, which was used as an emetic to make one vomit out the food not digested during the night), as well as *guarana* (a nervous tonic), *niopo* snuff (which was inhaled into the nose through the shank bone of the Oil-bird), and *caapi* (a vine which, when drunk in an infusion, caused hallucinations and which was in great demand by the witch-doctors). Besides these, there were bird feathers and animal skins, and, when wanted, *curare*, which when tipped on arrows caused almost instantaneous death.

The third coastal trade route to the cordilleras was the Pacatamú (now Pacasmayo)–Cajamarca route. A lesser but equally important one was that which bound Chan Chan, in Chimú times, to Cajamarca. Formerly called *Q'asa marka* (the town in the ravine – a very accurate description of it), Cajamarca, before the Inca conquest of *c.* 1450, was a powerful state which was closely allied with the Kingdom of Chimor, because of the fact that three of the largest rivers which watered the desert coast (Jequetepeque, Chicama, and Moche) had their origin in the mountains which Cajamarca controlled. It was visited by the ailing for hundreds of miles around and was highly venerated for its hot sulphur baths – the same baths which Atahualpa was enjoying when the Spaniards, under Pizarro, arrived to undertake his capture.

'This province of Cajamarca is fertile in the extreme,' averred Cieza de León. 'There is an abundance of corn and other edible roots, and all fruits … [the Indians] are very skilled at digging irrigation ditches and building houses, cultivating the land … and they work gold and silver expertly. And with their hands they weave as good tapestry as in Flanders from the wool of their flocks [vicunas]. The women are loving and some of them beautiful.' In addition, Cajamarca had numerous mines which yielded gold, silver, copper and tin. As it also tapped the upper Amazon, an ancient trade route and road ran to it, to the Marañón, and so down to Chachapoyas, for Cajamarca offered much in barter for coastal products.

The immense number of pre-Inca archaeological sites discovered in the last decades, all situated in the territory which was controlled by Cajamarca before its conquest by General Capac Yupanqui, the brother of the 9th Lord Inca Pachacuti, show how advanced this state was and how vast its trade potential was before it was drawn into the maw of the expanding Inca Empire. A vast area of well-built stone buildings, some three storeys in height, with weird and unusual *chulpa*-tombs, has

been found in those areas that lie in the valley made by the Rio Utcubamba.[76]

The fourth and perhaps the largest of the Mochica-Chimú trade
arteries, the Chan Chan-Otusco-Huamachuco lateral, traversed the valley
of the Rio Moche (whose waters gave life to the valley which harboured the
capital of Chan Chan and the temples of the Sun and the Moon) and led to
Otusco, itself a large pre-Inca settlement. Twenty-five miles beyond and
up was Huamachuco, a 'large province about eleven leagues [39 miles]
beyond Cajamarca,' says Cieza de León, 'which was in ancient times
thickly settled ... There used to be great Lords in this province of Huamachuco who, as they tell, were highly respected by the Incas.' The
remains of ruins suggest the same. Lying at 12,220 feet altitude, Huamachuco is almost on a direct line from Chan Chan which lies in the Moche
Valley.

The awe-inspiring Callejón de Huaylas, where most of the perennial
snow-covered mountains lay, formed by the immense Santa River, was
reached by the fifth trade route from the valley of Nepeña, considerably
south of the Moche Valley. It was settled in very early times by the Mochicas, who have left us one of their most impressive mural-covered
pyramids, called Pañamarca. The upper reaches of the valley, at the base of
the towering Andes, which rise with scarcely a geographical prelude, are
filled with ruins of palaces, fortresses, dams and *acequias*, all of which are
stone laid. The ancient trade route climbed, by means of a step-road, from
1,400 feet to 12,000 feet, passing the mountain village of Jumbi, then
travelled easterly over the Black cordillera to Huaylas, the titular village
of the Canyon – the Callejón de Huaylas.

The last and perhaps the most travelled of all trade routes between the
Mochica and Chimú cultures, since it was the easiest for ascent and
descent, was the natural pass (as much used as the Brenner in the Alps),
the Paramonga-Huaras route, which was formed out of the valley created
by the Rio Fortaleza. At the coastal end of this easily ascended lateral lay
Paramonga, the great Chimú-built and Inca-redesigned structure, which,
tradition says, marked the southern terminus of the Kingdom of Chimor.
This same route had been used for countless centuries before as one of the
routes of trade between coast and sierra.

The march to these markets was, one must presume, done with a
certain regularity, even though the orbit of the ordinary man was limited by
the very nature of the theocracy in which he lived. The Indians usually
set off to trade only after permission was granted by a local chieftain,

and, with the advent of the Incas, most paid tolls at bridges; travellers were also halted by guards when entering large towns. Markets and trading were bound up usually with holidays, and the traditional markets, where goods of exotic nature were offered by barter, were spaced in time and place so that vendors could reach most of them. 'In order', so wrote Garcilaso, 'that labour might not be continuous and thus oppressive, the Inca ordained that there should be three holidays monthly … that there should be three fairs every month.' And although this ordinance was Inca, it is fairly certain that these *catu*-markets were merely an official recognition of what had long been crystallized, for the economic interdependence of the various tribes did not require complex trade; what animated them was the desire for luxury goods, an exchange between the coastal and the mountain people on one side and between the mountain people and the denizens of the jungle on the other.

In these markets, then, the surpluses created by these communities were exchanged. Ideas, too, marched to the market, for diffusion by commerce has its roots deep in the ancient forms of barter. There was also ample time to compare methods of hunting, fishing, and growing, and to show new forms of weaving techniques and metallurgy. Diffusion is an essential dynamic in human progress, and from this resulted the many similarities found in cultural traits; borrowing and imitation resulted in the standardization of weapons, ideas, customs and beliefs – travel is the source of alertness. And, of course, things changed hands from market to market, so that often valuable commodities such as emeralds came from hundreds of miles away, from the Chibcha mines, passing from hand to hand until many of them came to final rest encrusted in the golden walls of the most sacred building in Cuzco, the Curicancha, the golden enclosure.

6 The Conquests

As THE Mochicas' mytho-history has it, they arrived fully born, as from the brows of a Peruvian Zeus, their king being fully provided even with trumpeters and cup-bearers. Precisely whom they displaced is not told. Archaeology, however, gives another version: that the Mochicas evolved in their environment out of earlier, less sophisticated cultures; later, as they became better organized, they spread out in both directions until they controlled six valleys, from Chicama to the Virú Valley. They developed between the years 300 BC and AD 1000; then something happened.

Tiahuanaco lies in the *altiplano* at 12,500 feet, on the Bolivian side of Lake Titicaca; the actual site – perhaps the most famous single one in Peru because of the historical enigmas it presents – lies back twelve miles from the lake itself. The milieu is bleak: treeless, forbidding, and glacially cold. On three sides are jagged peaks eternally snow-covered. Wendell Bennett has described it as follows:

The site of Tiahuanaco is certainly the most elaborate one, and the purest manifestation of the culture yet to be found. It is composed of a series of construction units spread out over an immense area. Although each unit is symmetrical within itself, no geometric system can be discovered in the over-all plan. The largest construction is a partially artificial, stepped pyramid, called Acapana, once stone-faced. The ground plan is 690 feet square and the height 50 feet. The flat top has house foundations and a large reservoir with a dressed-stone overflow. Acapana has every appearance of a fortified hill which could have served as a place of refuge in times of siege.

North-west of this hill is a large rectangular unit, called Calasasaya, which measures some 445 by 425 feet, and is outlined with dressed-stone uprights. Because it looks today like an enclosure, it has often been misnamed a 'stonehenge'. Actually, the enclosing rows of uprights are all that remain of the stone-facing of a raised platform or terreplain. The typical Tiahuanaco facing technique

153

employed stone uprights, set at intervals, and filled between with smaller blocks. These blocks have long since been removed and erosion plus years of ploughing have lowered the old platform surface. The original platform construction once contained a sunken court with a megalithic stairway at its eastern end. The famous monolithic stone gateway, called the 'Gate of the Sun', as well as several statues, are associated with this unit.[1]

The conclusion is that Tiahuanaco was not metropolitan; it did not have a large amount of permanent residents. Rather, it was a religious centre which was visited by pilgrims throughout the Andes. It seems to have been extant between AD 400 and 1000, and its influence, as will be seen, was immense. The earliest description of it is given by Pedro de Cieza de León:

Tiahuanacu is not a very large town, but it is famous for its great buildings which, without question, are a remarkable thing to behold. Near the main dwellings is a man-made hill, built on great stone foundations. Beyond this hill there are two stone idols of human size and shape, with the features beautifully carved, so much so that they seem the work of great artists or masters. They are so large that they seem small giants, and they are wearing long robes, different from the attire of the natives of these provinces. They seem to have an ornament on their heads. Close by these stone statues there is another building, whose antiquity and this people's lack of writing is the reason there is no knowledge of who the people that built these great foundations and strongholds were, or how much time has gone by since then, for at present all one sees is a finely built wall which must have been constructed many ages ago. Some of the stones are very worn and wasted, and there are others so large that one wonders how human hands could have brought them to where they now stand. Many of these stones are carved in different ways, and some of them are in the form of human bodies, and these must have been their idols. Along the wall there are many underground hollows and cavities. In another spot farther to the west there are other still greater antiquities, for there are many large gates with jambs, thresholds, and door all of a single stone. What struck me most when I was observing and setting down these things was that from these huge gateways other still larger stones project on which they were set, some of which were as much as thirty feet wide, fifteen or more long, and six thick, and this and the door, jamb, and threshold were one single stone, which was a tremendous thing. When one considers the work, I cannot understand or fathom what kind of instruments or tools were used to work them, for it is evident that before these huge stones were dressed and brought to perfection, they must have been much larger to have been left as we see them. One can see that these buildings were never completed, for all there is of them are these gateways and other stones of incredible size, some of them which I saw, cut and prepared to go into the building. A great stone idol, which they probably worshipped, stands a short distance away in a small recess. It is even said that beside this idol a quantity of gold was found, and around this shrine there were a number of other stones, large and small, dressed and carved like those already mentioned.

… In conclusion, I would say that I consider this the oldest antiquity in all Peru. It is believed that before the Incas reigned, long before, certain of these buildings existed, and I have heard Indians say that the Incas built their great edifices of Cuzco along the lines of the wall to be seen in this place. They even go farther and say that the first Incas talked of setting up their court and capital here in Tiahuanacu. Another strange thing is that in much of this region neither rocks, quarries, nor stones are to be seen from which they could have brought the many we see, and no small number of people must have been needed to transport them. I asked the natives, in the presence of Juan Varagas (who holds an *encomienda* over them) if these buildings had been built in the time of the Incas, and they laughed at the question, repeating what I have said, that they were built before they reigned, but that they could not state or affirm who built them. However, they had heard from their forefathers that all that are there appeared overnight. Because of this, and because they also say that bearded men were seen on the island of Titicaca and that these people constructed the building of Viñaque, I say that it might have been that before the Incas ruled, there were people of parts in these kingdoms, come from no one knows where, who did these things, and who, being few and the natives many, perished in the wars. As these things are so obscured, we can give thanks that writing was invented, which perpetuates memory for many centuries and spreads the fame of things that have taken place throughout the universe.[2]

From this Gateway of the Sun, which Cieza knew to be a tremendous thing – from this single monolithic doorway with the weeping Sun-God, the condor heads, and puma heads – came the trident and the step design: 'all of the designs represented in this frieze appear again and again in the pan-Peruvian spread of Tiahuanaco style, on ceramics, textiles, wood-carving, and other media'.[3] It had more influence on art and religion than any other single element in the Americas. And yet little is known about how it came about. In the centre of this frieze is the Sun-God, with the sunrays radiating from about his face in the form of puma heads. He holds two staffs adorned with puma and condor heads, and he weeps. (As this motif of the Weeping God makes its way throughout Peru, he weeps many types of zoomorphic tears: condor, puma, snake and human-headed tears.) Racing about the central figure are three rows of running Indians with staffs in their hands and with furled wings, the pinions being terminated by condor heads. A fret runs about the whole design: the visage of the Sun-God and stylized condor heads. Also associated with this Gateway of the

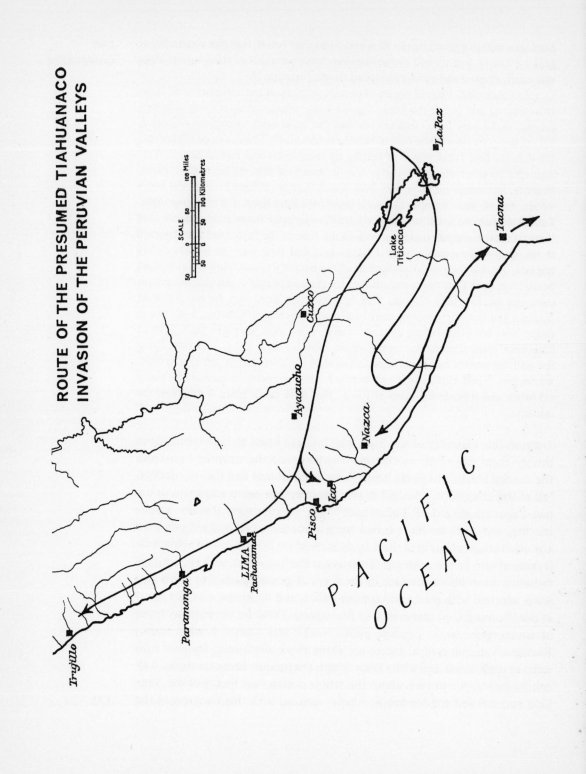

ROUTE OF THE PRESUMED TIAHUANACO
INVASION OF THE PERUVIAN VALLEYS

SCALE

100 Miles

100 Kilometres

La Paz

Tacna

Lake
Titicaca

Cuzco

Ayacucho

Nazca

Ica

Pisco

LIMA
Pachacamac

Paramonga

Trujillo

PACIFIC

OCEAN

Sun are pillar-like statues, twenty or more feet in height, with finely incised headbands representing woollen caps and again, the symbol of the Weeping God. The carvings of these figures are especially finely engraved, representing what was meant to be exquisite textile designs.

Tiahuanaco-inspired monuments appear in many places, notably at Pucara, at the northern extremity of Lake Titicaca, and still more so, at Huari, in the valley of Pacayccasa, hundreds of miles from the site of Tiahuanaco. The latter site, not over 8,000 feet in altitude and located near to Ayacucho, is strewn with volcanic stone; it is a meagre soil and filled with low scrub, a natural *cheval-de-frise* of cactus. There is a vague similarity between the ten stone carvings of figures found here and those of Tiahuanaco: the intricate patterns and tearful eyes. Also like those of Tiahuanaco, they were worked in stone. In addition to the figures, there are several immense subterranean galleries and stone basins, all carved from a single stone; there are immense walls of stone held together with adobe cement, and masses of superb polychromic potsherds which resemble the coastal Tiahuanaco style. However, if these resemble anything at all, it is the *general feeling* of the Tiahuanaco style and sculpture of Bolivia.[4]

Although there is no doubt about the impact of Tiahuanaco on South America, it would seem that one has to use 'Systematic Intuition' to see its direct influence, as did the late Arthur Posnansky, who would have it as 'The Cradle of American Man' – all over the Americas, even to the North American plains Indians, as well as down to the Arawaks of Brazil. 'The style of Tihuanacu', he says, 'evolved or rather became baroque, and in others it underwent an involution to the point of being absorbed and leaving no trace.' And, he adds, to find all this out one must go to the Tiahuanaco school: ' ... one must study in the "*primary school*" *which is Tihuanacu*, then in the "high school" which is *gran Peru*, finally to enter the "university", as represented by the study of man and his epic in Central America and especially in Mexico.'[5]

Nevertheless, something *did* happen, and one of our best scholars believed that 'the Tiahuanaco expansion was certainly strongly motivated by organized religion',[6] and that the cult of the Weeping God became – as also happened in the spread of Mohammed's faith – a religio-military invasion. Further, the reason that Huari looms large as the possible invasion point of highland to coast is that there was an ancient road near to it which led down into the Pisco Valley, the point where the Incas later built an elaborate road system, utilizing for the first time a pre-Inca road as a base on which to build their road. This point is the easiest route of access to the coast and is the closest one to Nasca, where Tiahuanaco influence was the strongest.

At the time that the Huari-Tiahuanaco invasion of the coast took place – generally accepted as about AD 1000 – there seem to have been considerable population shifts all over the Americas. Whether this was climatical, which is the essential basis for population shifts, or merely a result of the primary stimulus to move remains a question. Nevertheless, in the Mexican uplands there had been a prolonged drought in AD 900, and the great city of Teotihuacán (which was to Mexico in religious and art-style influence what Tiahuanaco was to South America) began to break up. After AD 900, the Mayas began to desert their stone cities, which were located in the cool, higher lands, and to make the 'great descent' to coastal Yucatán. In AD 987 Quetzalcoatl, who had ruled Tula for twenty years, was exiled from his capital; with his warriors he descended upon Yucatán and began a new phase of Maya history and culture. And throughout widely scattered areas in the Americas there was a similar breaking up of the old and mass invasions by the new.

The general effect of the Huari-Tiahuanaco invasion is in good part explained by archaeology. What was originally Nasca disappeared; pottery, wood-carving, and weavings became Tiahuanaco in style; the motif of the Weeping God became dominant. In one particular region, with the impossible archaeological designation of Pocheco, the grandiose pottery has designs which are almost exactly like the figure on the Sun Gate at Tiahuanaco – this even though the two areas are three hundred miles from one another, one being at sea-level and the other at 12,500 feet. The whole south coast was occupied by the Huari-Tiahuanaco, and their dominance of it was so strong that it could scarcely have been accomplished without first an actual military invasion and then social reorganization. The close uniformity of pottery styles over a spread of one thousand or more miles suggests, too, that this was relatively rapid. The strength of the religio-military invasion can be fully seen at Nasca, Ica, and most of the valley cultures to and beyond Chancay. And along with the Tiahuanaco invasion, there seems also to have been a change in architecture; having been used to working in stone in the Andes, but finding no such material on the coast, the invaders introduced a manner of moulding massive blocks of adobe, called *tapia*, and building their structures of this rather than of the small, hand-moulded, sun-dried bricks used by the previous cultures. And everywhere was stamped the Weeping God symbol of the Sun Gate, the very 'acme of religious symbolism'.[7]

It was at Virú that archaeologists were able to observe the social impact of the invasion and could see the 'tides of human events affecting all of the Peruvian coast and Andes which flowed and ebbed across Virú for many centuries'.[8] The Mochicas were in full command of that small and rather insignificant valley; they had large fortresses commanding the hills and scattered villages with ceremonial and administration centres. Archaeology suggests that the invasion in this valley was violent and abrupt;[9] the invaders built differently, buried differently, and made pottery differently – with the Weeping God motif always remaining dominant. Structures were studied to determine what change occurred in society, and there is no doubt that the sudden break-up and then disappearance of the Mochica ceramic style in Virú was the result of 'significant changes in the domestic politico-religious-military changes'.[10] All this is not wholly clear; nevertheless there is a good deal of significant evidence. The Mochicas apparently retreated into their traditional boundaries to the north. They were followed, and eventually they were pushed into the most northern pocket of the north coast, though not wholly extinguished.

The Tiahuanaco administration of the entire Peruvian coast lasted more or less three hundred years; then, something happened: the administrative apparatus failed or else they had dominion without dominance. Whatever the cause or causes, there followed an upsurge of particular cultures. The puzzling question is, then, what happened to the Tiahuanaco invaders? Were there enough of them to hold down a massive coastal population separated, as each valley was, by a vast hiatus of nothing? Since the Aymara-speaking populations about Lake Titicaca, who occupied the traditional lands of Tiahuanaco, were large – and the Inca annals are filled with their battles with them – it may be supposed that the population there was not drained for the coastal invasion. Then what happened to them? Also, what happened to the Incas when the Spaniards took over? If there are no historical records, then how much of an answer can be recovered from archaeological research? These questions are bound to remain unanswered for a long long while; years of archaeological toil in the field and in the laboratory might yield partial answers, but without written historical records, the pertinent question will remain unanswered. Only this is certain, that after about AD 1250, local coastal cultures began to emerge from Huari-Tiahuanaco domination and to regain their individuality.

THE SUCCESSORS OF THE MOCHICA-CHIMÚ

123 The gigantic stone head of a statue from Tiahuanaco near Lake Titicaca. About 900 AD the mountain tribes from this region invaded the whole of the southern coastal area and became the dominant civilization in Peru and Bolivia between 1000 and 1300.

124 The first drawing of the great ceremonial centre at Tiahuanaco, made by Léonce Angrand in 1847. The huge stone monoliths once formed a large walled square.

125 Calasasya, part of the structure at Tiahuanaco, as drawn by Léonce Angrand.

126 The Gateway of the Sun at Tiahuanaco, with the figure of the weeping god, the recurrent motif of Tiahuanacan culture, in the centre of an intricately carved frieze of running figures.

127 and 128 Two examples of vividly decorated pottery showing Tiahuanacan influence. The step design on the right-hand figure is characteristic of this culture.

129 The weeping god motif repeated on a bowl found in the Nasca valley showing the extent of the influence of Tiahuanacan culture.

130–37 A series of drawings from Theodor de Bry's *Americae* illustrating the Spanish conquest of the Incas.

130 Spanish soldiers felling a tree from which the Indians hurl a variety of missiles.

131 The cruelty of the Spaniards to their Inca slaves.

132 Spanish soldiers carrying off a group of Inca women whom they caught bathing.

133 Atahualpa, the Inca chieftain, entering Cajamarca with his retinue.

134 Incas bringing the Spaniards gold and silver vessels as a ransom for the captured Atahualpa.

135 The murder of Atahualpa on the orders of the Spanish leader Francisco Pizarro, despite his solemn promise to release the Inca chieftain for ransom.

136 Incas at work in a metal shop. They produced large quantities of beautifully worked gold and silver objects which were plundered by the Spaniards.

137 Inca funeral rites, showing how the dead were buried with provisions for the after-life.

Vue du Portique Occidental du Temple de Tiaguanaco.

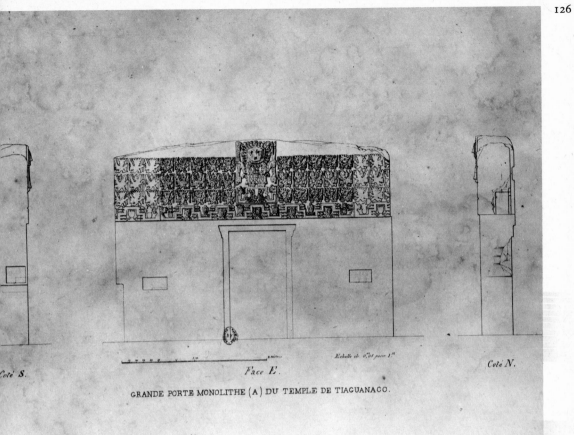

Face E.

Echelle de 0,^m01 pour 1^m.

GRANDE PORTE MONOLITHE (A) DU TEMPLE DE TIAGUANACO.

127

128

129

130

131

132

133

134

135

136

137

The Chimus emerged from the Huari-Tiahuanaco occupation and, with a modification of the Mochica culture, began their own imperial expansion. Of this, there is little archaeological doubt. They emerged as the Kingdom of Chimor from the gradual collapse of the Huari-Tiahuanaco invasion and mingled with the surviving elements of the Mochicas, who, from the evidence of the pottery, still survived in modified form in the far north during this occupation. The Chimús developed a massive imperial appetite and progressed from the temple-city stage through the conquering stage and into the tribute state, wherein, as in the other similar desert kingdoms in the Old World, they changed 'from a mechanical aggregate of persons, all doing much the same things but held together by feelings of kinship ... into an organic unit whose members perform complementary functions'[11] – in other words, into a highly regulated caste system.

And with this came conquest. By the year 1370, under the leadership of Nançen-pinco, the Chimús had taken over all the classical Mochica lands – the valleys from Saña to the Santa. They had extended the *acequia* system devised by the Mochicas, erected fortresses, and subdued the various 'lords of the valleys'. Their pottery – that which, above all, reflected their culture – was made in mass. Many of the old Mochica motifs were retained; many new ones were added. However, the pottery was no longer polychromic; instead, it was burned in a reducing kiln to jet, lustrous black (precisely why this was used, no one knows, but it does serve to give the sharp break between one régime and the other). Evidence shows, from the mass of metal objects created by them, that there was a guild of gold, silver and bronze workers, who produced all such objects as gold masks, pendants, arm bands, crowns, nose ornaments; silver goblets and cups (and one notable piece which was made half of gold, half of platinum), silver dishes and ear-spoons; bronze instruments, from delicate pincers to remove facial hair to immense crowbars; and the axe-halberds and all the other accoutrements of war. So famed were these gold-workers that, when that kingdom tumbled with the invasion of the Incas, one whole guild was sent to Cuzco; they were still there when Pedro de Cieza de León arrived in 1549. The mass of golden objects that the Chimús turned out was the greatest ever obtained by the Incas, and one scholar raises the interesting speculation as to how much of this golden cache later went into Atahualpa's ransom: 'It would be interesting to know what percentage of the loot (over $8,000,000 worth of gold) that the Spaniards took

L

from Cuzco in 1533 had been brought from Chimor seventy years before.'[12]

Archaeology confirms the sumptuousness of the Chimú rulers – the handsome feather weavings, the golden ornaments, the luxurious weavings, the elaborate graves. Even Cieza observed in 1548 (for some of this ritual still remained then) that 'the ancient rulers, before they were subdued by the Incas ... were feared and obeyed ... and served with great ceremony', that they 'were much given to their religion and performed great sacrifices', and further, that 'they were more self-indulgent and comfort-loving than the Andean dweller'. And so they had their gatekeepers and concubines, and there were doubtless, as their oral histories tell us, keepers of the royal face-paints, royal cup-bearers, and bathing masters: they were, in fact, surrounded by all the suffocating ritual which inevitably accompanies a theocracy.

By the year 1450, just preceding their fatal clash with the Incas, the dominions of the Kingdom of Chimor had been extended, under the 'Grand Chimú' named Minchan-çaman, through all the valleys to the north as far as Tumbes and down to Carabayllo (which is a valley near to Lima). They had then extended the informal alliance that the Mochicas had had with their Andean neighbours into a formal agreement, for the latter controlled the principal waterways that flowed into the valleys of the Chimú,[13] and they were also needed as buffer states against the expanding Incas. By this time, Chimor was an impressive kingdom: it controlled eighteen valley-oases, bridged by roads which ran over long stretches of desert of inhospitable sand and heat and through extreme waterless desolation. They had a population estimated at more than half a million, an extensive balsa-raft trade with the northern tribes of Ecuador, an extensive trade relationship with the highlands, and the previously mentioned alliance with their powerful Andean neighbours who controlled their water sources. The sea yielded an inexhaustible supply of fish, kelp, molluscs, and salt; agriculture was extensive, using elaborate techniques of irrigation; the army, like all others in the early Americas, was a well-trained and responsive militia.

But at the same time in the Andes, the Incas, under the impressive Lord Inca Pachacutic, were also expanding their empire – to the south, to the north, and on the coast. It was inevitable that these two civilizations would one day come into conflict, and when this finally occurred, it happened, as most wars do, in a way that no one had planned.

It was in 1461, after having conquered the southern coast up to Lima, that the Lord Inca sent his brother, Capac Yupanqui, on a raid in force to the north, far beyond Inca territory. The Inca's general, however, suffered great misfortune when the entire force of his Andean allies deserted; thus, in the hope of balancing this catastrophe with an easily won victory, he laid siege to the Cajamarca.

The capital of this tribe lay in a large, fertile valley at 10,000 feet altitude. It was a populous tribe, prosperous and secure in its treaty of alliance with the Grand Chimú. Their chieftain vigorously opposed the Incas and sent his runners to ask for the proffered military aid from the coast. When the Inca's ambassadors, who were always sent as a prelude to attack arrived in Cajamarca, the inhabitants 'replied with great arrogance that they did not need either new gods or a foreign lord, and that they had inherited a sufficient number of laws from their ancestors not to desire any new ones: the Incas, they concluded, should be content with those who had already agreed to obey them, or seek elsewhere if they wanted more subjects, because none here was willing to hear them.'[14]

The Incas attacked and defeated the combined forces of Cajamarca and Chimor. The chieftain was killed, and the city was occupied by a strong Inca garrison. Then, expecting to be received in triumph, the general sent his *chasqui* runners ahead to bring the news to Pachacutic, the Lord Inca, but instead of being accorded a victor's welcome, he was executed for disobeying orders, for having led a whole Inca army five hundred miles into unsubdued territory. The Topa Inca then ordered his son, successor to the Incaship, to prepare a large army to subdue all the intervening territory between Cuzco and Cajamarca and to reinforce the Inca garrison at Cajamarca. And thus it was that the Chimús and the Incas came to war.

The Chimús, even though they had lost their Andean allies at Cajamarca, continued to attack in the highlands. Then the Incas, in combination with the coastal allies of the Chuqimancu troops and those of Cuismancu, who controlled the valleys around Lima, began the coastal attack on the outward bastions of the Kingdom of Chimor. At first, the Incas were defeated at Paramonga, in a battle so violent that 'the dead on both sides were so numerous that they were a hindrance to the living'. But then the troops of 20,000 reinforcements poured down from Cuzco, and the Chimús were forced to give up Paramonga, and to retreat north to the next valley of

Huarmey (anciently Huallmi), and later even further north to take up strong positions on the Santa, where the fortress built for this defence still remains. 'The inhabitants of Santa,' remembers Garcilaso,[15]

were particularly brave, and they fought with such ardour that they won the respect of their own adversaries. Their lord, the great Chimú, was so elated and hopeful as a result that he persuaded himself that Prince Yupanqui would be the first to grow weary of this cruel war and would soon return to the comforts of his court life, with the result that he refused to listen to the peace proposals that the Incas continued to make to him. On the contrary, he levied fresh troops in the other valleys of his kingdom, and the war became more and more pitiless; each one saw no other end than his own victory; there were quantities of dead on both sides; and indeed, it was the most costly campaign the Incas had yet conducted.

Then the Inca tried a new strategy. He marched his troops into the north, where they swung around and proceeded to attack the Chimús from the direction of Tumbes. The Chimús, still holding the Santa Valley, presumed that the weight of the attack would fall either there or else down from the heights of Cajamarca; thus, they were unprepared for this new eventuality. The Inca invasion was three-pronged: one force, under the Topa Inca, came down from the mountains; the other two, under the generals Auqui Yupanqui and Tillca Yupanqui, moved southward from Tumbes, conquering as they went, and soon entered Chan Chan, the capital of the Kingdom of Chimor. Now all Peru was Inca, and the last serious threat to the Inca hegemony had been eliminated. Their territory extended throughout Ecuador, Peru, now Bolivia, and much of Chile.

'Inca administration of the conquered kingdom was very shrewd,' writes John Rowe.[16] 'At first, its integrity and constitution were respected; Minchan-çaman was kept in honoured exile at Cuzco, and a son of his was appointed to the throne as Inca puppet. This son was named Chumun-caur; he was living at Huaura with his mother, Chanquir-guanguan, at the time of the Inca conquest. Chumun-caur was succeeded by his son Guaman-chumo whose name is part Quechua (*waman* means falcon) and who was probably educated in Cuzco, that being the normal Inca policy. His son Anco-cuyuch succeeded him at Chimor, but by his time the unity of the kingdom had been subverted by the ingenious policy of setting up each son of the old dynasty as hereditary lord of a town or valley. The valleys that did not receive new princely lords continued under the families that the kings of Chimor had appointed in the old days, but these families learned to look directly to Cuzco instead of to Chimor, and by the time the Spaniards came the old kingdom was only a memory. Lambayeque and Jayanca were ruled by families of this latter type.'

Following the death of the 11th Lord Inca, Huayna Capac, in 1527, a struggle began between Atahualpa and Huascar over the Inca Empire; this occurred after the Incas had exercised lordship over the Kingdom of Chimor for only fifty years. It was a disaster for the coastal yuncas, as many were dragged away from their daily tasks to fight in the Andes at unaccustomed altitudes. Thus, the depopulation of the valleys began. Then, too, Tumbes suffered considerably from the raids of the Punas, who lived on an island of that name at the mouth of the Rio Guayas and were the principal suppliers of balsa rafts. During the resulting *mêlée*, much of Tumbes was destroyed. Then, to put the final quietus on the whole long history of the coastal yuncas, the Spanish arrived for their conquest, just at the moment that Atahualpa – the victor in the struggle for the Incaship – was resting at the baths in Cajamarca, while waiting to be called to Cuzco to receive the royal fringe, or crown.

1532: THE YEAR OF THE SPANIARDS

The Spanish had originally arrived in 1527 with a small ship of seventy tons, piloted by Bartolome Ruiz and carrying aboard Francisco Pizarro and his famous thirteen men of Gallo, those who agreed on the Isla of Gallo, off the coast of Colombia, to remain with Pizarro until he discovered the 'kingdom of gold'. They made their landfall at Tumbes, which they could see from the sea, and Pedro de Candia, 'one of the thirteen', clad in full armour and armed with sword and arquebus, made his entry alone into the city. At that time, Huayna Capac still lived, the Sun Temple was resplendent in gold ornaments; the people were curious and friendly.[17] The new arrivals exchanged some Spanish geegaws for food – potatoes, tomatoes, squash, and corn; then, indicating in sign language that he would return, Pizarro weighed anchor and they made their way, in leisurely fashion, down the coast. Sailing as far south as the Santa Valley, and 'everywhere received with the same spirit of generous hospitality', Pizarro then returned to Tumbes.

While at Tumbes, two from the ship decided to remain there; they were Alonso de Molina and a freed negro slave from Panama named Gines. They were to stay in Tumbes to search out information for Pizarro's return. In exchange, the natives of Tumbes yielded up several of their own people to go along with Pizarro back to Spain, one of whom would turn out to be the Indian-turned-Christian-cum-traitor, Felipillo, 'little Philip', who was to play his part in the death and destruction of Atahualpa. So, with his Indians, llamas, weavings, and gold and silver ornaments, Pizarro took off for Panama, then to Spain, where he would eventually sign the Capitulation of Toledo, his contract for the conquest of Peru.

There is no precise history of the fate of the two who remained in Tumbes (although they are the subject of a baroque eighteenth-century novel[18]). What is known is that soon after their arrival, Huayna Capac is said to have sent for them, as he was then in Tumipampa, which was linked by direct road to Tumbes. Somewhat later, the Inca took sick and died, 'from a pestilence', says one, 'that hung over the land, carrying away thousands of Indians'. Whether or not this disease was Spanish-transmitted is mere surmise. In any case, however, he died, as also did Alonso de Molina. According to one source, Molina died in Tumbes in 1532, Gines in Cinto, deep in Chimú territory. And one conquistador-chronicler[19] says that when his group neared Puna in 1532, they saw 'a high cross, a painted crucifix' near to a house of about thirty boys and girls, 'who shouted upon seeing their white skins and beards, *loado sea Jesucristo, Molina, Molina*'.

When the Spaniards returned in 1532, they came to deal out *blut und eisen*. They were attacked on landing, and subsequently dealt out reprisals that made the *tallanes*, who had been conquered successively by the Mochicas, the Chimús, the Incas and now by these new arrivals, realize that they would soon be less than nothing. Francisco Pizarro and his small army of foot-soldiers and mounted troops then moved along the fringe of the ancient Mochica and Chimú territory. They travelled along the coastal road – 'fifteen feet wide with strong walls on both Sides above the Height of a Man ... and in each of these Vales the Incas had stately Apartments for themselves and Magazines for their Soldiers,' and it was in these stately Apartments, or *Tampus*, that Francisco Pizarro and his company took their ease. The former Kingdom of Chimor was bypassed, for Pizarro's main object was the Inca. This object was ultimately attained, and on the 29th August, 1532, Atahualpa was led out to be garrotted, in spite of the ransom which he had paid for his life and even before all that gold and silver had been melted down and sent to Spain.[20]

There was no need for any concerted Spanish conquest of the coastal yuncas; they meekly submitted to the yoke of peace, and in the civil wars that followed – those fought between the Spanish victors over the carcass of the Inca Empire – they were ultimately decimated, as Pedro de Cieza de León testified: 'Now all is in ruins ... Time and wars have so wasted all that the only thing to be seen in proof [of their former greatness] ... are the many large burial places of the dead and how the many fields that lie in the valley were planted and cultivated by them when they were alive.'

What man had left undone, nature continued. Unprecedented rains fell; next, locusts swarmed over what was left. And still 'their Spanish *encomenderos* tried to collect tribute as if nothing had happened, even levying the tribute of the dead'. Yet the yuncas still spoke their language and in secret worshipped their gods, thus setting off in 1620 a great campaign against idolatry. That which had survived wars, conquest, and rains was now destroyed by religious zeal,[21] although these practices still persisted to some extent until the late eighteenth century, when they were recorded by the native artists developed under the direction of Bishop Martínez de Compañón.

Today the coast is dotted with the material remains of the Kingdom of Chimor, but the sands have covered much. Erosion, the interplay of sun and *garva*, wind and sand, has acted as an abrasive on the once highly colourful murals that clothed the bare walls; immense holes, where treasure-hunters search for gold, have so disfigured the once proud pyramids and temples that they have lost all form. First, man here made his conquest of nature; then, each culture in turn was the aggressor or victim of conquest. For history is neither good nor evil, altruistic nor egoistic; it is an ensemble of forces in which one force gives away to another under superior pressure. It is now sand and time that have made the final conquest of the Kingdom of Chimor.

Notes

I THE REDISCOVERY OF THE KINGDOMS

1 Unpublished with the exception of *Trujillo del Peru a fines del siglo XVIII*, edited by Jesús Dominquez Bordona (Madrid, 1936), in which there was produced with an uncritical text, a few hundred of these 1400 illustrations.

2 Philip Ainsworth Means, *Baltasar Jaime Martínez de Compañón y Bujando, a Great Prelate and Archaeologist. Hispanic American Essays*, University of North Carolina Press (Chapel Hill, N.C., 1942), pp. 67–77; Rubén Vargas Ugarte, *Martinez y Compañón, Revista histórica*, vol. X (Lima, 1936), pp. 161–191.

3 Marshall Saville lists in his *Bibliographic Notes on Palenque* (Museum of the American Indian Publications, vol. VI, no. 5, New York, 1928) the publications which were the outcome of his discovery: Waldeck, Frederic de, *Voyage pittoresque et archéologique* (Paris, 1838); Waldeck and Brasseur de Bourbourg, *Recherches sur les ruines de Palenqué* (Paris, 1866); John Herbert Caddy, *City of Palenqué*, 36 pp. of MS. with 24 sepia paintings and a folded map, dated 1840 (unpublished and lost); John L. Stephens, *Incidents of Travel in Central America*, 2 vols. (New York, 1841); Catherwood's *View of Ancient Monuments* (London, 1844).

4 Tacunga, properly Llactacunga, approximately forty miles south of Quito, near the active volcano of Cotopaxi. The Inca ruins of Callao were close to Llactacunga, erected by Tupac Yupanqui and Huayna Capac after the conquest of Quito (*c.* 1475). Alexander von Humboldt, in *Views of Nature*, has given the only description of the edifice on the Royal Road (between Quito and Cuzco). The building formed a square, the sides of which were thirty-five yards long; four great trapezoidal doors were distinguished in 1801. There were eight apartments, the walls nearly five yards high and one yard in thickness. There were eighteen niches (the leitmotif of Inca architecture), 'distributed', said Humboldt, 'with the greatest symmetry'. *Pedro de Cieza de León*, p. 56.

5 Markham's first published book was *Cusco & Lima* (London, 1856), a period piece. A shorter work on the *Geographical positions of the Tribes which formed the Empire of the Incas* is notable and led later to the publication of *The Incas of Peru* (London, 1910). Markham is best known for his translations of sixteenth-century Spanish authors in the Hakluyt Society publications.

1 *Parte primera de la Chrónica del Perú...* (Seville, 1553). Antwerp, 1554 edition: *La Chrónica del Perú*. The other histories that survived were not published until 1880 and thereafter.

2 José de Acosta, *The Naturall and Morall Historie of the East and West Indies*, Book III, Chapter 3 (London, 1608).

3 Excavated by Dr Junius Bird, the most knowing of the dirt-archaeologists. Junius Bird, *Preceramic Cultures in Chicama and Viru*, Society of American Archaeology, Memoir 4 (Menasha, 1948), pp. 21–28.

4 This mytho-history first appears in the manuscripts of Miguel Balboa Cabello, who was born in Malaga, Spain, and who was in the Americas as early as 1566. Of him we know nothing, not even the date of his death; but we do know that he travelled widely in the highlands and jungles. His belief, which came to him in Quito (1576), that the American Indians were descended from Noah through Shem gives one the first note of caution when consulting him. His manuscript *Antarctica* gives the most detailed account of the coastal peoples, which, since there was nothing of this before, he must have gathered himself. In his history of Ñaymlap it reads that he 'came from the far south'. (What he must have meant is north, since there are no balsa trees south of Tumbes.) The green stone would have been an emerald, obtained by trade from the muzo or chimor regions in the Chibcha realm in Colombia.

5 Harold B. Osborne, *Indians of the Andes: Aymares and Quechuas* (London, 1952).

6 Junius Bird's Carbon 14 reading of associated material with Mochica artifacts.

7 Rafael Larco Hoyle, *A Cultural Sequence for the North Coast of Peru, Handbook of South American Indians*, vol. II (Washington, 1946), pp. 149 *et seq.*

8 Heinrich Ubbelohde-Doering, *Kunst im Reiche der Inca* (Tübingen, 1952), p. 17.

9 *The Incas of Pedro de Cieza de León*, edited with introduction by Victor W. von Hagen, University of Oklahoma Press (Norman, Oklahoma, 1959).

10 Antonio de la Calancha, *Cronica moralizada* (Barcelona, 1638), p. 556. Padre Antonio de la Calancha was born in Chuquisaca (now Sucre), Bolivia, in 1584. As his father came from Andalucia and his mother was Spanish, he was presumably a chapetón. Educated at the University of San Marcos in Lima, he journeyed widely throughout Peru and was one of those padres assigned to the northern coastal regions of Peru – sometime around 1628 – for the extirpation of idolatry. While, as a zealous missionary, he was destroying *huacas* and effigies of tribal gods among the yuncas, he was also noting down their history, polity and customs. His book is, as P. A. Means writes, 'a fund of precious information not to be found elsewhere'. In particular, chapters 1 and 2, folios 545–557, are crammed with detail on the coastal history and ethnography of the yuncas.

11 Pedro de Cieza de León, *The Incas*, translated by Harriet de Onis, edited by Victor Wolfgang von Hagen, University of Oklahoma Press (Norman, Oklahoma, 1959).

12 Cieza, *op cit.*, p. 303.

13 *History of Technology*, vol. I (New York & London, 1954), pp. 407–408.

14 From the Old Testament: Onan and Thamar; his offence being masturbation, so

that masturbation in either sex is known as onanism. Richard Lewisohn, *A History of Sexual Customs*, Longmans, Green & Co. (London, 1956).

15 See 'The Cure of Disease', p. 97.

16 A brilliant exception is the Tarascan culture of north-western Mexico.

17 The carob, hispanized from the Arabic *kharrubah*, a North African evergreen, was confused by the early Spaniards with the Peruvian coastal mimosa – the *Prosopis horridus* of the botanists of the African species.

18 John H. Rowe, *Inca Culture before the Spanish Conquest, Handbook*, III, pp. 282–287.

19 So quickly did one event follow the other that Cieza avers that 'there were regions where most of them never were able to learn the language of Cuzco (*Quechua*)'.

20 *Relacion de las Cosas de Yucatán* ('Account of the Things of Yucatan'), written in 1566, is the principal source of late Maya history. 'The details Landa gives of Maya lives, the description of food, history, and tribal *mores*, the delineation of the *katuns*, or twenty-year periods, of Maya history (which made possible the modern reduction of Maya dates), and his insistence that the Mayas in his time were the very same people who built the stone cities found in the jungles (which even then were ascribed to Roman, Greeks, and Jews) – these have given him a unique place in the literature on the Mayas.' – V. W. von Hagen, *The Ancient Sun Kingdoms of the Americas*, p. 201.

21 Archbishop Toribio de Mogrovejo, while making a general survey of the northern coast, including the languages then being spoken, observed that Muchic was spoken only in Lambayeque; whereas, in Moche, Illimo, Túcume, Chiclayo, Rerue Callance, Jauanca, Monséfu, Mocupe Chepen, Jequetepeque, and Chicama, the spoken language was *yunca* (equated with *quingnam*); and that in Éten and Cao they spoke the Pescadora, the fisherman's language. However, W. B. Stevenson, who was twenty years on the coast, serving as Secretary to Lord Cochrane, and an official in Esmeraldas, Ecuador, stated that 'the village of Éten is the only one where Chimú dialect is spoken'.

22 *La Lengua Yunca o Mochica* (Lima, 1921), pp. 122–127. Larco Hoyle, *Los Mochicas*, vol. II (Lima, 1939), pp. 77–82.

23 In 1604 Fray Luis Jerónimo de Oré published *Rituale seu manuale Peruanum*, in which various Christian prayers appeared translated in Quechua, *aymara*, Mochica and *guaran*.

24 John Howland Rowe, *The Kingdom of Chimor, Acta Americana*, vol. VI, nos. 1–2 (1948).

25 M. S. Drower, *Water-supply, Irrigation and Agriculture, History of Technology*, vol. I (London, 1954), pp. 520 *et seq.*

26 *Herodotus*, translated by A. D. Godley, vol. I, Loeb Classical Library (London, 1960).

27 *Ibid.*, p. 397.

28 John H. Rowe, *op. cit.*, p. 34.

29 John V. Murra, *Land Tenures in the Inca State*, Vassar College. This paper was read at the symposium on Land Tenures in the High Civilizations of the Americas, at the annual meeting of the American Anthropological Association in Mexico, D.F., December, 1959.

30 *Herodotus*, vol. I, p. 399.

31 *Ibid.*, p. 189.

32 Victor W. von Hagen, *The Bitter Cassava Eaters, Natural History Magazine* (March, 1949).

33 'So far as the Incas were concerned, its use seems to have been limited to the nobility, the priests (for divination), perhaps old people, and mayhap the *chasqui* couriers to aid their running in high altitudes. The Indians make a quid of the leaves, about the size of a walnut, which they hold in the sides of their cheeks; lime is added to it, quickening the process of leaf disintegration; the juice alone is swallowed. The average daily consumption of cocaine is minute, 300–700 mg. It seems to dull the senses, making the coca chewer less hungry, cold, and thirsty. Its effect on the Indians over a period of time has been argued for four centuries; there is still no firm medical conclusion.' (*The Incas of Pedro de Cieza de León, op. cit.*, p. 260.)

34 'In trueth the trafficke of coca in Potosi doth yearely mount to above a halfe million of peeces [pesos] ... for they use fifteene thousand baskets every yeare. It is a kind of merchandise, by which all their Markets and Faires are made with great expedition. The Indians esteeme it much and in the time of their Incas it was not lawfull for any of the common people to use this coca ... They say it gives them great courage, and is very pleasing unto them. Many grave men hold this as supersition & a meere imagination: for my part, and to speak the truth I persuade not myself that it is an imagination; but contrariwise, I thinke it works and gives force and courage to the Indians ... They willingly imploy their money therein, and use it, as money: yet all these things were not inconvenient, were not the hazard of the trafficke thereof, wherein so many men are occupied. The Inguas used Coca as a delicate and royall thing, which they offered most in their sacrifices, burning it in honor of their idolls.' (José de Acosta, *The Naturall and Morall Historie of the West Indies* [written *c.* 1570].)

35 *The Incas of Pedro de Cieza de León, op. cit.*, pp. 259–260.

36 Robert Cushman Murphy, *Oceanic Birds of South America*, 2 vols. (New York, 1936).

37 Garcilaso de la Vega, *Primera Parte de los Commentarios reales* (Lisbon, 1609).

III MOCHICA AND CHIMU CRAFTS

1 Wendell C. Bennett, *Ancient Arts of the Andes*, The Museum of Modern Art (New York, 1954).

2 Gerdt Kutscher, *Arte Antigue de la Costa Norte del Perú*, Gebr Mann (Berlin, 1955).

3 Wendell C. Bennett and Junius B. Bird, *Andean Cultural History* (New York, 1949), pp. 246 *et seq.*

4 Bennett and Bird, *op. cit.*, pp. 201–209.

5 The published results of the Inca Highway Expedition, which under the auspices of the American Geographical Society explored the highland and coastal

roads of Peru, and parts of Ecuador, Chile and Bolivia, is still incomplete. A popular account, *Highway of the Sun* (Gollancz, London, 1956), gives an overall picture of the road.

6 Bennett and Bird, *op. cit.*

7 Cotton is so much of a botanical puzzle that it causes botanists genetic nightmares, for American varieties show that the chromosomes of cotton point to a trans-Pacific passage west to east by an Asiatic parent. It must have been distributed by birds, if not man, who in the early history of the Americas 'brought' cotton from the Old World, then several millennia later picked up the American cotton, which had developed new chromosome patterns, and brought it back again to Eurasia.

8 William B. Stevenson, *A Historical and Descriptive Narrative of Twenty Years' Residence in South America* (London, 1825), 3 vols.

9 Alexander von Humboldt, *Views of Nature* (London, 1858), pp. 404–410.

10 The Aguarunas ('waterpeople'), who are Shuara-Jivaro, still live on the Marañón River. When the Incas wanted to control these gold-producing areas and invaded the jungle, the Shuaras fought with the troops of Huayna Capac and defeated them.

11 This route was, when conquered by the Incas, made into a stone-laid lateral connecting the Andean royal road with the coastal highway. Huancabamba was visited by Hernando de Soto after the Cajas adventure, who found it 'larger than Cajas with better buildings and a fortress built entirely of stone'; it was one day's journey from Cajas along the royal road. It had in addition to the fortress a sun temple and a *Aclla-huasi* – house of the Chosen Women. It was an important region before the Inca conquest; the name itself is Quechua, meaning 'valley-of-the-field guardian'. Little is known of this tribe in pre-Inca times except that its influence extended down into the jungles about the Marañón; This author, with the Inca Highway Expedition (1954) found evidence of the road that had been built by the Huancas and enlarged by the Incas to exploit the jungles about Jaén. However, the Incas were repulsed by the people called Aguarunas. They were (and still are) head-hunters, sharing the same culture and language as the Shuara tribes of Ecuador. The Jívaros [Shuaras] are scattered over a vast territory approximating 25,000 square miles; language, appearance, beliefs, and customs are closely interrelated; those on the Marañón called Aguarunas are actually Huambizas.

'After the conquest of northern Peru, including Huancabamba, the Inca ordered a lateral road to extend down to the Marañón, from which the conquered people obtained gold, feathers, and wood. Topa Inca began the assault some time after 1470. The army met with disaster, as Cieza gathered from firsthand information.' (*The Incas of Pedro de Cieza de León, op. cit.*, footnote p. 92.)

12 Bird and Bennett, *op. cit.*, p. 251.

13 The *Voyages* of De Bry have been the subject of numerous studies by bibliographers; none, however, are in agreement as to what constitutes the proper contents of a set of *La Collection des Grands et Petits Voyages*.

14 Benzoni, *History of the New World*, p. 150. (As reprinted by S. K. Lothrop, *Inca Treasure As Depicted by Spanish Historians. Publications of the Frederick Webb Hodge Anniversary Publication Fund*, vol. II [Los Angeles, 1938], pp. 15–16.)

15 Garcilaso de la Vega, *Royal Commentaries*, Lib. 2, Cap. 28. (As reprinted in Lothrop, *op. cit.*, pp. 16–17.)

16 These techniques were echoed elsewhere: the metallurgists of the Jordan Valley took advantage of the prevailing north winds and orientated their smelting ovens near Elath in order to gain the high temperatures sufficient to smelt copper.

17 From Albrecht Dürer's notebook. He was in Brussels at the time of the arrival of the ship from Vera Cruz bringing Charles V the first fruits of conquest. Although his references were actually directed to Aztec and Totonaca gold-work, they would have applied just as well to Mochica or Chimú artifacts, had he seen them.

18 S. K. Lothrop *et al.*, *Pre-Columbia Art*, Phaidon Publishers (New York, 1957), p. 64.

19 *The Incas of Pedro de Cieza de León*, *op. cit.*

20 Victor W. von Hagen, *The Search for the Gilded Man*, Natural History, vol. 61 (September, 1952), pp. 312–321.

21 W. B. Stevenson, *op. cit.*, vol. II.

IV TRIBAL LIFE

1 Published in part in Madrid, 1936. *Trujillo del Perú … a fines del Siglo XVIII*, prólogo Jesús Dominguez Bardona … Selected 208 examples. Some of the dances include the following: Vol. II, p. 143: Dance de los Parlampanes; p. 145: Dance de los Diablicos; p. 146: Dance de Carnestolendas; p. 147: Dance del Chimo; p. 148: Dance del Chimo; p. 149: Dance de Pallas; p. 151: Dance Chimo; p. 152: Dance Pallas; p. 153: Dance Huacos; p. 154: Dance del Purap; p. 159: Dance del Chusco; p. 162: Dance de Pájaro; p. 163: Dance de Huancamayos; p. 164: Dance de Monos, Cóndores, Osos, Leones, Carneros, Venados.

2 *The Incas of Pedro de Cieza de León*, *op. cit.*, footnote pp. 296–297. Of this sarsaparilla [*Similax medica*] and the cure the famous botanist Richard Spruce wrote (see Victor W. von Hagen, *South America Called Them*): 'Piura [in Perú] is considered the sovereignest place on earth for the cure of "rheumatic" (*lege* "syphilitic") affections. Many wonderful cures are reported; but the treatment is rather severe. It is as follows: First, you pay the priest to say "novenas" – that is, masses on nine consecutive days – on your behalf; on each of these days you drink copiously of a warm decoction of sarsaparilla towards midday, and then your friends take you outside the town and bury you up to the neck in the burning sand, shielding your head with a broad straw hat and an umbrella. There you perspire in such a way as to bring out all the mercury you may have taken, and to reduce your swollen joints to their proper dimensions. Now you may see the use of the masses, for if you survive the operation (which is not always), they serve to express your thankfulness; and if you die under it, you will need not only those nine masses, but several additional ones – for which you make due provision in your last will and testament – to secure the repose of your soul.'

3 The full original title of this work is as follows: Hieronymi Fracastorii / Syphilis /sive Morbvs Gallicvs / Veronae, MDXXX, mense Augusto. / Non sine

Priuilegio, mulctáq; pecuniaria, & excõ- / municationis pœna: pro ut in Príulegijs Continetur.

4 Works on the origins of syphilis include the following: Ivan Block, *Der Ursprung der Syphilis* (Jena, 1911); Karl Sudhoff, *Der Ursprung der Syphilis* (Leipzig, 1913); Karl Sudhoff (ed.), *Earliest Printed Literature on Syphilis*, Monumenta medica, Vol. III (Florence, 1925).

5 *Niopo*, which is an acacia, was classified as *Piptadenia niopo H*(umboldt); we owe our knowledge of it to this explorer, who was the first to collect it, describe it, and to give out its medicinal virtues.

6 See André Thevet, *Les Singularitez de la France antarctique, autrement nommée Amerique, & de plusieurs Terres & Isles decouuertes de nostre temps* (Paris, 1558).

7 *The Incas of Pedro de Cieza de León*, *op. cit.*, pp. 308–310.

8 Pedro de Cieza de León, *op. cit.*, pp. 311–313.

9 'For in these valleys it was the custom to bury with the dead his wealth and the things he most prized, and many women and servants of those who were closest to the lord when he was alive. And it was the custom in olden times to open the tombs and renew the clothing and food that had been buried in them.' (Pedro de Cieza de León, *op. cit.*, p. 312.)

10 Herodotus, *op. cit.*, Book II, p. 371.

11 Norman Douglas, *South Wind* (London, 1917), p. 223.

V TRIBAL ORGANIZATION

1 Pedro de Cieza de León, *op. cit.*, p. 307.

2 Rowe, *op. cit.*, p. 39.

3 Philip Ainsworth Means, *Biblioteca Andina*, Part I, Transactions of the Connecticut Academy of Arts and Sciences, vol. 29, pp. 271–525 (New Haven, Connecticut; May, 1928), p. 317.

4 It is very important, however, to examine the man and the personal equations that cloud his observations, his collections and his musings – especially so since many parts of his work have been seized upon by the Heyerdahl balsa-migration school.

5 Means, *Biblioteca Andina*, p. 318.

6 *Ibid.*, p. 323.

7 Calancha, *op. cit.*, p. 547.

8 John Murra, *op. cit.*, p. 9.

9 *Ibid.*, p. 7.

10 Garcilaso de la Vega, *The Incas: The Royal Commentaries of the Inca, Garcilaso de la Vega*, ed. by Alain Gheerbrant, The Orion Press (New York, 1961), p. 262.

11 Garcilaso de la Vega, *Royal Commentaries*, pp. 313–314. This narrative was reported to Garcilaso de la Vega, who further explains that Pedro de Candia 'was a strong, brave man, a good Christian and of unusual stature. I did not know him, but I well remember his son, who went to grammar school with me [in Cuzco, in the years 1548–1549].'

12 Alonso Enríquez de Guzmán. From *The Great City Called Tumpiz*, his account written in 1536.

13 The road, in fact, is really 25½ feet in width, and it preserves this width more or less down its entire length to Chile, which is 2,520 miles.

14 Motupe, which lies 90 miles south of the Serran Valley, is a small developed oasis created out of the river of the same name. Pizarro's scribe, Francisco de Xérez, wrote in 1532 how they 'came to a place called Motuc, rested there four days', and found the place fertile and the population extensive. Cieza de León, who followed in 1578, wrote that 'once in the valley of Motupe, one comes to the highway of the Incas, wide and well constructed ... there were great lodgings for the Incas in these parts.'

15 Pedro de Cieza de León, *op. cit.*, p. 320.

16 Perhaps called 'Sayanca', or 'Chayanca'. The titles of the land that contained this ancient site go back to 1711. It is now the Hacienda La Viña, and the Inca road, on its way to Batan Grande, runs through the vast estate two and a half miles west of the Hacienda house.

17 A. L. Kroeber (*The North Coast*, Archaeological Explorations in Peru, Part II, Field Museum of Natural History, Anthropology Memoirs, vol. 2, no. 7 [Chicago, 1930]) gives a map of it.

18 The *Huaca Chotuna* is located at Lambayeque, or Pimental, near to the village of San José, which lies a few miles to the north; its frieze was found by *huaqueros* in 1941.

19 Richard Schaedel, *Major Ceremonial and Population Centers in Northern Peru*, The Civilizations of Ancient America (Chicago, 1951).

20 Pedro de Cieza de León, *op. cit.*, pp. 320–321.

21 *Ibid.*, p. 321.

22 See V. W. von Hagen, *Highway of the Sun, op. cit.*, p. 220.

23 Squier, *op. cit.*; also Weiner, *op. cit.*, plate facing p. 98.

24 *Huaca*, a Quechua word (the Mochica word was *tuné*), meant a holy place, and while many things could be and were *huaca*, the word was mostly applied to the pyramids, which were often the burial place of chieftains. *Huaco* is the general term for a ceramic, and a *huaquero*, Spanish-Quechua derivation, is one who digs out *huacos* – a tomb-rifler, in fact. Although they have been immensely destructive, still, these *huaqueros* – who are, in fact, an institution – have found most of the material which later led archaeologists to those areas.

25 Such as the *Huaca del Dragon*, found only a few feet from the modern Pan American highway. See Richard Schaedel, *Uncovering a Frieze on the Peruvian Coast, Archaeology*, vol. 2, no. 2 (Summer, 1949), pp. 73–75.

26 Max Uhle, *Die Ruinen von Moche, Journal Société des Americanistes de Paris* (Paris, 1913), pp. 95–117.

27 Neither was Egyptian architecture all done in carved stone. The mastaba tombs of the early kings are of sun-dried brick – adobe, in short. Dwellings of the lesser men and even those of rulers were of 'interminable mud-brick' and the Egyptians themselves did not begin to use kiln-bricks until very late in their empire; so, it can be seen that construction with sun-dried materials has a long, honourable and classical background.

28 Seton Lloyd, *Building in Brick and Stone, A History of Technology*, vol. I, pp. 456–490 (New York and London, 1954), p. 459.

29 Seton Lloyd, *op. cit.*, p. 461.

30 Robert Shippee, *The 'Great Wall of Peru'*, *The Geographical Review*, vol. XXII, no. 1, pp. 1–29 (New York, January, 1932), pp. 1–2.

31 This river is so large, in fact, that in full flood it is often 1800 yards across and causes immense destruction when it leaves its banks.

32 Pedro de Cieza de León, *op. cit.*, p. 325.

33 See the Isometric projection of the reconstruction of the Temple of Ur-nammu, as given in Seton Lloyd, *op. cit.*, figure 298.

34 See Victor von Hagen, *Highway of the Sun*.

35 Pedro de Cieza de León, *op. cit.*, pp. 305–306.

36 Garcilaso de la Vega, *Royal Commentaries*, pp. 179–180.

37 Nobody knows when the first camel appeared in the recorded history of man. There are no records of any in a wild state, yet they have a longer heredity of variation and adaptation than any of the cattle. They do not appear on the early monuments of Egypt, and Julian Huxley has recently confirmed that they did not appear in Egypt until 300 BC (see his *From an Antique Land* (New York and London, 1954). Camels were apparently still relatively new to the Fertile Crescent, since, when Xerxes in 480 BC started on his invasion of Greece, Herodotus says that vast army had only one camel corps: 'The Arabians equipped ... on riding camels which in speed are not inferior to horses', but they 'brought up the rear to avoid spreading panic amongst the horses who cannot endure the presence of camels'.

38 Typical is a recent's writer's verdict that 'the llama is a typical beast of the high-lands and did not thrive on the coast'. (See Hermann Leicht, *Realm of the Incas* [London, 1961], p. 62.)

39 The La Gasca, *Pizarro Papers*, Huntington Library Collection, Catalogue p. 324.

40 Herodotus, who travelled the Susa-Babylonian route, wrote that 'there is nothing in the world which travels faster than these Persian couriers, the whole idea is a Persian invention'. He explains how the mounted riders were stationed along the road at intervals in post-houses and then messages passed in relays from rider to rider.

41 Garcilaso de la Vega, *Royal Commentaries*, p. 157.

42 It seems incredible that even Indians could run at such high altitudes without collapsing from anoxia, but the Inca Highway Expedition, experimenting over a still extant Inca highway at 11,000 feet with modern, untrained Indians, proved that they could run on average a mile in 6½ minutes even at these altitudes, so that the *chasquis*, as averred by Pedro de Cieza, could have been able to run 250 miles during the twenty-four hours in relay system.

43 Yet history, too, was transmitted with their aid. 'Suppose', wrote Padre Calancha in 1638, 'that a functionary wishes to express that before Manco Capac, the *first Inca*, there was neither king, chief, cult or religion; that in the *fourth* year of his reign this emperor subdued *ten* provinces, whose conquest cost him a certain number of men; that in one of them he took a *thousand* units of gold, and *three thousand* units of silver, and that in thanksgiving for the victory he had celebrated

a festival in honor of the god, Sun.' (Calancha, *op. cit.*) All this, then, would be done on a *quipi*, tying knots symbolizing 'gold', 'Inca', or 'Sun'.

44 Pedro de Cieza de León, *op. cit.*, p. 174.

45 An authority on writing believes this *pictography* to be 'the first important step beyond embryo-writing in that it is no longer restricted to the recording of single, disconnected images, but is capable of representing the sequential stages or ideas of a simple narrative. The action is recorded by a series of more or less straightforwardly representational pictures of sketches, each one of which is called a *pictogram*. Picture-writings can be expressed orally in any language without alteration of content, since the pictures do not stand for specific sounds.' (David Diringer, *Writing* [London, 1962], p. 21.)

46 Rafael Larco Hoyle, *La escritura peruana sobre pallares, Relaciones de la Sociedad Argentina de Antropologia*, IV, pp. 57 *et. seq.* (Buenos Aires, 1944).

47 Such as Diego de Landa, *Relación de las Cosas de Yucatán*, ed. with notes by Alfred M. Tozzer, Papers of the Peabody Museum of American Archaeology and Ethnology, vol. XVIII (Cambridge, Mass., 1941). Landa wrote his *Relación* in Spain in 1566, and took the manuscript back to Yucatán in 1573. After his death the work was kept in the convent at Mérida. It was first published by Brasseur de Bourbourg (Paris, 1864). There were later editions by Jean Genet and William Gates. Alfred M. Tozzer's is the sixth edition and the most authoritative to date. Bernardino de Sahagún also came early to Mexico (1595) while the Aztec traditions were still alive. His work, *A History of Ancient Mexico* (trans. by Fanny R. Bandelier [Nashville, Tenn., 1932]), is wonderfully detailed (there are accompanying illustrations which do not appear in all the publications) and it is an honest attempt at reportage. The edition in English was prepared by Fanny Bandelier, the widow of Adolph Bandelier, one of the pioneers in American Indian studies.

48 Ruiz, a native of Moguer in Andalucía, was the principal pilot of the conquest and the first to sail below the equatorial line in the Pacific. In the 'Capitulation of Toledo', when Pizarro was given his contract for the discovery and conquest of Peru, Ruiz was titled an *hijo de algo*, *Piloto Mayor de la Mar del Sur*, with an annual salary of 75,000 maravedises.

49 Spielbergn in 1615; Frézier in 1712 (Amédée François Frézier voyaged along the coast of Peru between the years 1712 and 1714. Not long after his return, his book was published first in French and then in English. Frézier's picture and plan of a sealskin boat seen by him at Arica appears in Plate 18); Juan and Ulloa in 1748; Humboldt in 1801; and others.

50 Garcilaso de la Vega, *Royal Commentaries*, p. 68.

51 José de Acosta, a Jesuit, was born in Medina del Campo in 1540 of wealthy parents. He reached intellectual maturity early and took his novitiate in the Society of Jesus at eighteen. At the age of thirty he travelled widely in Mexico, then passed on to Peru. He had a vivacious, independent spirit; he condemned the burning of the Maya books at Mani Yucatán by Diego de Landa in 1562 ('this followed from some stupid zeal when without knowing or wishing to know the things of the Indies they say as in a sealed package that everything is sorcery'), and he refused to swallow any of the Indians-are-descendants-of-Noah theory

M

then being widely voiced. The last years of his life were spent at Salamanca, where he wrote his great work (previously mentioned), the English title of which is *The Naturall and Morall Historie of the Indies.* Philip A. Means rightly calls it 'one of the greatest books in the whole field of Andean bibliography'; and the number of editions which were printed in Spain (1588, 1590, 1591, 1598; and finally published in English in 1604) indicate the high regard his contemporaries had for it.

52 Garcilaso de la Vega, *Royal Commentaries,* pp. 69 and 73.

53 Philip A. Means, *Pre-Spanish Navigation Off the Andean Coast, The American Neptune,* vol. II, no. 2 (1942).

54 S. K. Lothrop, *Aboriginal Navigation Off the West Coast of South America, Journal of the Royal Anthropological Institute,* vol. LXII (1932), pp. 229–256 and especially pp. 238–239.

55 'In the days of the Inca,' wrote Cieza, 'there used to be a toll-taker who received tribute from those who passed over the bridge, which is made of bundles of stalks in such a way that it is strong enough to allow men and horses to cross over it.' (Pedro de Cieza de León, *op. cit.,* p. 243.) This famous floating pontoon bridge was to endure for over eight hundred years and was still in place in 1864, when the American explorer-diplomat, Squier, came upon it: fortunately for us, he sketched it.

56 Thor Heyerdahl and Arne Skjolsvold, *Archaeological Evidence of Pre-Spanish Visits to the Galápagos Islands,* Supplement to *American Antiquity,* vol. XXII, no. 2, Part 3, The Society for American Archaeology (October, 1956).

57 Father Miguel Cabello de Balboa, one will recall, came early to the Americas and, speculating on the origins of the American Indians, insisted that they were Jews descended through Ophir, great-grandson of Noah. Therefore, any legend of people arriving by raft fitted into his preconceived theory of origins.

Capitán Pedro Sarmiento de Gamboa was in Perú from 1557 to 1579 and wrote a *History of the Incas* (translated and edited by Sir Clements Markham [London, 1907]) under the patronage of the Viceroy Francisco de Toledo. He was interested in establishing that Wawa Chumpi and Nina Chumpi were the Galápagos Islands, since he wanted the Viceroy to sponsor his voyage of discovery to the Pacific (it was he who discovered the Solomon Islands).

58 In sixteenth-century Spanish vocabulary, a *legua,* or league, was 7,416 Spanish yards, or about 2.76 nautical miles.

59 Means, *Pre-Spanish Navigation,* pp. 17–18.

60 Robert Cushman Murphy, *The Earliest Spanish Advances Southward from Panama Along the West Coast of South America, The Hispanic American Historical Review,* vol. XXI, no. 1 (February, 1941), p. 9.

61 *Ibid.,* p. 9.

62 There was, however, the early legend current in Peru of Tici Viracocha, the creator-god, who, having been dissatisfied with his handiwork, had set off into the sea – to return some day. (The same legend hovers about the person of Quetzalcoatl, the plumed serpent god of Middle America.)

63 Means, *Pre-Spanish Navigation.*

64 Heyerdahl, *op. cit.*

65 Heyerdahl, *op. cit.*

66 *Ibid.*, p. 57.

67 Albemarle Island?

68 Letter from Tomás de Berlanga to the King of Spain, *Archivo fr. Indies Patronato Esta à cajón 2 leg.*, dated April 6, 1535.

69 This author spent seven months in the Galápagos Islands, from August, 1935 to March, 1936, for the Darwin Memorial Expedition, during which time a monument was erected to Charles Darwin and all the islands were painstakingly explored in order to gain, among other things, a precise idea of the state of the wildlife so that a programme of conservation could be prepared (as it later was). All the areas which were visited (albeit only for a few days) by the Heyerdahl group were intimately known to our expedition for several months.

    We lived on the very island of Indefatigable where Heyerdahl's group found an archaeological cache of potsherds. Yet, while this author's group found no evidence of pre-Spanish habitation in seven months, Thor Heyerdahl found it within several days.

70 Heyerdahl, *op. cit.*, p. 61.

71 Herman Melville, *The Encantadas, or Enchanted Isles* (William P. Wreden: Burlingame, California, 1940), p. 5.

72 Melville, *op. cit.*, p. 5.

73 See Victor W. von Hagen, *Ecuador and the Galápagos Islands* (Norman, Oklahoma, 1949).

74 Heyerdahl, *op. cit.*, p. 61.

75 Zarran (now Serran), lying midway on the Inca Coastal highway between Tumbes and Batan Grande, was a large coastal administrative centre controlled by the Incas through a local koraka. From this Zarran ran a stone-paved lateral road to Huancabamba (then to the Upper Amazon). After receiving intelligence that the Inca himself may have been there, Pizarro despatched Hernando de Soto, with forty men. This was reported in great detail by Diego Trujillo. In June of 1532 de Soto arrived with forty mounted soldiers at Huancabamba, and then he went on to Chulucanas (called Caxas), a village surrounded by mountains. It was here that they saw for the first time tangible evidence of the great wealth of the Incas – 'fine edifices,' wrote Trujillo, 'and a fortress built entirely of cut stones and a wonderful road made by hand and broad enough for six men on horseback to ride abreast'.

76 Something of the unusual archaeological and historical problems that this area presents may be seen from a reading of the following: Henry and Paule Reichlen, *Recherches Archéologiques dans Les Andes de Cajamarca, Journal de la Société des Américanistes*, N. S., t. XXXVIII (Paris, 1949), pp. 137–174. And by the same authors: *Recherches Archéologiques dans Les Andes du Haut Utcubamba, Journal de la Société des Américanistes*, N. S., t. XXXIX (Paris, 1950), pp. 219–246.

1 Wendell C. Bennett, *Ancient Arts of the Andes* (The Museum of Modern Art, New York, 1954), pp. 67–68.

2 Pedro de Cieza de León, *op. cit.*, pp. 282–284.

3 Bennett, *Ancient Arts of the Andes*, p. 27.

4 Cieza, who made the classic comments on Tiahuanaco, also saw this Huari, then called Viñaque. Of it he said the following: ' ... [it] is called Viñaque, where there are some large and very old buildings which, judging by the state of ruin and decay into which they have fallen, must have been there for many ages. When I asked the Indians of the vicinity who had built that antiquity, they replied that other bearded, white people like ourselves, who, long before the Incas reigned, they say came to these parts and took up their abode there. This and other ancient buildings in this kingdom seem to me not of the sort the Incas built or ordered built, for this building was square, and those of the Incas, long and narrow.' (Pedro de Cieza de León, *op. cit.*, pp. 123–124.)

Huari (which seems never to have been mentioned again until 1929) is important to the history of the Mochicas, as to all other coastal cultures, for it is doubtless from this point that the often-repeated (although incorrectly so) Tiahuanaco 'invasion' of the coast occurred.

5 Ing. Arthur Posnansky, *Tihuanacu, The Cradle of American Man*, trans. by James F. Shearer, vol. III (La Paz, Bolivia, 1896), pp. 10–11.

6 Bennett, *Ancient Arts of the Andes*, p. 76.

7 *Ibid.*

8 Gordon R. Willey, *Prehistoric Settlement Patterns in the Virú Valley, Peru*, Smithsonian Institution *Bulletin*, no. 155 (1953), p. 400.

9 James A. Ford, '*The History of a Peruvian Valley*', *Scientific American* (August, 1954), p. 32.

10 *Ibid.*

11 V. Gordon Childe, *Early Forms of Society, A History of Technology*, vol. I, p. 52.

12 Rowe, *op. cit.*, pp. 44–45.

13 The Niepos tribe controlled the upper reaches of the Rio Chancay, which river watered the city of Pacatamú; next, the Cajamarcas, a larger tribe, controlled the Jequetepeque River, which also nurtured the valley and city of Pacatamú; and finally, the Huamachuco tribe controlled the headwaters of the Moche where Chan Chan was situated.

14 Garcilaso de la Vega, *Royal Commentaries*, p. 169.

15 *Ibid.*, pp. 200–201.

16 Rowe, *op. cit.*, p. 45.

17 All of this is described in more detail in William H. Prescott's *The Conquest of Peru*.

18 Jean François Marmontel, *The Incas; or, the Destruction of the Empire of Peru*, 2 vols. (London, 1806). Alonso de Molina is the hero of this tragedy.

19 Diego de Trujillo, who wrote *Relación del Desubrimento del Reyno del Perú* in 1532; *Edicion, prólogo y notas de Raul Porras Barranechea* (Seville, 1948).

20 Atahualpa's ransom yielded 1,326,539 pesos of pure gold; the gold averaged

$22\frac{1}{2}$ carats. At that time 100 gold pesos equalled 190 silver pesos. At today's value, the silver of the ransom reached $8,818,876.99. Gold at the value of today ($35.02 an ounce) would bring the total gold ransom to $19,851,642.07. Thus Atahualpa paid $28,670,519.06, but failed to ransom himself.

21 And yet, sometimes the right things happen for the wrong reasons, for in their destruction of the remnants of this culture, the Church made an invaluable ethnological documentation; beliefs, customs, and *mores* were recorded and the reports drawn up by Padre Calancha (much cited in this book), as well as by Padre Carrera, who produced his work on the Muchic grammar.

Bibliography

Acosta, José de, *The Naturall and Morall Historie of the East and West Indies.* London, 1604.

Anonymous History of 1604. (See Vargas Ugarte 1936 and 1942).

Bennett, Wendell C., *Ancient Arts of the Andes.* New York, 1954.

Bennett, Wendell C., and Bird, Junius B., *Andean Culture History.* American Museum of Natural History, Handbook Series, no. 15. New York, 1949.

Bennett, Wendell C., *The Archaeology of the Central Andes, Handbook of South American Indians*, vol. 2. *The Andean Civilizations.* Washington, 1946.

Bennett, Wendell C., *Archaeology of the North Coast of Peru, AMNH-AP*, vol. 37 (1939), 1–153.

Benzoni, Girolamo, *La Historie del Monde Nuovo.* Venice, 1565. (See also Theodore de Bry, *La Collection des Grands et Petits Voyages*, Part V.)

Bird, Junius B., *Pre-ceramic Cultures in Chicama and Viru, American Antiquity*, vol. XIII, no. 4, Part 2 (April, 1948), 21–28.

Bruning, Enrique E., *Estudios monogràficos del Departamento de Lambayeque: Fasciculo I: Lambayeque; Fasciculo II: Olmos.* Libreria e Imprenta de Dionisio Mendoza. Chiclayo, 1922.

Cabello Balboa, Miguel, *Miscelanea Antartica.* (Original written in 1586. An 18th-century copy in the New York Public Library.)

Calancha, Antonio de la, *Cronica moralizada del orden de San Augustín en el Perú* (Barcelona, 1638.)

Carrera, Fernando de la, *Arte de la Lengua Yunga* (1644), ed. by Radames A. Altieri. Publicaciones Especiales del Instituto de Antropología, no. 3. Universidad Nacional de Tucumán, Tucumán, 1939.

Childe, V. Gordon, *Early Forms of Society*, in Singer *et al.* (eds.), *A History of Technology*, vol. I. New York and London, 1954.

Cieza de León, Pedro de, *The Incas of Pedro Cieza de León*, trans. by Harriet de Onis and ed. by Victor W. von Hagen. University of Oklahoma Press, Norman, 1959.

Codex Mendoza, 2 vols. Mexico, 1925.

Doering, Heinrich U., *Kunst im Reiche der Inca.* Tübingen, 1952.

Drower, M. S., *Water-Supply, Irrigation and Agriculture, A History of Technology*, vol. I. New York and London, 1954.

Feyjoo y Sosa, *Descrición del Valle de Chimo*. Madrid, 1760.

Ford, James A., *The History of a Peruvian Valley*, *Scientific American*, vol. 191, no. 12 (August, 1954), 28–34.

Garcilaso de la Vega, *The Royal Commentaries of The Inca Garcilaso de la Vega*, ed. by Alain Gheerbrant and trans. from the French by Maria Jolas. New York, 1961.

Gillin, John, *Moche. A Peruvian Coastal Community*. Smithsonian Institution, Institute of Social Anthropology, Publication no. 3. Washington, 1947.

Herodotus, Books I and II, trans. by A. D. Godley. Loeb Classical Library. London, 1960.

Heyerdahl, Thor, and Arne Skjolsvold, *Archaeological Evidence of Pre-Spanish Visits to the Galápagos Islands*, Supplement of *American Antiquity*, vol. XXII, no. 2, Part 3 (October, 1956), 1–69.

Holstein, Otto, *Chan Chan: Capital of the Great Chimú*, *Geographical Review*, vol. 17, no. 1 (New York, 1927), 36–61.

Horkeimer, Hans, *La Cultura Mochica*. Las Grandes Civilizaciones del Antiguo Peru, Tomo I. Lima, 1961.

Horkheimer, Hans, *Vistas Arqueológicas del Noroeste del Perú*. Libreria e Imprenta Moreno. Trujillo, 1944.

Humboldt, Alexander von, *Tagesbücher*, 30 vols. Humboldt Universität, East Berlin.

Humboldt, Alexander von, *Views of Nature*. London, 1858.

Humboldt, Alexander von, *Vues des Cordilléres et Monuments des Peuples Indigènes de l'Amérique*. Paris, 1810.

Huxley, Sir Julian, *From an Antique Land*. London and New York, 1954.

Kroeber, Alfred Louis, *The North Coast*. Archaeological Explorations in Peru, Part II. Field Museum of Natural History, Anthropology Memoirs, vol. 2., no. 2. Chicago, 1930.

Kroeber, Alfred Louis, *The Uhle Pottery from Moche*. University of California Publications in American Archaeology and Ethnology, vol. 21, no. 6 (Berkeley, 1925), 235–264.

Kutscher, Gerdt, *Arte Antigue de la Costa Norte del Perú*. Berlin, 1955.

Kutscher, Gerdt, *Chimu, eine altindianische Hochkultur*. Berlin, 1950.

Kutscher, Gerdt, *Iconographic Studies as an Aid in the Reconstruction of Early Chimu Civilization*, *Transactions of the New York Academy of Sciences*, Series II, vol. 12, no. 6 (1948), 194–203.

Kutscher, Gerdt, *Nordeperuanische Keramik*, *Monumenta Americana*, vol. I. Berlin, 1954.

The La Gasca–Pizarro Papers. Huntington Library Collection. Catalogue, Maggs Bros. London, 1927.

Landa, Diego de, *Relación de las Cosas de Yucatán*, ed. with notes by Alfred M. Tozzer. Papers of the Peabody Museum of American Archaeology and Ethnology, vol. XVIII. Cambridge, Mass., 1941.

Larco Hoyle, Rafael, *A culture sequence for the North Coast of Peru*, *Handbook of South American Indians*. Bureau of American Ethnology, Bulletin 143, vol. 2 (Washington, 1946), 149–175.

Larco Hoyle, Rafael, *La Escritura Peruana Sobre Pallares*, *Revista Geográfica Americana*, Ano 11, vol. 20, nos. 122–123 (1943), 93–103.

Larco Hoyle, Rafael, *Los Mochicas. Casa Editoriales La Crónica y Rimac*, 2 vols. Lima, 1938–1939.

Lloyd, Seton, *Building in Brick and Stone*, in Singer *et al.* (eds.), *A History of Technology*, vol. I. New York and London, 1954.

Lothrop, Samuel K., *Aboriginal Navigation Off the West Coast of South America*, *Journal of the Royal Anthropological Institute*, vol. LXII (1932), 229–256.

Lothrop, Samuel K., *Inca Treasure as Depicted by Spanish Historians*. Publications of the Frederick Webb Hodge Anniversary Publication Fund, vol. 2. Los Angeles, 1938.

Lothrop, Samuel K., W. F. Foshag, and Joy Mahler, *Pre-Columbian Art*. New York, 1957.

Mangelsdorf, Paul, *The Origin of Indian Corn and its Real Relatives*. College Station, Texas, 1939.

Markham, Sir Clements R., *Cuzco: A Journey to the Ancient Capital of Peru*; and *Lima: A Visit to the Capital and Province of Modern Peru*. London, 1856.

Martínez y Compañón, in *Trujillo del Perù … a fines del Siglo XVIII*, prólogo by Jesús Dominguez Bardona. Madrid, 1936 (This contains only a selection of the otherwise yet unpublished works by Martínez de Compañón.)

Means, Philip Ainsworth, *Ancient Civilizations of the Andes*. New York and London, 1931.

Means, Philip Ainsworth, *Baltasar Jaime Martinez de Compañón y Bujando, A Great Prelate and Archaeologist*, *Hispanic American Essays*. Chapel Hill, North Carolina, 1942.

Means, Philip Ainsworth, *Biblioteca Andina*, Part I. Transactions of the Connecticut Academy of Arts and Sciences, vol. 29 (May, 1928), 271–525.

Means, Philip Ainsworth, *Pre-Spanish Navigation on the Andean Coast*, *American Neptune*, vol. II, no. 2 (1942).

Middendorf, E. W., *Peru*, 3 vols. Berlin, 1893–1895.

Murphy, Robert Cushman, *The Earliest Spanish Advances Southward from Panama Along the West Coast of South America*, *The Hispanic American Historical Review*, vol. XXI, no. 1 (February, 1941), 1–28.

Murphy, Robert Cushman, *Oceanic Birds of South America*, 2 vols. New York, 1936.

Murra, John V., *Land Tenures in the Inca State*, Vassar College. This paper was read at the symposium on Land Tenures in the High Civilizations of the Americas, at the annual meeting of the American Anthropological Association, in Mexico, D. F. (December, 1959).

Osborne, Harold, *Indians of the Andes: Aymares and Quechuas*. London, 1952.

Paulsson, Gregor, *The Study of Cities*. Copenhagen, 1959.

Pizarro, Pedro, *Relación del Descubrimiento y Conquista de los Reinos del Perù* (written in 1570–1571), in *Col. Docs. ineds. Historia de Espana*, vol. V: 201–388. Madrid, 1844.

Pizarro, Pedro, *Relation of the Discovery and Conquest of the Kingdoms of Peru*, trans. and ed. by P. A. Means, 2 vols. Cortez Society. New York, 1921.

Posnansky, Arthur, *Tiahuanacu, the Cradle of American Man*, trans. by James F. Shearer, 2 vols. New York, 1945–1957.

Prescott, William H., *Conquest of Peru*, ed. and abridged by V. W. von Hagen New York, 1961.

Reichlen, Henry and Paule, *Recherches Archéologiques dans les Andes de Cajamarca, Journal de la Société des Américanistes*, N. S., t. XXXVIII (Paris, 1949), 137–174.

Reichlen, Henry and Paule, *Recherches Archéologiques dans les Andes du Haut Utcubamba, Journal de la Société des Américanistes*, N. S., t. XXXIX (Paris, 1950), 219–246.

Rowe, John H., *The Kingdom of Chimor, Acta Americana*, vol. VI, nos. 1–2 (1949), 26–59.

Rowe, John H., Donald Collier, and Gordon R. Willey, *Reconnaissance Notes on the Site of Huari, Near Ayacucho, Peru, American Antiquity*, vol. 16, no. 2 (October, 1950), 120–137.

Sansevero, Raimondo di Saugro, *Lettera Apologetica* ... Naples, 1750.

Schaedel, Richard, *Major Ceremonial and Population Centers in Northern Peru.* The Civilizations of Ancient America. Chicago, 1951.

Schaedel, Richard, *Monolithic Sculpture of the Southern Andes, Archaeology*, vol. I, no. 2 (June, 1948), 1–66.

Schmidt, Max, *Kunst u. Kultur von Peru*. Berlin, 1929.

Scott, Sir Lindsay, *Pottery, A History of Technology*, vol. I. New York and London, 1954.

Shippee, Robert, *The 'Great Wall of Peru' and other Aerial Photographic Studies by the Shippee-Johnson Peruvian Expedition, The Geographical Review*, vol. XXII, no. 1 (January, 1932), 1–29.

Singer, Charles, E. J. Holmyard, and A. R. Hall (eds.), *A History of Technology*, vol. I. New York and London, 1954.

Squier, E. George, *Peru: Incidents of Travel and Exploration in the Land of the Incas*. New York, 1877.

Stevenson, William B., *A Historical and Descriptive Narrative of Twenty Years Residence in South America*, 3 vols., London, 1825.

Strong, William Duncan, *Finding the Tomb of a Warrior God, National Geographic Magazine*, vol. 91, no. 4 (Washington, 1947), 453–482.

Trujillo, Diego de, *Relación del Descubrimento del Reyno del Perù* (written in 1532), *Edicion, prólogo y notas* by Raul Porras Barrenechea. Sevilla, 1948.

Uhle, Max, *Die Ruinen von Moche, Journal de la Société des Américanistes*, vol. X (Paris, 1913), 95–117.

Vargas Ugarte, Rubén, *La Fecha de la Fundación de Trujillo, Revista Histórica*, vol. X, no. 2 (Lima, 1936), 229–239.

Vargas Ugarte, Rubén, *Martínez de Compañón, Revista Histórica*, vol. X, (Lima, 1936).

Vargas Ugarte, Rubén, *Los Mochicas y el Cacicazgo de Lambayeque*. Actas y Trabajos Científicos del XXVII° Congreso Internacional de Americanistas, vol. II (Lima, 1942), 475–482.

von Hagen, Victor Wolfgang, *The Ancient Sun Kingdoms of the Americas.* Cleveland and New York, 1961.

von Hagen, Victor Wolfgang, *The Bitter Cassava Eaters, Natural History Magazine* (March, 1949).

von Hagen, Victor Wolfgang, *Ecuador and the Galápagos Islands.* Norman, Oklahoma, 1956.

von Hagen, Victor Wolfgang, *The Search for the Gilded Man, Natural History Magazine,* vol. 61 (September, 1952), 312–321.

von Hagen, Victor Wolfgang, *South America Called Them: Explorations of the Great Naturalists: La Condamine, Humboldt, Darwin, Spruce.* New York, 1945.

Willey, Gordon, R., *Prehistoric Settlement Patterns in the Virú Valley, Peru,* Smithsonian Institution *Bulletin,* no. 155 (1953).

Willey, Gordon R., *The Virú Valley Program in Northern Peru, Acta Americana,* vol. 4, no. 4 (Mexico, 1946), 224–238.

Index